# DATA ANALYTICS 2019

The Eighth International Conference on Data Analytics

September 22 - 26, 2019

Porto, Portugal

**DATA ANALYTICS 2019 Editors**

Sandjai Bhulai, Vrije Universiteit Amsterdam, the Netherlands

Hesham H. Ali, UNO Bioinformatics Core Facility, College of Information Science and Technology, University of Nebraska at Omaha, USA

Les Sztandera, Thomas Jefferson University, USA

**Printed from e-media with permission by:**

Curran Associates, Inc.
57 Morehouse Lane
Red Hook, NY 12571

**Some format issues inherent in the e-media version may also appear in this print version.**



Printed with permission by Curran Associates, Inc. (2020)

International Academy, Research, and Industry Association (IARIA)
412 Derby Way
Wilmington, DE 19810

Phone: (408) 893-6407
Fax: (408) 527-6351

petre@iaria.org

**Additional copies of this publication are available from:**

Curran Associates, Inc.
57 Morehouse Lane
Red Hook, NY 12571 USA
Phone: 845-758-0400
Fax: 845-758-2633
Email: curran@proceedings.com
Web: www.proceedings.com

## Table of Contents

# DATA ANALYTICS 2019

## Forward

The Eighth International Conference on Data Analytics (DATA ANALYTICS 2019), held between September 22-26, 2019 in Porto, Portugal, continued the series on fundamentals in supporting data analytics, special mechanisms and features of applying principles of data analytics, application-oriented analytics, and target-area analytics.

Processing of terabytes to petabytes of data, or incorporating non-structural data and multi-structured data sources and types require advanced analytics and data science mechanisms for both raw and partially-processed information. Despite considerable advancements on high performance, large storage, and high computation power, there are challenges in identifying, clustering, classifying, and interpreting of a large spectrum of information.

The conference had the following tracks:

- Application-oriented analytics
- Big Data
- Sentiment/opinion analysis
- Data Analytics in Profiling and Service Design
- Fundamentals
- Mechanisms and features
- Predictive Data Analytics
- Transport and Traffic Analytics in Smart Cities

We take here the opportunity to warmly thank all the members of the DATA ANALYTICS 2019 technical program committee, as well as all the reviewers. The creation of such a high quality conference program would not have been possible without their involvement. We also kindly thank all the authors that dedicated much of their time and effort to contribute to DATA ANALYTICS 2019. We truly believe that, thanks to all these efforts, the final conference program consisted of top quality contributions.

We also gratefully thank the members of the DATA ANALYTICS 2019 organizing committee for their help in handling the logistics and for their work that made this professional meeting a success.

We hope that DATA ANALYTICS 2019 was a successful international forum for the exchange of ideas and results between academia and industry and to promote further progress in the field of data analytics. We also hope that Porto provided a pleasant environment during the conference and everyone saved some time to enjoy the historic charm of the city.

**DATA ANALYTICS 2019 Chairs**

**DATA ANALYTICS Steering Committee**
Sandjai Bhulai, Vrije Universiteit Amsterdam, the Netherlands
Dimitris K. Kardaras, Athens University of Economics and Business, Greece
Ivana Semanjski, Ghent University, Belgium / University of Zagreb, Croatia
Eiko Yoneki, University of Cambridge, UK
Andrew Rau-Chaplin, Dalhousie University, Canada
Rudolf Berrendorf, Bonn-Rhein-Sieg University, Germany
Les Sztandera, Philadelphia University, USA
Kerstin Lemke-Rust, Hochschule Bonn-Rhein-Sieg, Germany
Prabhat Mahanti, University of New Brunswick, Canada

**DATA ANALYTICS Industry/Research Advisory Committee**
Alain Crolotte, Teradata Corporation - El Segundo, USA
Tiziana Guzzo, National Research Council/Institute of Research on Population and Social Policies - Rome, Italy
Thomas Klemas, SimSpace Corporation, USA
George Tambouratzis, Institute for Language and Speech Processing - Athena Research Centre, Greece
Azad Naik, Microsoft, USA

# DATA ANALYTICS 2019

# COMMITTEE

**DATA ANALYTICS Steering Committee**
Sandjai Bhulai, Vrije Universiteit Amsterdam, the Netherlands
Dimitris K. Kardaras, Athens University of Economics and Business, Greece
Ivana Semanjski, Ghent University, Belgium / University of Zagreb, Croatia
Eiko Yoneki, University of Cambridge, UK
Andrew Rau-Chaplin, Dalhousie University, Canada
Rudolf Berrendorf, Bonn-Rhein-Sieg University, Germany
Les Sztandera, Philadelphia University, USA
Kerstin Lemke-Rust, Hochschule Bonn-Rhein-Sieg, Germany
Prabhat Mahanti, University of New Brunswick, Canada

**DATA ANALYTICS Industry/Research Advisory Committee**
Alain Crolotte, Teradata Corporation - El Segundo, USA
Tiziana Guzzo, National Research Council/Institute of Research on Population and Social Policies - Rome, Italy
Thomas Klemas, SimSpace Corporation, USA
George Tambouratzis, Institute for Language and Speech Processing - Athena Research Centre, Greece
Azad Naik, Microsoft, USA

**DATA ANALYTICS 2019 Technical Program Committee**

Mohd Helmy Abd Wahab, Universiti Tun Hussein Onn Malaysia, Malaysia
Bilal Abu Salih, Curtin University, Australia
Danial Aghajarian, Georgia State University, USA
Rajeev Agrawal, US Army Engineer Research and Development Center, USA
Ana Alves, University of Coimbra, Portugal
Ioannis Athanasiadis, Wageningen University, Netherlands
Cecilia Avila, Universitat de Girona, Spain / Corporación Tecnológica Industrial Colombiana – TEINCO, Colombia
Valerio Bellandi, Università degli Studio di Milano, Italy
Rudolf Berrendorf, Bonn-Rhein-Sieg University, Germany
Nik Bessis, Edge Hill University, UK
Sanjay Bhansali, Google, Mountain View, USA
Jabran Bhatti, Televic Rail NV, Belgium
Sandjai Bhulai, Vrije Universiteit Amsterdam, The Netherlands
Yaxin Bi, Ulster University, UK
Amar Budhiraja, IIIT-Hyderabad, India
Ozgu Can, Ege University, Turkey
Juan Vicente Capella Hernández, Universitat Politècnica de València, Spain
Darlinton Carvalho, Federal University of Sao Joao del-Rei (UFSJ), Brazil
Miguel Ceriani, Queen Mary University of London, UK
Julio Cesar Duarte, Military Institute of Engineering (IME), Brazil
Lijun Chang, University of New South Australia, Australia

Daniel B.-W. Chen, National Sun Yat-Sen University, Taiwan
Xi Chen, GEIRI North America, USA
Alain Crolotte, Teradata Corporation - El Segundo, USA
Ernesto William De Luca, Georg Eckert Institute, Germany
Corné de Ruijt, Endouble, Amsterdam, Netherlands
Varuna De-Silva, Loughborough University London, UK
Ma. del Pilar Angeles, Universidad Nacional Autonoma de Mexico, Mexico
Konstantinos Demertzis, Democritus University of Thrace, Greece
Damiano Di Franceco Maesa, Istituto di Informatica e Telematica - Consiglio Nazionale delle Ricerche (CNR), Pisa, Italy
Mohand Djeziri, Aix Marseille University (AMU), France
Atakan Dogan, Anadolu University, Turkey
Dmytro Dosyn, Karpenko Physico-Mechanical Institute of the Nas of Ukraine, Ukraine
Suleyman Eken, Kocaeli University, Turkey
Nadia Essoussi, University of Tunis - LARODEC laboratory, Tunisia
Muhammad Fahad, Centre Scientifique et Technique du Batiment CSTB (Sophia-Antipolis), France
Yixiang Fang, University of Hong Kong, Hong Kong
Panorea Gaitanou, Ionian University, Greece
Diego Galar, Luleå University of Technology, Sweden
Wensheng Gan, Harbin Institute of Technology, Shenzhen, China
Amir H Gandomi, Stevens Institute of Technology, USA
Tiantian Gao, Stony Brook University, USA
Catalina García García, Universidad de Granada, Spain
Filippo Gaudenzi, Università degli Studi di Milano, Italy
Felix Gessert, University of Hamburg, Germany
Ilias Gialampoukidis, Information Technologies Institute | Centre of Research & Technology - Hellas, Thessaloniki, Greece
Ana González-Marcos, Universidad de La Rioja, Spain
Gregor Grambow, Aalen University, Germany
Geraldine Gray, Technological University Dublin - Blanchardstown Campus, Ireland
Luca Grilli, Università degli Studi di Foggia, Italy
William Grosky, University of Michigan, USA
Jerzy Grzymala-Busse, University of Kansas - Lawrence, USA
Ruchir Gupta, IIITDM Jabalpur, India
Tiziana Guzzo, National Research Council/Institute of Research on Population and Social Policies - Rome, Italy
Mohamed Aymen Ben HajKacem, University of Tunis, Tunisia
Houcine Hassan, Universitat Politècnica de València, Spain
Felix Heine, Hannover University of Applied Sciences and Arts, Germany
Carlos Henggeler Antunes, INESCC | University of Coimbra, Portugal
Jean Hennebert, University of Applied Sciences HES-SO, Switzerland
Béat Hirsbrunner, University of Fribourg, Switzerland
Tzung-Pei Hong, National University of Kaohsiung, Taiwan
Babak Hosseini, CITEC - Bielefeld University, Germany
LiGuo Huang, Southern Methodist University, USA
Sergio Ilarri, University of Zaragoza, Spain
Olaf Jacob, Neu-Ulm University of Applied Sciences, Germany
Nandish Jayaram, Pivotal Software, USA

Zbigniew W. Ras, University of North Carolina, Charlotte, USA / Warsaw University of Technology, Poland / Polish-Japanese Academy of IT, Poland
Andrew Rau-Chaplin, Dalhousie University, Canada
Yenumula B. Reddy, Grambling State University, USA
Manjeet Rege, University of St. Thomas, USA
João Rocha da Silva, INESC TEC / FEUP-DEI, Portugal
Alessandro Rozza, Waynaut, Italy
Gunter Saake, Otto-von-Guericke-University Magdeburg, Germany
Anatoliy Sachenko, Ternopil National Economic University, Ukraine
Donatello Santoro, Università della Basilicata, Italy
Anni Sapountzi, Amsterdam Center of Learning Analytics - Vrije Universiteit, Netherlands
Anirban Sarkar, National Institute of Technology, Durgapur, India
Burcu Sayin, Izmir Institute of Technology, Turkey
Ivana Semanjski, Ghent University, Belgium / University of Zagreb, Croatia
Salman Ahmed Shaikh, University of Tsukuba, Japan
Piyush Sharma, Army Research Laboratory, USA
Sujala D. Shetty, Birla Institute of Technology & Science, Pilani, India
Rong Shi, Facebook, USA
Rouzbeh A. Shirvani, Howard University, USA
Leon Shyue-Liang Wang, National University of Kaohsiung, Taiwan
Jaya Sil, Indian Institute of Engineering Science and Technology, Shibpur, India
Josep Silva, Universitat Politècnica de València, Spain
Marek Śmieja, Jagiellonian University, Poland
Dora Souliou, National Technical University of Athens, Greece
María Estrella Sousa Vieira, University of Vigo, Spain
Christos Spandonidis, Prisma Electronics R&D, Greece
Les Sztandera, Philadelphia University, USA
George Tambouratzis, Institute for Language and Speech Processing, Athena, Greece
Mingjie Tang, Hortonworks, USA
Farhan Tauheed, Oracle research labs, Zurich, Switzerland
Marijn ten Thij, Vrije Universiteit Amsterdam, Netherlands
Ioannis G. Tollis, University of Crete, Greece / Tom Sawyer Software Inc., USA
Juan-Manuel Torres-Moreno, Université d'Avignon et des Pays de Vaucluse, France
Li-Shiang Tsay, North Carolina A&T State University, USA
Chrisa Tsinaraki, EU Joint Research Center - Ispra, Italy
Aditya Tulsyan, Massachusetts Institute of Technology, USA
Murat Osman Unalir, Ege University, Turkey
Roman Vaculin, IBM Research, USA
Genoveva Vargas-Solar, French Council of Scientific Research | LIG-LAFMIA, France
Sebastián Ventura, University of Cordoba, Spain
J. J. Villalobos, Rutgers Discovery Informatics Institute, USA
Sirje Virkus, Tallinn University, Estonia
Haibo Wang, Texas A&M International University, USA
Liqiang Wang, University of Central Florida, USA
Wolfram Wöß, Institute for Application Oriented Knowledge Processing | Johannes Kepler University, Linz, Austria
Yubao Wu, Georgia State University, USA
Eiko Yoneki, University of Cambridge, UK

Fouad Zablith, Olayan School of Business | American University of Beirut, Lebanon
Bo Zhang, Watson and Cloud Platform - IBM, USA
Yichuan Zhao, Georgia State University, USA
Angen Zheng, University of Pittsburgh, USA
Qiang Zhu, University of Michigan, USA

**Copyright Information**

# Improve Operations of Real-Time Image Classification Utilizing Machine Learning and Knowledge Evolution

David Prairie
*Electrical and Computer Engineering Dept.*
*University of Massachusetts Dartmouth*
Dartmouth, Massachusetts United States
Email: dprairie@umassd.edu

Paul Fortier
*Electrical and Computer Engineering Dept.*
*University of Massachusetts Dartmouth*
Dartmouth, Massachusetts United States
Email: pfortier@umassd.edu

*Abstract*—**This paper delves into the generation and use of image classification models in a real-time environment utilizing machine learning. The ImageAI framework is used to generate a list of models from a set of training images and also for classifying new images using the generated models. Through this paper, previous research projects and industry programs are analyzed for design and operation. The basic implementation results in models that classify new images correctly the majority of the time with a high level of confidence. However, almost a quarter of the time the models classify images incorrectly. This paper attempts to improve the classification accuracy and improve the operational efficiency of the overall system as well.**

*Index Terms*—**Machine Learning, Tensor Flow, Image Classification**

## I. INTRODUCTION

Presented in this research paper is a new and novel approach to machine learning design that maximizes the balance between accuracy, efficiency, solution justification, and rule evolution. This research attempts to improve four factors of machine learning within a single design. Different components of the system design shall aim to improve one of the four factors compared to traditional designs. During this research, traditional open source machine learning methodologies are altered to improve different aspects of machine learning, tested against one application. These traditional methodologies will be integrated using ensemble methods for enhancing the performance along with providing justifications for the classification results. This paper will discuss the preliminary results, data used, the analysis, and validation methodologies used.

During this research the Identifiable Professionals (IdenProf) Dataset was used for training and validating models. The dataset contains ten image sets of distinguishable professions, each set containing 900 images for training and 200 images for validation per profession. The expected outcome of this research is a two part system capable of analyzing a real-time feed and perform profession classification based on a remotely generated model.

This paper is broken up into a Background section, where high-level aspects of machine learning and knowledge-bases will be discussed. The Methodology will be discussed following the Background section. Following the Methodology section the preliminary results will be discussed in the Data Analytics and Results sections. Finally the conclusion will discuss planned future work and recommended further work.

## II. BACKGROUND

Knowledge base systems enable problems to be quickly and accurately solved based on previous cases. Knowledge base systems also allow for problem solving of very complex situations at speeds humans alone would not be able to achieve at such accuracies. Throughout the last 20 years, knowledge bases have grown in applications to assist in everyday tasks. More recently, IBM's Watson, an Artificial intelligence supercomputer, is in the limelight through its uses in the medical arena and in personal taxes with H&R Block. Other applications of machine learning have been completed or are being developed include detecting insider threats, big data analytics, market analysis for proposals, condition-based maintenance, and diagnostics in the medical field.

In the medical industry, Watson has proven capable of making the same recommended treatment plans as doctors 99% of the time. Unlike traditional human doctors, Watson can use all available medical resources when making a patient's diagnosis. By having such vast amounts of knowledge, Watson can provide treatment options doctors may miss. Watson utilizes powerful algorithms and immense computing resources to analyze all medical relevant data to find "... treatment options human doctors missed in 30 percent of the cases." [2] Since Watson has so much computing power it is able to determine treatment plans for patients faster than human doctors could, allowing doctors to put patients on treatments faster with the intervention of Watson. Watson is one example of how knowledge base systems positively benefit society by efficient and accurate problem solving of complex problems. Additional research into knowledge bases will allow them to problem solve faster, with more accuracy, and with less compute power requirements.

Condition-Based Maintenance is the method of monitoring a system's components to determine what level of maintenance is required for the system to remain functioning. Using a Condition-Based Maintenance system for managing maintenance events allows professionals to be proactive with performing maintenance activities versus being reactive. Reactive maintenance involves replacing components after they already failed, causing system downtime. When a system goes down for unscheduled maintenance or repairs, many different repercussions can occur depending on the affected system's role. Using air traffic control centers as an example, any unplanned downtime has the potential to disrupt hundreds of flights and cost a significant amount of money due to flight delays [11]. Machine learning can be used to assist professionals to determine optimal maintenance schedules while minimizing system down time.

Although some of the described applications may not be as drastic as life or death medical decisions, all still can greatly affect society. Utilizing machine learning allows organizations to detect threats, conduct predictive maintenance, and perform many repeatable decision-making tasks consistently and efficiently. By allowing a machine to learn over time through historical cases and building a knowledge base, the machine allows operators to make informed decisions by providing every available piece of information. Systems are able to make decisions in a fraction of the time compared to a human expert attempting to come to the same decision, however additional advancement is needed to make machine learning more accurate and efficient. Areas needing additional inquiries include indexing algorithms, storage solutions, and finally the decision-making algorithms themselves. Machine learning is important because of the wide range of applications and benefits provided through the decision making and predictions capable. As the field advances, machines will create predictions and perform decision making faster and more completely.

### A. *Deep Learning Frameworks - Tensor Flow*

Tensor Flow is a deep learning framework built on the first generation framework called DistBelief. Both frameworks were developed by Google to advance technology for the public and for use in Google's wide range of data products [13]. One of TensorFlow's major improvements over DistBelief is its ability to scale up onto large distributed hardware platforms utilizing multiple CPUs and GPUs. Tensor Flow utilizes a master orchestrator to distribute work across the number of hardware platforms available, each individual platform then breaks the work down to be solved across each system's available CPUs and GPUs.

Benchmarks conducted by Google researchers showed the Tensor Flow framework performs, as well as other popular training libraries. However, Tensor Flow did not have the best performance statistics as other libraries in the study when tested on a single machine platform

### B. *Rule Evolution IB1 & IB2 Algorithms*

The IB1 and IB2 algorithms are used to evolve a system's rules used for classification by incorporating new cases. The addition of more instances over time causes the machine to alter its rules to improve the probability of giving a correct prediction on future instances. Instances can either enforce existing rules or go against existing rules. Over the course of a training period, the IB1 algorithm will converge to the actual results based on altering its rules. IB1 requires data to have specific attributes, making cases distinct enough for the algorithm to learn over time. If the data does not have distinct attributes then the machine will not learn, since no strong points of comparison are available between cases [1].

A downside of the IB1 algorithm is the need to store all correct and incorrect classifications over the lifetime of the machine. The IB2 algorithm is a branch of the IB1 algorithm that does not require the storage of all classifications, only the incorrect classifications. The trade off of saving storage space is the increase in time required for the IB2 algorithm to learn to predict with strong accuracy [1].

During the evaluation of both the IB1 and IB2 algorithms, researchers determined both algorithms are able to achieve acceptable prediction accuracies in some situations. However, IB1 attains greater accuracies on each scenario when compared to the IB2 algorithm. The increase in accuracy for IB1 could be attributed to the storing of all classification events versus only the incorrect classifications.

## III. Methodology/Theory

This section discusses the methodology used in the completion of this research. The research processed followed the system engineering v-diagram during development. This section is further broken into a system architecture and software architecture sections.

### A. *System Architecture*

The implementation, which is shown in Figure 1, is broken into four sections; a workstation computer, web server, raspberry pi, and a shared storage box. The workstation computer contains a NVidia GTX 980ti and is used for generating models based on the training images. Once the models are generated they are stored on a centralized shared storage array. The raspberry pi is used as the real-time image capture device and performs classifications utilizing the models.

The web server is the middle point between the workstation and the raspberry pi, by serving the models generated for the Pi to download. To enable future learning from real imaging, the Pi will upload classified images to the web server for the Desktop to use in future model generation.

### B. *Software Architecture*

The following software packages and frameworks are used to generate the models for real-time image classifications and for classifying new images:

- Python 3.6
- Tensorflow-GPU
- Numpy
- SciPy
- OpenCV
- Pillow
- Matplotlib
- H5py

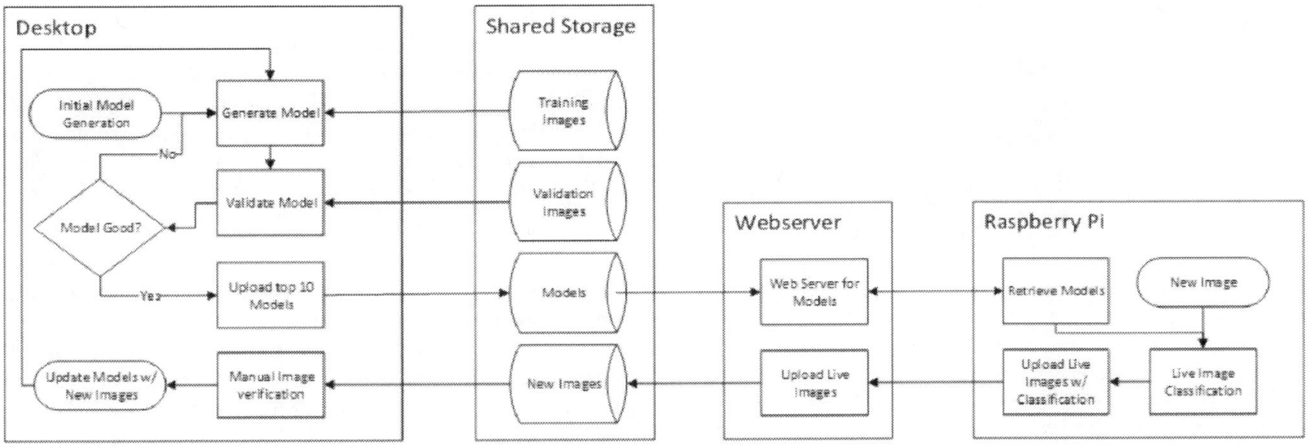


Fig. 1. System Flow Diagram.

- Keras
- ImageAI [10]

ImageAI is an API that can generate models based on an image set and perform image classifications based on the generated models. The API can generate models using the Desenet, Inveption v3, Resnet, and Squeezenet algorithms.

The workstation utilizes the above listed software when generating the initial models used for classification. ImageAI is a wrapper framework for the rest of the libraries, simplifying the development process. The same ImageAI framework is used on the raspberry pi for real-time image classification utilizing an add-on camera board. The raspberry pi is capable of handling the classification algorithms because the model generation and model evolution is offloaded to the workstation [9]. This heavily reduces the compute requirements, enabling the mobile real-time classification.

The web server is a repository for the raspberry pi to retrieve the latest generated models and to upload classified images for further analysis. Real-time images are uploaded to the webserver for manual verification of the image's classification and are then loaded into the desktop as additional training images to evolve the models. The combination of the Desktop and Raspberry Pi enables an overall system supporting model evolution while increasing the efficiency of the real-time classifier [9].

A future implementation adds a system capability of justifying the classifications provided. The current design behind the justification uses the built in confidence levels provided when classifying images. An alternative approach includes providing sample images that were classified using the same models and produced the same results.

## IV. Data Analytics

During this research, the Identifiable Professionals (IdenProf) dataset [14] is used for evaluating the proposed changes to the ImageAI algorithm. IdenProf contains 10 distinguishable professions, listed in Table I. The dataset consists of over 900 images per profession used for training the system's models and an additional 200 images per profession for validating the models. All images are sized to a common pixel dimensions of 224 by 224 for uniformity. The image set has a make up of mostly white males from the top 15 most populated countries [14], compared to other genders or nationalities. During the duration of this research project additional images can be gathered by pulling images from Google's search engine.

TABLE I. Training Images Classifications

| Training Images Classifications | |
|---|---|
| **Profession** | **Accuracy** |
| Chef | 74.5% |
| Doctor | 76.5% |
| Engineer | 86.0% |
| Farmer | 89.5% |
| Firefighter | 90.5% |
| Judge | 92.0% |
| Mechanic | 84.5% |
| Pilot | 87.5% |
| Police | 87.5% |
| Waiter | 72.0% |

Current experiments include testing the base algorithms against the training and validation images. These 200 images will allow analysis and validation of the models generated at all three stages of development. Additional experiments will be planned utilizing the raspberry pi and camera for real-time image classification. The models used in classifications are selected based on the assigned accuracy defined during model generation. For these experiments the models select have over eighty percent accuracy.

Figure 2 depicts one of the test images for a pilot, one of the professions used in this research project. When running a classification against image, the system provides three results. Each result comes with a probability that the answer is correct. Typically the models generate one answer with a probability of over 95% and then the remaining two answers will make up the remaining percentage. In this case, the following probabilities are produced when classifying Figure 2: Pilot: 99.9527%, Chef: 0.0457%, and Mechanic: 0.0015%.

Fig. 2. Sample Profession Image - Pilot

## V. RESULTS

Initial runs for the system produced expected results, as shown in "Table I". Two professions to take note of are the Chef and Waiter. From reviewing the Chef and Waiter images, there are many images where its difficult to distinguish which profession the image is of. Incorporating additional models for classification and using a voting scheme (described in the next section) could produce more accurate classifications.

When reviewing the model's perceived accuracy on classification, the top profession is consistently listed as 95% or higher. This shows although the models are not able to reach the correct classification every time, the model produces a high level of certainty on the correct answer. When reviewing the raw data, a pattern arose showing when the models classified an image incorrectly, the probability produced tends to be significantly lower.

## VI. CONCLUSION

At this stage in development the system has only been implemented using base algorithms and libraries with no other design improvements. The next step in development is to implement a voting scheme where the system will utilize multiple generated models to classify new images. Then the system will use the prediction from multiple models and use a voting method incorporating the model probability to determine a classification. The voting result is not necessary equal votes per model, the votes can be based on the model's confidence in the answer the individual model is providing. For instance, if one model has a 98% confidence in the answer provided and the second model only has a 80% confidence, then chances are the first model would be the better of the two results to go with.

Upon completing the accuracy improvements, the system implementation will be broken up into the same format discussed in Figure 1. Currently the implementation has all model generation and model validation being conducted locally on Desktop. This is done to simplify the process, while ensuring the base algorithms are operating correctly. Once the remaining design are implemented a deeper system analysis will be completed. The analysis will include determining the reliability of the overall system and determining the theoretical versus actual efficiency of the algorithm.

Beyond the implementations and the analysis, additional work should be done collecting real-time images. The majority of the images used in this research project are collected from international researchers. A collection of images from additional countries, like the United States or United Kingdom, should be done to see if models are capable of classifying images correctly from other nations. This can also incorporate utilizing the raspberry pi at an event or walking around in pubic to do real-time classifications.

This research project attempts to incorporate common open source algorithms to enable real-time image classification using minimal processing power. By enabling the system to operate on minimal processing power at the user level, the system can be applied to new applications without relying on massive compute infrastructures at the endpoint. The base algorithms used will be modified to increase the operational efficiency and accuracy of the overall system.

The end result of this project can be applied to applications, such as security checkpoints or even used for field classifying insects and animals. As each component is implemented into the overall design, systems analysis for efficiency and reliability will be conducted to ensure the system is improving.

## REFERENCES


[1] D. Aha, D. Kibler and M. Albert, "Instance-Based Learning Algorithms," Machine Learning, vol. 6, no. 1, pp. 37-66, 1991

[2] D. Galeon, "Paging Dr. Watson," 28 October 2016. [Online]. Available: https://futurism.com/ibms-watson-ai-recommends-same-treatment-as-doctors-in-99-of-cancer-cases/. [Accessed 22 February 2019].

[3] Dtex Systems, "The Hidden Security Threat," Dtex Systems, 2016. [Online]. Available: https://dtexsystems.com/portfolio-items/infographic-findings-from-the-2016-costs-of-insider-threats-report/. [Accessed 21 March 2019].

[4] Q. Althebyan and B. Panda, "A Knwoledge-Base Model for Insider Threat Prediction," Proceedings of the 2007 IEEE Workshop on Information Assurance, vol. June, pp. 20-22, 2007.

[5] P. Bakkum and K. Skadron, "Accelerating SQL Database Operations on a CPU with CUDA," University of Virginia, Charlottesville, 2010.

[6] J. Jean, G. Dong, H. Zhang, X. Guo and B. Zhang, "Query Processing with An FPGA Coprocessor Board," in Proceedings of the International Conference on Engineering and Reconfigurable Systems and Algorithms, 2001.

[7] Martín Abadi et al, "TensorFlow: A System for Large-Scale Machine Learning," in 12th USENIX Symposium on Operating Systems Design, Savannah, 2016.

[8] D. Patil and P. Jayantrao. "Malicious URLs Detection Using Decision Tree Classifiers and Majority Voting Technique." Cybernetics and Information Technologies. 18. 11-29. 10.2478/cait-2018-0002.

[9] S. Jain, "How to easily Detect Objects with Deep Learning on Raspberry Pi", medium.com, Mar. 20, 2018. [Online]. Available: https://medium.com/nanonets/how-to-easily-detect-objects-with-deep-learning-on-raspberrypi-225f29635c74. [Accessed May. 11, 2019].

[10] DeepQuest AI, "Official English Documentation for ImageAI!" DeepQuest AI. [Online]. Available: https://imageai.readthedocs.io/en/latest/. [Accessed: Feb. 11, 2019].

[11] C. Nichols, "How many flights come in and out of LAX every day?," Los Angeles Magazine, 1 May 2011. [Online]. Available: http://www.lamag.com/askchris/how-many-flights-come-in-and-out-of-lax-every1/. [Accessed Mar. 20, 2018].

[12] Homeland Security, "Combating the Insider Threat," Homeland Security, 2014.

[13] Google, "Tensor Flow" Google, [Online]. Available: https://www.tensorflow.org/. [Accessed Apr. 20, 2019]

[14] M. Olafenwa, "IdenProf Datasheet" Olafenwa, [Online]. Available: https://github.com/OlafenwaMoses. [Accessed Mar. 16, 2019]

# Johann Sebastian Bach's Music is Speeding Up: Fake News?

David van Erkelens

Information Studies
Institute for Informatics
University of Amsterdam
Email: d.vanerkelens@student.uva.nl

Daan van den Berg

Minor Programmeren
Institute for Informatics
University of Amsterdam
Email: d.vandenberg@uva.nl

***Abstract*—This study in cultural informatics investigates the claim made in 2018 by several news media that performances of Johann Sebastian Bach's *Double Concerto in D Minor*, his compositions in general, and of classical music as a whole are becoming ever faster. Data for a total number of 19,660 releases in five of Bach's compositional categories from between 1950 and 2019 are retrieved from online database Discogs, of which 2,999 are analyzed historically for speed increase. For the Double Concerto, we do find a slight speedup, but surprisingly enough, West European recordings speed up much more than non-West European recordings. And whereas the *Brandenburg Concertos* and several cantatas do speed up significantly, the Trio Sonatas for Organ and Suites for Cello Solo actually tend to *slow down*. We review the original claims in light of this new evidence, and contextualize our findings by relating to studies on musical development, the pace of life in urbanized communities, and begin to construct a scientific hypothesis for explaining our findings.**

***Keywords*–Music; Tempo; Violin Concerto; BWV 1043; Bach; Data Analysis; Online Data Retrieval; Fake News.***

## I. Introduction

Johann Sebastian Bach (1685-1750) is undoubtedly one of most revered classical composers in our time. Spanning nearly 1100 compositions ranging from huge oratoria such as the *Saint Matthew Passion, BWV 244* through *Brandenburg Concertos, BWV 1046 - 1051* to works as small as the *Sonatas and Partitas, BWV 1001 - 1006* written for a single violin only, many regard these works as the best that classical music has to offer. Today, all of Bach's compositions have been conventiently indexed by a BWV (Bach-Werke-Verzeichnis, literally *Bach works catalogue*) numbering, categorizing the late master's work in different genres like cantatas, concertos, or harpsichord works. But the details of everyday performance are not undisputed; many classical compositions have separate *movements*, which are often annotated with a 'tempo' or 'style' indication. Traditionally, in Italian (even for German composers), annotations, such as *presto* ('rapidly'), *adagio* ('slowly'), *vivace* ('lively') and *allegro* ('cheerful') leave plenty of room for interpretation on behalf of the musician (see Figure 1).

Late 2018, several news articles appeared claiming that the compositions of Bach, and classical music in general, are being performed ever faster. First published by the *Rolling Stone*, the article featured a record label's study showing "performances of Bach are almost 30 percent faster than they were 50 years ago" [1]. From there, the news spread like wildfire. An article on *iNews - Britains Most Trusted Digital News Brand* claimed that "performances of classical music [...] are now one third quicker than they were 50 years ago" [2]. They also cite a highly positioned music scholar when giving an explanation: "It's a basic change in taste from the rather weighty concert style of previous years towards something that is more light, airy and flexible." Or, as the international radio station *Classic FM* so aptly phrased it: "classical music performances are taken at a greater lick" [3]. Even more confident was broadcaster *WQXR*, stating that "Bach is undoubtedly getting faster" and like Rolling Stone, they also provide an explanation for the speedup: "Society speeds up? Music speeds up." But even research institutions like the *Smithsonian Institution*, administered by the US Government, reported the news [4]. "Johann Sebastian Bach's music may be timeless, but [...] even the compositions of [Bach] are not immune to todays breakneck speed of life." and "Clock the last 40 years and you'll find the beat getting relentlessly faster."

So Bach's music, or classical music in general, is speeding up because life is speeding up. Interesting find, but the problem is that it isn't true. Or partially, at best. Or for some recordings of some concertos released at some places only, to be precise. The news published by *Classic FM*, *WQXR* and *Smithsonian* all refer back to Rolling Stone, which appears to be the source of the news, but the lack of (academic) references, the apparently thin basis for the conclusions (three recordings of Bach's *Double Violin Concerto in D Minor, BWV 1043*) and the seemingly reckless adoption of the news by other media raises questions about the scientific validity of the claims. Is Bach's music really speeding up lately, or is this another prime example of *fake news*?

*Fake news* is a denomination that has seen a rapid increase since the 2016 United States presidential election, even though it conceptually existed long before [5]. Historically, the term has been used to describe disinformation serving different goals than objective reporting, such as political gains or social unrest. In the ages of digitization, fake news seems to find its way to people much easier, with visits to fake news sites originating from social media at a much higher rate than visits to real news sites [6]. It is estimated that in the months prior to the 2016 U.S. elections, every American adult had been exposed to at least one fake news story [7].

Even though fake news only reaches a small part of the overall audience [6] [8], Facebook and other social media started tagging and removing fake news in order to combat the distribution of mis- and disinformation [9]. Despite these efforts, scientists Gordon Pennycook and David Rand found that tagging fake news stories creates an *implied truth effect*:

Figure 1. **Left:** the only known genuine portrait German composer of J.S. Bach, painted by E.G Haussmann. **Middle:** cutouts from the manuscript of Bach's Double Violin Concerto show tempo indications "Vivace" ("lively") and "Allegro" ("cheerful") which leave plenty of room for interpretation. **Right:** the article from Rolling Stone claiming enormous speedups in performances of Bach's work (image edited for size purposes).

once a story is *not* tagged as fake news, it is more likely to be deemed reliable [10]. An earlier study at McMaster University found that a statement, whether true or false, is more likely to be believed if it expresses information that 'feels familiar' [11]. But repetition also results in something like an implied truth effect: in an experiment by Frederick Bacon, people were given a number of statements and told that half of these were false. Even with this explicit aforehand instruction, people rated the repeated statements to be more reliable [12]. In Danielle Polage's experiment "Making up History: False Memories of Fake News Stories", half of the subjects were given a fake news story to read [13]. Five weeks later, the exposed subjects did not only find it to be more believable than the control group, but they were even more likely to believe that they actually heard the story from a source *outside* of the experiment. But most famous in this context might be the groundbreaking work by American psychologist Elizabeth Loftus. Her team has done extensive research on 'false memories', and found that people's recollection of an episode might be corrupted even from hearing disinformation afterwards [14]. These studies collectively show that human memory is dynamic, susceptible to disinformation, and can easily integrate fake news as genuine facts – even to the extent of one's personal history.

Regrettably though, efforts of verification seldomly find their way to the audience most susceptible to fake news [8]. Fact checking, dismissing false claims and disposing of mis- and disinformation are at the core of scientific practice. It is therefore hard to overstate the shock that went through the academic world when Dutch social psychologist Diederik Stapel was found to have engaged in large scale fact fraud, and as of 2019, almost 60 of his publications have been retracted [15] [16]. Since then, verification and the replicability of research is seriously gaining traction, as witnessed in the expansive work described in a publication by 24 authors reproducing 21 social science studies from *Nature* and *Science* [17]. But also economic disciplines do not escape scrutiny and more recently, even famous computer science experiments are being rigorously replicated, and even extended [18] [19]. An interesting related development is the observation by Sacha Epskamp from University of Amsterdam, that shows fast-paced development of methodological developments and software implementations might both facilitate and undermine replicability [20]. Though Epskamp does not explicitly quantify the term 'fast-paced', it is an interesting observation that the pace of development appears to be speeding up in scientific replicability too.

With a much more light-hearted objective, we aim to contribute to the practice of fact finding by checking whether Bach's Double Violin Concerto is indeed being performed at an ever faster pace, such as reported by Rolling Stone and others. We will also investigate the more general claim that Bach's other compositions (or indeed all classical music) are speeding up by analyzing his other two Violin Concertos, the six Brandenburg Concertos, six well-known cantatas, the six Trio Sonatas for Organ and the six Suites for Cello Solo. Together, these categories cover a broad variety of compositions with variations in ensemble sizes, instrumentations and 'compositional details', such as polyphony, the number of movements, and whether dedicated to liturgical service or attaining a more secular occasion. We retrieve data for a total of 19,660 Bach recordings released between 1950 and 2019 and analyze the historical development of their duration.

The rest of this paper is organized as follows: in Section II, the methods for retrieving and analyzing the releases of Bach's works are detailed. The results of this analysis are presented in Section III, where we also discuss possible explanations for the found results. Finally, the conclusions of our research are laid out in Section IV.

## II. Methods

The growth of the Internet and public availability of data is both a blessing and a curse for scientists. *Discogs* is a community-driven online database owned by Zink Media

TABLE I. THE NUMBER OF RELEASES IN THE DATA SET RETRIEVED FROM DISCOGS ('TOTAL') AND AFTER FILTERING ('USED') FOR EACH COMPOSITION IN THIS STUDY.

| | Composition | Total | Used | Percentage |
|---|---|---|---|---|
| Violin | BWV1041 | 893 | 149 | 16.685% |
| | BWV1042 | 901 | 149 | 16.537% |
| | BWV1043 | 1120 | 169 | 15.089% |
| Brandenburg | BWV1046 | 1008 | 227 | 22.520% |
| | BWV1047 | 1279 | 284 | 22.205% |
| | BWV1048 | 1257 | 275 | 21.877% |
| | BWV1049 | 1019 | 223 | 21.884% |
| | BWV1050 | 1116 | 263 | 23.566% |
| | BWV1051 | 911 | 205 | 22.503% |
| Cantatas | BWV106 | 918 | 34 | 3.703% |
| | BWV131 | 414 | 28 | 6.763% |
| | BWV140 | 756 | 45 | 5.952% |
| | BWV170 | 309 | 24 | 7.767% |
| | BWV173 | 549 | 10 | 1.821% |
| | BWV208 | 525 | 6 | 1.143% |
| Organ Trio S. | BWV525 | 713 | 61 | 8.555% |
| | BWV526 | 410 | 47 | 11.463% |
| | BWV527 | 346 | 47 | 13.584% |
| | BWV528 | 684 | 53 | 7.749% |
| | BWV529 | 368 | 54 | 14.674% |
| | BWV530 | 462 | 53 | 11.472% |
| Cello Suites | BWV1007 | 748 | 110 | 14.706% |
| | BWV1008 | 514 | 99 | 19.261% |
| | BWV1009 | 635 | 102 | 16.063% |
| | BWV1010 | 520 | 89 | 17.115% |
| | BWV1011 | 635 | 100 | 15.748% |
| | BWV1012 | 650 | 93 | 14.308% |

containing more than 11 million Digital Data Locations (DDL) for audio recordings such as CD's, vinyl, digital bootlegs and promotional releases [21]. It is publicly accessible and offers an open Application Programming Interface (API), which can be used to query the database, making it suitable for quantitative analysis of historical releases [22]. Since Discogs offers a large quantity of different types of recordings, this source forms a valid representation of recordings from this era.

In order to retrieve the DDLs from Discogs, a search query is first sent to the API containing a search term (e.g., *"BWV 1043"*) which then returns a list of DDLs. Each DDL contains a pointer to the information from exactly one release, which can then be downloaded separately to obtain details about the recording.

Since Discogs is widely accessible without central moderation, the retrieved data might be invalid, incorrect or incomplete. One can therefore hardly escape the laborious task of manually sifting through the data returned by the API after issuing a query. To be suitable for analysis, the DDL has to meet three requirements:

- The DDL's data must include a **year** of release;
- The DDL's data must contain the **entire work**, and not just a single movement;
- Every used track in the DDL's data must contain a valid value in their **duration** field.

In order to (in)validate the results research reported by the various news media from Section I, we retrieved a total of 1120 releases from between 1958 and 2018 of Bach's Double Violin Concerto. After manually filtering the DDLs, 169 valid, complete and correct data records were used for linear regression, plotting duration against year of release (see Table I). The applied method is as follows: for dataset $D$, containing the DDLs with their years of release $x$ and associated durations $y$, a straight line

$$f(x) = a \cdot x + b \tag{1}$$

is fitted, where $x$ denotes the year for which the fit is calculated. Values for $a$ and $b$ are calculated by

$$a = \frac{\sum_{i\in D}((x_i - mean(\mathbf{x}) \cdot (y_i - mean(\mathbf{y}))}{\sum_{i\in D}((x_i - mean(\mathbf{x}))^2)} \tag{2}$$

$$b = mean(\mathbf{y}) - a \cdot mean(\mathbf{x}). \tag{3}$$

For the Double Violin Concerto, the three movements (*Vivace, Largo ma non tanto* and *Allegro*) were also analyzed separately. To compare results to Bach's other two violin concertos, 893 and 901 releases for *BWV 1041 and BWV 1042* from between 1955 and 2018 were retrieved, from which 149 and 149 suitable data records were analyzed in similar fashion (see Table III).

Widening the scope, we extended the investigation to four more compositional categories, some of which are very different from the violin concertos. The second category, the six *Brandenburg Concertos, BWV 1046 - 1051* are compositions of ensemble sizes comparable tot the violin concertos, but with very different instrumentations including oboes, fagottos, trumpets, horns and "echo flutes". For this category, we retrieved 6590 DDLs of which 1477 (equalling 22.41%) were usable after manually filtering the data.

Third was a collection of six popular cantatas (BWV 106, 131, 140, 170, 173 and 208), compositions that involve vocal soloists, duets and choirs. Though ensemble sizes can vary considerably from one recording to the next, cantatas are usually performed by significantly more musicians than both the violin and Brandenburg concertos. This specific selection of cantatas was partially enforced by the Discogs API which does not facilitate prefix free queries, and by the number of DDLs available for each cantata, which might reflect its popularity (see Table I). Although very many of the retrieved cantata DDLs contained a value for 'year', very few of those also had a value for 'duration', thereby still resulting in high dismissal; of 3471 retrieved DDLs, only 147 yielded suitable data, a mere 4.24%.

The fourth category was made up by the six *Trio Sonatas for Organ, BWV 525 - 530*. Although performed by only one musician, Bach's organ compositions can be considered to be of 'near-equal complexity' to his concertos; in fact, organ-solo arrangements exist for several of Bach's concertos, including BWV 1043. For this category, we retrieved 2983 DDLs of which 315 were usable after filtering, corresponding to a post-filter usability of 10.56%.

The fifth and final category is made up by data records for the six *Cello Suites, BWV 1007 - 1012*. These works, written for a single cellist only, largely consist of isolated melody lines accompanied by the accidental harmonization. Though Bach somehow managed to weave a sophisticated polyphonic style even in these sparse compositions, they are undoubtedly belong to the 'smallest' of Bach's works. This category holds

TABLE II. THE NUMBER OF RELEASES PER CONTINENT FOR EACH OF THE VIOLIN CONCERTOS BWV 1041 & 1042, AND THE DOUBLE CONCERTO BWV 1043.

| Composition | Continent | Number of releases |
|---|---|---|
| BWV1041 | West-Europe | 119 |
| | East-Europe | 9 |
| | North America | 12 |
| | Australia | 3 |
| | Asia | 1 |
| | South America | 1 |
| | Unknown | 4 |
| BWV1042 | West-Europe | 114 |
| | East-Europe | 8 |
| | North America | 17 |
| | Australia | 4 |
| | Asia | 1 |
| | South America | 1 |
| | Unknown | 4 |
| BWV1043 | West-Europe | 126 |
| | East-Europe | 5 |
| | North America | 25 |
| | Australia | 3 |
| | Asia | 3 |
| | South America | 2 |
| | Unknown | 5 |

593 data points after filtering, which corresponds to 16.02% of 3702 retrieved DDLs.

A subset of the retrieved entries from the filtered data set contained a value in the "country" field, indicating where the release was originally issued. Even though many individual countries are too thinly represented for significant analysis, collectively the values might provide some additional insight into our data (see Table II). We separately analyzed the West European releases, and categorized all others as either non-West European or 'unknown'. Finally, all data used for the calculations in this section has been made publicly available for reproduction, replication and further investigation of our results [23].

## III. Results and Discussion

From the analysis as reported in Section II, it appears out that the reported speedup of the Double Violin Concerto contains a grain of truth, be it a tiny one. With a 5.31% decrease in duration over 169 recordings from between 1958 and 2018, performances of the work have indeed sped up slightly in the past 60 years (see Table III). This effect is not confined to any single one of its movements, with the duration of the *Vivace* decreasing by 5.09%, the *Largo* decreasing by 3.63% and the final *Allegro* movement decreasing by 8.45%. The speedup of this concerto however, is much more prominent in West European releases (10.74%) than in non-West European releases (4.85%) (see Figure 2). But the pattern is not entirely uniform across the violin concertos as a category. Although like the Double Concerto, recordings of the *Violin Concerto in E Major, BWV 1042* sped up, by an average of 7.40% between 1955 and 2018, recordings the *Violin Concerto in A Minor, BWV 1041* are actually *slowing down* on average, with a duration increase of 0.40% over the same period.

The Brandenburg Concertos are the only category in this investigation which have consistently been speeding up in recent history. But whereas the recordings of all concertos show a decrease in duration between 1953 and 2018, there are significant differences between the individual concertos, with BWV 1048 showing a double-digit decrease in duration and BWV 1047 a mere 3.19%. But in this category too, the speedup appears to be mainly a West European phenomenon, with two of the concertos slowing down in non-West European releases. The six cantatas of this study show a rather eccentric pattern; although BWV 106, 131, 140 and especially BWV 173 show significant speedups, the other two (BWV 170 and 208) show a moderate slowdown in the period from 1957 to 2018.

Quite contrarily to the Violin and Brandenburg Concertos, recordings of the Trio Sonatas for Organ have slowed down considerably around the world. Showing an average increase in duration of 7.15% between 1950 and 2018, the only outlier in this category is BWV 529, which shows a slight decrease of 3.98% in duration. Similarly, the Cello Suites have also slowed down up in recent history. On average, the duration recordings of these works have increased by 3.30%. Here, only BWV 1008 shows a decrease in duration of 8.29%, whereas BWV 1012 slowed down 10.87%. Moreover, the only speedups of these works are found in West European recordings; the rest of the world is actually slowing down.

The geographical origin of the releases appears to be an important indicator for its tempo development. Of the 27 compositions we analyzed, 18 compositions (66.6%) have increased in speed of performance in West European releases. However, the non-West European releases of the same 27 compositions, less than half (13 performances, 48.1%) could be confirmed speeding up. Three cantatas have insufficient non-European data though; excluding these brings the total to 13 out of 24 (54.2%). These numbers give rise to the interesting question if (or why) the speedups and slowdowns are related to the specific location, demographic or culture in which a release is being issued. But still, even for the works with the largest speedup across all categories in this investigation, cantata *"Erhöhtes Fleisch und Blut", BWV 173*, the decline in duration (18.39%) is nowhere near the 30% figure reported by the Rolling Stone and others.

The root of the difference might be the sparsity of the source data. The findings as presented by Rolling Stone were based on just three releases of BWV 1043: the version by David & Igor Oistrakh (1961, 17:15), one by Arthur Grumiaux & Herman Krebbers (1978, 15:42) and most recently Nemanja Radulovic & Tijana Milosevic (2016, 12:34), indeed showing a 27.06% decrease in duration. However, if we cherry pick three different releases from Discogs roughly covering the same era (Milstein & Morini (1965, 15:40), Suske & Kröhner (1980, 16:42), Menuhin & Oistrakh (2016, 18:41)), the duration actually shows an *increase* of 19.19%. So, it seems that a set of three data points is simply too small for any definitive conclusions.

Music is changing though. A paper by Serra et al. [24] studied contemporary popular music between 1955 and 2010 using the Million Song Dataset [25]. By analyzing pitch, loudness and timbre, the researchers conclude that contemporary popular music develops towards less variety in pitch transitions and a more uniform timbre. Especially the loudness of pop songs has increased between 1965 and 2005, a trend which is sometimes dubbed the "loudness war, a terminology that is used to describe the apparent competition to release recordings with increasing loudness, perhaps with the aim of catching potential customers attention" [24].

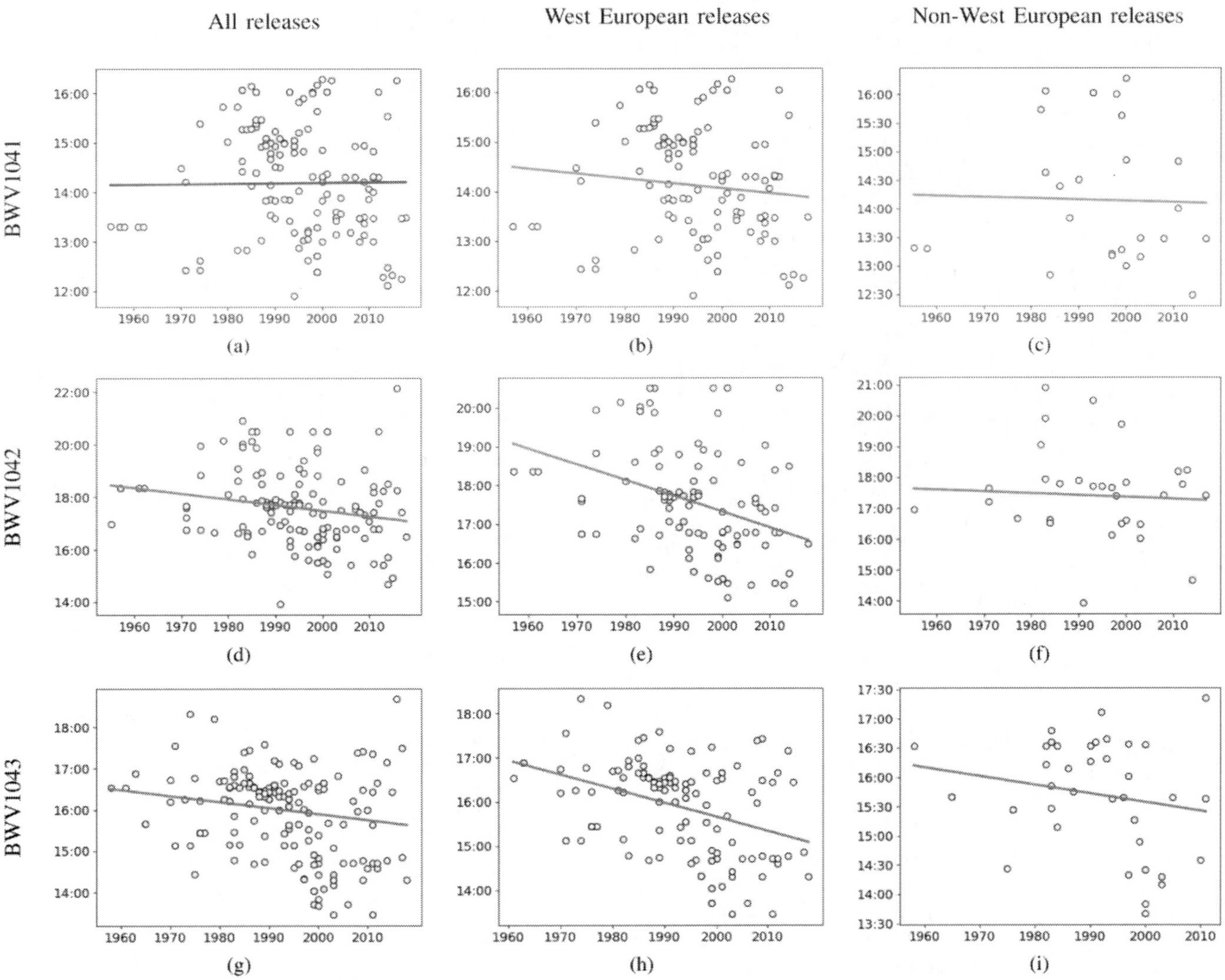


Figure 2. Speed development in Bach's (Double) Violin Concertos over the period 1955 - 2018. Generally speaking, both for the Double Concerto (Figures 2g, 2h and 2i) and the Violin Concerto in E Major (Figures 2d, 2e and 2f), newer releases tend to be faster, but the effect is much stronger in Western Europe than elsewhere. The Violin Concerto in A Minor (Figures 2a, 2b and 2c) actually slows down a bit, even though both regional subsets speed up slightly.

In a report by Hubert Léveillé Gauvin, 303 U.S. top-10 singles from the period between 1986 and 2015 have been compared on various temporal properties like overall tempo (measured in BPM), time before the first lyrics, and time before the title is first mentioned. The study found that "attention-grabbing [tempo] principles" such as overall speed increased significantly, possibly driven by the "attention economy" [26]. But the speedup here is different, because classical music involves new recordings of the same old 'songs', whereas for most U.S. pop songs are first releases. Furthermore, their data set covers *American* pop songs, which are technically speaking from a different culture than West European classical music, so a definite relation is hard to forge. Still, the speedup in pop songs for the hypothesized purpose of attention-grabbing is too alluring to be left unnoticed in light of our findings.

And how could demographics play a role in the speedup of some of Bach's works? Is the "pace of life" or the "speedup of society" to blame, as mentioned by the (experts in) various news media? There is some relevant scientific research. In a study by Levine and Norenzayan, the average pace of life, measured in walking speed, working speed, and the accuracy of clocks, has been investigated for 31 countries [27]. The researchers found significantly higher values in both Japan and the countries of Western Europe. The famous study "Growth, Innovation, Scaling, and the Pace of Life in Cities" by Bettencourt et al. shows that the population size of a city is positively related to its pace of social life [28]. With ever increasing numbers living in urban areas over the last century, especially in Western Europe, this would imply that the regional pace of social life is increasing accordingly [29]. The recent explosive growth of urbanization now has 80% of the European population living in urban areas, especially in Northern and Western parts [30]. A particularly interesting detail about this study, by Marc Antrop from University of Ghent, is that it covers an era

TABLE III. THE INCREASE IN DURATION FOR RELEASES IN ALL FIVE COMPOSITIONAL CATEGORIES. $I_{TOTAL}$ IS THE INCREASE IN DURATION FOR ALL RELEASES, WHEREAS $I_{WEST}$ DENOTES THE SAME VALUES FOR WEST EUROPEAN RELEASES ONLY, AND $I_{NONWEST}$ FOR NON-WEST EUROPEAN RELEASES ONLY.

| | Work | Years | $I_{total}$ | $I_{west}$ | $I_{nonwest}$ |
|---|---|---|---|---|---|
| Violin | BWV1041 | 1955 - 2018 | 0.404% | -4.212% | -1.017% |
| | BWV1042 | 1955 - 2018 | -7.400% | -13.097% | -2.141% |
| | BWV1043 | 1958 - 2018 | -5.314% | -10.743% | -4.853% |
| Brandenburg | BWV1046 | 1954 - 2018 | -8.434% | -11.552% | 7.467% |
| | BWV1047 | 1953 - 2018 | -3.194% | -4.691% | 4.683% |
| | BWV1048 | 1953 - 2018 | -10.451% | -11.412% | -6.626% |
| | BWV1049 | 1954 - 2018 | -6.178% | -7.854% | -2.408% |
| | BWV1050 | 1954 - 2018 | -4.124% | -3.584% | -3.472% |
| | BWV1051 | 1954 - 2018 | -9.266% | -10.372% | -11.145% |
| Cantatas | BWV106 | 1967 - 2017 | -13.517% | -13.352% | -8.199% |
| | BWV131 | 1973 - 2016 | -13.962% | -4.527% | - |
| | BWV140 | 1967 - 2014 | -11.902% | -15.950% | -3.136% |
| | BWV170 | 1957 - 2018 | 3.620% | 4.748% | -15.208% |
| | BWV173 | 1979 - 2009 | -18.387% | -16.504% | - |
| | BWV208 | 1995 - 2012 | 3.573% | 4.313% | - |
| Organ Trio S. | BWV525 | 1954 - 2016 | 19.631% | 18.323% | 7.484% |
| | BWV526 | 1950 - 2014 | 4.153% | 2.503% | 10.498% |
| | BWV527 | 1959 - 2018 | 7.638% | 7.975% | -3.468% |
| | BWV528 | 1950 - 2013 | 4.617% | 5.891% | 1.366% |
| | BWV529 | 1950 - 2013 | -3.981% | -2.180% | -2.283% |
| | BWV530 | 1960 - 2014 | 10.864% | 10.219% | -2.719% |
| Cello Suites | BWV1007 | 1960 - 2018 | 0.957% | -2.903% | 5.522% |
| | BWV1008 | 1960 - 2019 | -8.285% | -12.835% | 1.907% |
| | BWV1009 | 1960 - 2018 | 6.349% | 7.626% | 8.703% |
| | BWV1010 | 1960 - 2018 | 5.481% | -5.618% | 20.339% |
| | BWV1011 | 1960 - 2018 | 4.412% | -6.836% | 9.299% |
| | BWV1012 | 1960 - 2018 | 10.865% | 3.649% | 5.802% |

from 1950, which largely coincides with ours. These findings therefore provide an interesting hypothesis, worthy of further exploration in future work.

## IV. CONCLUSION

In this paper, we explored the historical tempo development in performances of Bach's Double Violin Concerto, and of his compositions in general, following several online news reports which claimed significant speedups. We found these claims to be questionable on several points. Even though the Double Concerto has sped up slightly during the last decades, several other compositions slowed down, so there is no general trend for Bach's work, let alone for classical music as a whole. Interesting discovery is that the speedup of this concerto is most prominent in West European releases, but the pervasiveness of this pattern across musical genres is yet to be confirmed. Future work could therefore entail similar investigations for other composers, such as Palestrina, Haydn, Mozart, Beethoven, Chopin, Brahms, Tchaikovsky and Rachmaninoff, covering a broader range of styles, historical periods and topographical provenance. If sufficient amounts of data are available, such an investigation could shed more light on the ubiquity of the findings from this investigation.

Summarizing, some categories of Bach's music tend to speed up somewhat, but predominantly, sometimes even exclusively, in West European releases. Could this phenomenon be related to the high pace of life in cities, and therefore simply ride along the increasing urbanization since the fifties? Or is it the intensifying race for attention that increases the meter of the metronome? Our lives are moving faster, our attention spans shorter, and our music tries to keep the pace. It seems like a plausible theory, but more evidence is needed to not dismiss this hypothesis as *fake news*.

## REFERENCES


[1] Rolling Stone, "Even Classical Music Is Getting Faster These Days," October 2018, https://www.rollingstone.com/music/music-news/even-classical-music-is-getting-faster-these-days-748385/, Last accessed on 2019-08-06.

[2] iNews, "Classical music performances are speeding up by 30 per cent, Bach analysis finds," October 2018, https://inews.co.uk/culture/music/bach-333-classical-music-speeding-up/, Last accessed on 2019-08-06.

[3] Classic FM, "New study into performances of Bach reveals classical music is speeding up," October 2018, https://www.classicfm.com/music-news/classical-music-is-getting-faster/, Last accessed on 2019-08-06.

[4] Smithsonian, "Are Classical Music Performances Speeding Up?" October 2018, https://www.smithsonianmag.com/smart-news/study-bach-compositions-suggests-classical-music-performances-are-speeding-180970667/, Last accessed on 2019-08-06.

[5] W. Weir, History's Greatest Lies: The Startling Truths Behind World Events Our History Books Got Wrong. Fair Winds Press, 2009.

[6] J. L. Nelson and H. Taneja, "The small, disloyal fake news audience: The role of audience availability in fake news consumption," new media & society, vol. 20, no. 10, 2018, pp. 3720–3737.

[7] H. Allcott and M. Gentzkow, "Social media and fake news in the 2016 election," Journal of economic perspectives, vol. 31, no. 2, 2017, pp. 211–36.

[8] A. Guess, B. Nyhan, and J. Reifler, "Selective exposure to misinformation: Evidence from the consumption of fake news during the 2016 US presidential campaign," European Research Council, vol. 9, 2018.

[9] N. Wingfield, M. Isaac, and K. Benner, "Google and Facebook take aim at fake news sites," The New York Times, vol. 11, 2016, p. 12.

[10] G. Pennycook and D. G. Rand, "The implied truth effect: Attaching warnings to a subset of fake news stories increases perceived accuracy of stories without warnings," SSRN (Elsevier), 2017.

[11] I. M. Begg, A. Anas, and S. Farinacci, "Dissociation of processes in belief: source recollection, statement familiarity, and the illusion of truth." Journal of Experimental Psychology: General, vol. 121, no. 4, 1992, p. 446.

[12] F. T. Bacon, "Credibility of repeated statements: Memory for trivia." Journal of Experimental Psychology: Human Learning and Memory, vol. 5, no. 3, 1979, p. 241.

[13] D. C. Polage, "Making up History: False Memories of Fake News Stories." Europe's Journal of Psychology, vol. 8, no. 2, 2012.

[14] E. F. Loftus and H. G. Hoffman, "Misinformation and memory: The creation of new memories." Journal of Experimental Psychology: General, vol. 118, no. 1, 1989, p. 100.

[15] W. J. Levelt, P. Drenth, and E. Noort, "Flawed science: The fraudulent research practices of social psychologist Diederik Stapel," Report commissioned by the Tilburg University, University of Amsterdam and the Rijksuniversiteit Groningen, 2012.

[16] Retraction Database, "Retraction Watch Database: Diederik Stapel," May 2019, http://retractiondatabase.org/RetractionSearch.aspx?AspxAutoDetectCookieSupport=1#?auth%3dStapel%252c%2bDiederik%2bA, Last accessed on 2019-08-06.

[17] C. F. Camerer et al., "Evaluating the replicability of social science experiments in nature and science between 2010 and 2015," Nature Human Behaviour, vol. 2, no. 9, 2018, p. 637.

[18] ——, "Evaluating replicability of laboratory experiments in economics," Science, vol. 351, no. 6280, 2016, pp. 1433–1436.

[19] G. van Horn, R. Olij, J. Sleegers, and D. van den Berg, "A Predictive Data Analytic for the Hardness of Hamiltonian Cycle Problem Instances," Proceedings of Data Analytics, Athens, Greece, 2018, pp. 91–96.

[20] S. Epskamp, "Reproducibility and Replicability in a Fast-paced Methodological World," PsyArXiv, September, vol. 15, 2018.

[21] Discogs, "Discogs," May 2019, https://www.discogs.com, Last accessed on 2019-08-06.

[22] ——, "Discogs API Documentation," May 2019, https://www.discogs.com/developers/, Last accessed on 2019-08-06.

[23] https://www.bachspeedup.com, Last accessed on 2019-08-06.

[24] J. Serrà, Á. Corral, M. Boguñá, M. Haro, and J. L. Arcos, "Measuring the evolution of contemporary western popular music," Scientific reports, vol. 2, 2012, p. 521.

[25] T. Bertin-Mahieux, D. P. Ellis, B. Whitman, and P. Lamere, "The Million Song Dataset," Columbia University Libraries, 2011.

[26] H. Léveillé Gauvin, "Drawing listener attention in popular music: Testing five musical features arising from the theory of attention economy," Musicae Scientiae, vol. 22, no. 3, 2018, pp. 291–304.

[27] R. V. Levine and A. Norenzayan, "The pace of life in 31 countries," Journal of cross-cultural psychology, vol. 30, no. 2, 1999, pp. 178–205.

[28] L. M. Bettencourt, J. Lobo, D. Helbing, C. Kühnert, and G. B. West, "Growth, innovation, scaling, and the pace of life in cities," Proceedings of the national academy of sciences, vol. 104, no. 17, 2007, pp. 7301–7306.

[29] U. Nations, "2018 revision of world urbanization prospects," 2018.

[30] M. Antrop, "Landscape change and the urbanization process in Europe," Landscape and urban planning, vol. 67, no. 1-4, 2004, pp. 9–26.

# Analyzing the Structural Health of Civil Infrastructures using Correlation Networks and Population Analysis

Prasad Chetti and Hesham H. Ali
College of Information Science and Technology
University of Nebraska at Omaha
Omaha, NE 68182, USA
email:pchetti@unomaha.edu and hali@unomaha.edu

*Abstract* — **Traditional Structural Health Monitoring (SHM) methods require bridge inspectors to manually inspect each bridge periodically (usually every two years) and recommend maintenance or rehabilitation services to the bridge if necessary. As limited manpower and budget constraints are the two major shortfalls in traditional SHM methods, in addition to potential human errors and lack of consistency, more rigorous and frequent solutions are needed to assess the health levels of bridges and provide needed recommendations. In this work, we process a new population-based approach that employs the concept of Correlation Networks to evaluate the status of each bridge based on general parameters as well as how it compares to other similar bridges. We propose a Correlation Network Model (CNM) that builds a network of bridges, based on time-series data on sufficiency ratings, for a population of 9,546 "steel bridges with stringer/multi-beam or girder design," taken from the U.S. National Bridge Inventory (NBI) database. We apply Markov Clustering Algorithms to produce clusters of bridges with similar features associated with their fitness ratings over user-defined periods of time. The top five clusters are identified and further analyzed using population analysis algorithms. We were able to identify three clusters with lower fitness ratings and suggest that the bridges in these clusters need to be serviced sooner than those included in the other clusters. Experimental results show that the proposed model provides an efficient approach that allows domain experts to assess the structural health of bridges/civil infrastructures in a robust way that can guide rehabilitation services for all bridges and identify potentially unsafe bridges that need urgent attention.**

***Keywords* — *Structural Health Monitoring; Population Analysis; Correlation Networks; Markov Clustering; Sufficiency Rating; National Bridge Inventory database.***

## I. INTRODUCTION

The National Bridge Inventory (NBI) database consists of information on more than 600,000 bridges of the United States of America (USA), with each bridge dataset comprising 116 parameters. After each inspection cycle, usually every two years, the bridge inspectors develop condition ratings of the bridges as specified by the U.S. Federal Highway Administration (FHWA) [1]. Sufficiency Rating (SR) is an outcome parameter/measure which reflects the overall fitness rating of the bridge and is derived from over 20 NBI data fields/parameters grouped in four factors, i.e., Structural Evaluation, Functional Obsolescence, Essentiality to the Public Use, and Special Reductions as described in the FHWA coding guide [2]. SR ranges between 0% and 100 % or between 0 and 1000. Lower percentages/ratings indicate that the bridge fitness is low and higher percentages/ratings indicate that the bridge is highly fit. SHM is a process of implementing a damage detection and characterization strategy for engineering structures [3]. Traditional SHM methods require bridge inspectors to manually inspect each bridge over a period of time and recommend maintenance or rehabilitation services to the bridge if necessary. As limited manpower, budget constraints, and lack of consistent and continuous monitoring are the major shortfalls in traditional SHM, research communities are interested in new solutions to assess the structural health of civil infrastructures while taking advantage of the massive data available in the NBI database. In this work, we propose the use of Correlation Network Models (CNMs). CNM is a powerful big-data tool that has recently been used to analyze and visualize complex systems having large data with multiple dimensions/parameters in various domains [12], [17], [18]. We propose to employ CNM to create a correlation network of bridges, based on the time-series data of bridges' overall fitness rating, such as SR for a population of 9,546 "steel bridges with stringer/multi-beam or girder design" obtained from the NBI database. These bridges are taken from three US states: California, Iowa, and Nebraska, which come from three different climatic regions as shown in Figure 1. We then apply a Markov Clustering algorithm, such as MCL to obtain clusters of bridges that have similarity in their fitness ratings (such as SRs) over a certain period of time.

Our basic hypothesis is that the bridges with similar fitness characteristics are included in common groups or clusters. MCL is a graph-based efficient algorithm designed based on the random walks property of the graphs. As every clustering method groups elements with similar attribute values together [16], when applied to the bridge correlation network, MCL finds clusters of bridges with similar behavior in terms of SRs. We identified the top clusters produced by the algorithm for further analysis. We were able to identify clusters with lower fitness ratings that need to be serviced relatively soon compared to bridges in other groups. Our experimental results show that the proposed approach provides a new efficient tool that allows bridge owners to evaluate the structural health of bridges/civil infrastructures and identify the structures that need immediate attention. This may serve as the main component of a new SHM decision support system.

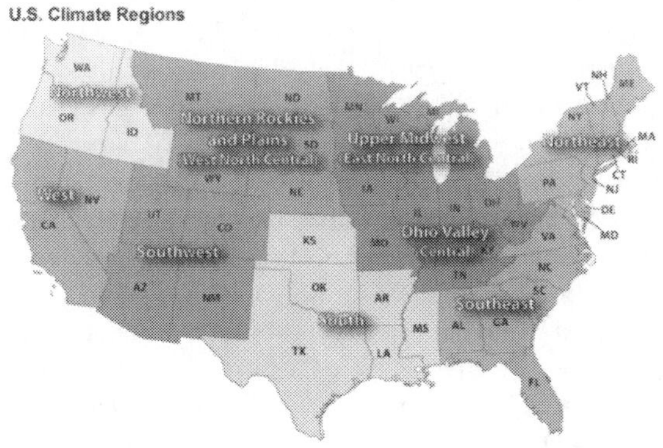


Figure 1. Map of nine USA climate regions ( image courtesy NOAA). [8]

The remainder of this paper is organized as follows. Section II provides a general background, where the need for creating a Correlation Network of bridges with time-series data of SRs is discussed. Section III discusses the key concepts used for creating Correlation Networks and the population analysis approach, followed by a discussion on how network models are used in various application domains. Section IV includes the complete methodology used to implement the proposed approach. Section V discusses the experimental results of the study. Conclusions and future directions are summarized in Section VI.

## II. BACKGROUND

Several researchers have recently attempted to develop deterministic and stochastic deterioration models for various bridge components, such as Deck, Superstructure and Substructure, and Average Daily Traffic [4]. Several studies have used Two-Step clustering, a powerful data mining tool, to study concrete deck parameters in the NBI database to identify the order in which bridges need to be serviced [5]. While there are some deterioration models that are based on temporal data [4], [6], but they usually consider only one or few input ratings, such as Deck Rating or Superstructure Rating, for their analysis. Since they did not consider a holistic approach or compound rating measures such as SR (which is a complex measure based on multiple parameters), their models are somewhat limited and lack robustness and consistency. For example, such models can explain how Deck Rating changes over a period of time but fail to measure the overall safety of bridges as a whole. To estimate the overall fitness ratings of bridges, we are proposing a population analysis model that is based on the complex SR measure. Again, as various models consider temporal data of selected input ratings, they are useful in estimating ratings of individual elements but fail in estimating the overall fitness ratings of bridges [4], [5], [6].

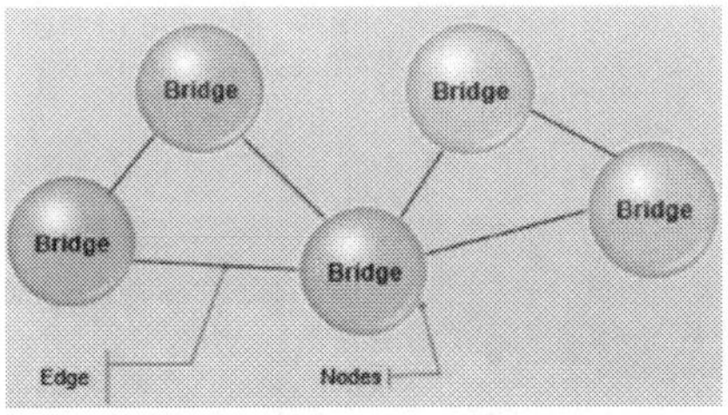


Figure 2. Graph model representation with bridges.

On the other hand, there are models, that could consider the overall fitness rating as their measure in predicting the health of civil infrastructures [7], [18], but they do not utilize time series data. Hence, obtained predictions may not be accurate or do not really characterize the overall behavior of the bridges over a period of time. Therefore, there is a need for a model that considers bridges' overall behavior or fitness ratings over a period of time and identifies the categories of bad bridges with respect to their fitness ratings.

### A. *Correlation Network Model (CNM)*

As mentioned earlier in the introduction section, the NBI database has information on more than 600,000 bridges, each with 116 parameters. The big-data associated with these bridges can easily be analyzed or visualized using a powerful tool such as CNM. CNM [17], [18] is a graph- based model which would allow the correlated bridges to be connected by an edge in the Correlation Network Graph. Creation of a Correlation Network is explained in our methodology section. CNM is relevant for this research as the highly correlated bridges or bridges with dense connections (usually we call them clusters) would give us information about bridges that have the same kind of behaviors or characteristics.

For example, bridges with similar patterns in their SRs over a long period of time may be highly correlated and will have an edge between them in the CNM. Hence, all the highly correlated bridges will have dense edges among them and form as a cluster. The population analysis allows us to compare two or more clusters of bridges with respect to one or more enrichment parameters. This analysis will allow us to discover what parameters are significantly affecting a particular cluster. For example, if one particular cluster is highly enriched by Structurally Deficient (SD) bridges, then we can identify other parameters that are similar to these bridges and hence, we can control them. If this structural deficiency is due to the deterioration of deck rating, then we can advise the bridge authorities to implement deck-related rehabilitation measures.

*B. Correlation Networks in Various Disciplines*

In the past decade, Correlation-based Network Analysis has become a powerful analysis tool in biological studies and have been used by other researchers in various disciplines because of their ability

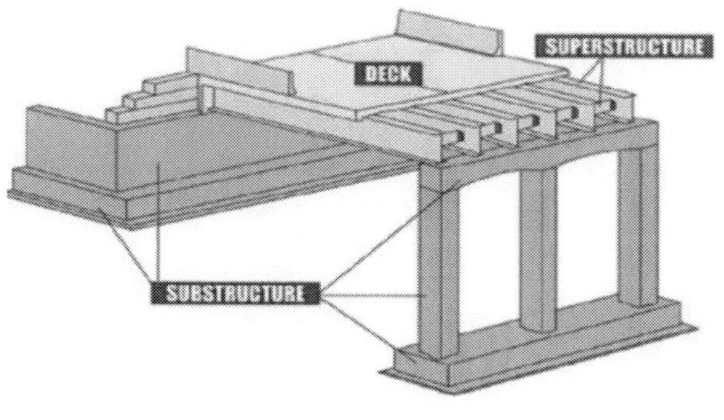


Figure 3: Structural elements of a bridge [21].

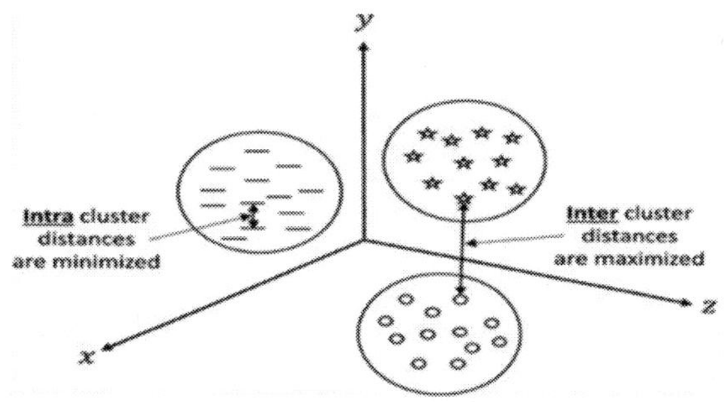


Figure 4. Representation of clustering.

to show generalization, visualization, and analysis capabilities [12]. CNA was successfully applied in biological systems to determine plant growth and biomass in Arabidopsis thaliana Recombinant Inbred Lines (RIL) and introgression lines (IL) [13], [14]. It was also applied to evaluate the effects of hypoxia on a tumor cell biochemistry [15]. Correlation networks are powerful and provide us the opportunity to measure changes in temporal datasets, and there are clusters which are highly enriched by a few Gene Ontology (GO) terms [17].

*C. Correlation Networks to Monitor Structural Health*

Recently, researchers have applied CNM to monitor the structural health of civil infrastructures and have also analyzed the safety issues with respect to various parameters such as inventory rating and deck rating [18]. One of the advantages of using CNM in civil infrastructures is that the bridges can be clustered based on some similarity, and visualized as healthy and unhealthy clusters of bridges [18], using any existing visualization tools, such as Cytoscape [19] and Gephi [20]. As CNM is a new approach for SHM, it can be used to display critical bridges and find an efficient way to improve bridge inspection schedules [18]. However, one of the limitations of the latter study is that it did not consider the temporal-data of SRs; hence, it cannot accurately predict a future overall fitness rating behavior of the bridges. Hence, creating a Correlation Network model that could deal with temporal-data is one of the objectives of this paper. The motivation of this paper is to develop a CNM that could consider bridges' overall behavior (i.e., SR) over a period of time and analyze highly correlated clusters of bridges to predict bridges' future behavior. The research question of this paper is to determine what parameters are enriched for each cluster of bridges in the population, if the bridges are clustered using the correlations of temporal data of SRs. The research objective of this paper is to provide a CNM-based Decision Support System for bridge owners to enable them to find out which bridges need to be serviced first. As a result, we developed a novel CNM that considers the temporal data of SRs of the bridges for the last 25 years (from 1992 to 2016), so as to exactly characterize the overall fitness behavior of the bridges over a period of time and hence, predict the future fitness behavior accurately.

## III. GRAPH MODEL, CORRELATION COEFFICIENT, AND CLUSTERING

This section talks about the graph model, correlation coefficient and Markov clustering.

*A. Graph Model*

The graph model (denoted by G= (V, E), where V is a set of vertices/nodes, and E is a set of edges) used in this paper is undirected and unweighted. An example of an undirected and unweighted graph is shown in Figure 2 with five vertices and six edges, where every vertex represents a bridge/civil infrastructure and any two bridges are connected by an edge if and only if they have some correlation. Various colors of bridges may represent various status of bridges while visualizing them. For example, a green-colored bridge may represent a structurally sufficient bridge, whereas a red-colored bridge could be a SD bridge.

*B. Correlation Coefficient*

A Pearson's correlation coefficient [10] between any two variables is a real value that ranges between -1 and +1, and which expresses the strength of linkage or co-occurrence. This strength is called Pearson's $r$ or Pearson product-moment correlation coefficient if the correlation is between two continuous–level variables [10], [11]. This paper uses bivariate (Pearson's) correlation analysis to show the relationship between any two bridges.

### C. *Markov Clustering*

Clustering groups objects with similar attribute values together [16]. The objects are grouped together in such a way that distances among the clusters are maximized and the distances within the clusters are minimized, as shown in Figure 4. The MCL algorithm [9] with default parameters is used in this paper to cluster the bridges, as the MCL is more suitable to graph-based networks. MCL is a fast and efficient algorithm that is designed based on the random walks property of the graphs. A random walk in a strongly connected cluster usually visits almost all the nodes in the cluster. MCL was applied on various protein-protein interaction networks and proved to be remarkably robust to graph alternations and superior in extracting complexes from interaction networks [26]. Since our correlation network with civil bridges is also a kind of protein-protein interaction network, we used MCL to extract the clusters of bridges that behave similarly.

## IV. METHODOLOGY

The following are the four phases of the CNM we are proposing.

i. Data acquisition and filtering
ii. Creating a correlation network and applying MCL algorithm
iii. Analyzing various clusters with respect to both input parameters, and output parameters, and comparing various clusters (population analysis)
iv. Developing a decision support system

The first two phases are explained in this section and the last two sections are explained as part of the next section. The novelty of this method is that the similar bridges are connected together into one cluster and the individual clusters are analyzed to see what input or output ratings are highly enriched for that cluster. The population analysis allows us to compare various clusters with respect to various rating parameters and then the decision support system allows us to make decisions about various clusters.

### A. *Data Acquisition and Filtering*

Bridge data of California, Iowa, and Nebraska, from the years 1992 to 2016, was obtained from the NBI database. Each bridge description is an alpha-numeric string of 432 characters in the database. There are 45,397 (California-15123, Iowa-16513, and Nebraska-13761 bridges) common bridges from 1992 to 2016 (based on the structure number entry in the database) in these three states. A total of 7,038 bridges out of 45,397 are culverts (Alpha-Numeric character string position 262! ='N') and 38,359 are non-culverts, according to the 2016-database. As the data was processed for any kind of anomalies, we found that there are 2,285 of these 45,397 common bridges that have inconsistent entries. In some years, they were recorded as culverts and in some years they were non-culverts. These 2,285 bridges were omitted from consideration. The remaining 43,112 common bridges consisted of 5550 culverts and 37,562 non-culverts (bridges). The majority of non-culverts (9,546 out of 37,562) were coded with main-structure type-302 (Item 43 from the NBI coding guide). In the coding 302, the first digit 3 represents the kind of material, i.e., "Steel," and the last two digits, 02, represent the type of design, which is, "Stringer/Multi-beam or Girder."

Our method takes a population of this 9,546 steel-stringer/multi-beam or girder bridges across three states of the USA (California, Iowa, and Nebraska), which come from three different climatic regions (as shown in Figure 1). The following items/parameters extracted from the FHWA coding guide [2] were considered for our analysis.

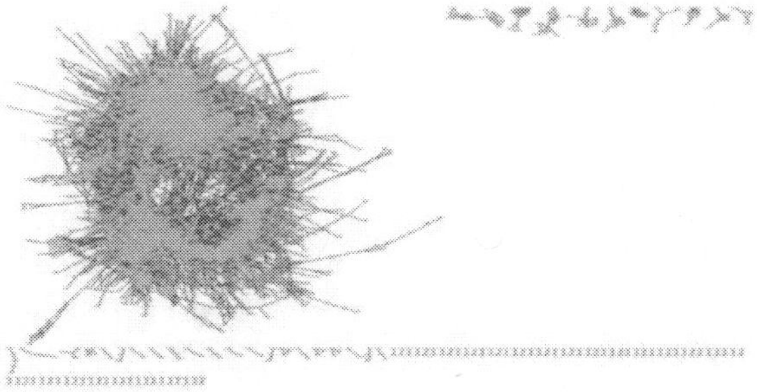

Figure 5. Correlation Network (correlation $\rho >= .90$) with 9,546 nodes and 767542 edges (Average degree=89.14, and 101 Connected components).

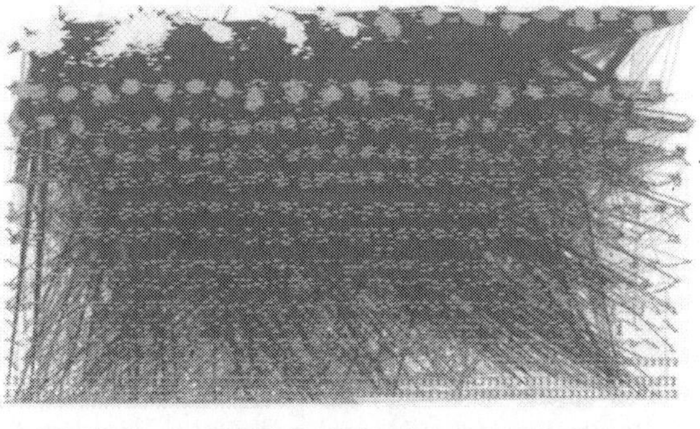

Figure 6. Clusters produced by MCL algorithm. Top-5 clusters are indicated by yellow color. Figure 5 and 6 were generated using Cytoscape [19].

i. Item 58 - Deck Rating (DR)
ii. Item 59 - Superstructure Rating (SPSR)
iii. Item 60 - Substructure Rating (SBSR)

iv. Item 67 - Structural Condition Rating (SCR) / Structural Evaluation Rating (SER)
v. Item 71 - Water Adequacy Rating (WAR)
vi. Status of the bridge as defined in [22]
vii. Sufficiency Rating

*B. Creating a Correlation Network*

The SRs of each of the 9,546 bridges from 1992 to 2016 (25 years) are recorded as an input matrix (say, SR matrix) with each row (i.e., each bridge) of the matrix having 25 years' SRs in it. So, there are 9,546 rows in the matrix, with each row as a vector of 25 years' SRs. A Pearson correlation coefficients matrix (say, Correlation-matrix) was then obtained over the SR matrix. The resultant Correlation-matrix is of size 9546 times 9546. Assuming each bridge as a node (vertex) in the graph model, two nodes are connected by an undirected edge if and only if their correlation coefficient $\rho >= 0.90$ and significance value $p <=.01$. This creates a Correlation-Network with bridges as nodes along with highly correlated nodes connected by edges as shown in Figure 5. We applied the MCL algorithm with all default parameters in Cytoscape [19] on the obtained Correlation Network, in order to produce clusters. These clusters are basically sub-networks of nodes and edges. Each cluster was further analyzed to see which input parameters were enriched for that cluster. As the clusters are formed with high correlations among the nodes, we can infer that the overall behavior of the nodes within each cluster is the same. This is the hypothesis of this research. MCL has produced 8610 nodes in various clusters and 3865 nodes are present in the Top 5 clusters and shown in Figure 6. These Top 5 clusters are considered for further analysis. Various experiments are conducted on the Top 5 clusters produced by the MCL algorithm, and the results are shown below.

## V. EXPERIMENTAL RESULTS

This section demonstrates various experimental results with respect to various network properties of the Top-5 clusters, SR, and other input ratings.

*A. Network Properties of Top 5 Clusters*

Figure 5 shows the correlation network (correlation $\rho>=0.90$) formed with 9546 nodes, 767542 edges, and 101 connected components. This is a scale-free network and follows a power-law node degree distribution. In a power-law node degree distribution, there are many nodes with fewer degrees and fewer number of nodes with more degrees. The top 5 clusters (yellow colored clusters) produced by the MCL algorithm are shown in Figure 6. These clusters' statistics are shown in TABLE 1, with the top- most cluster having the highest number of nodes 1496 and 354939 edges, and the least cluster having 255 nodes and 13922 edges. The lower the diameter, the closer the nodes are. Hence, almost all the nodes in all the clusters are around the center node(s). The higher the clustering coefficient [23], the higher the degree to which nodes in a graph are inclined to cluster together. The higher values of the average clustering coefficient for each cluster / subnetwork indicate that the nodes inside each cluster tend to be part of that cluster only. Therefore, the Top 5 clusters with higher clustering coefficients are considered for further analysis. TABLE 1 shows that cluster 5 has the highest clustering coefficient, which is 0.838. The cluster density describes the potential number of edges present in the sub-network compared to the possible number of edges in the sub-network. From TABLE 1, we see that cluster 3 has the highest density (0.533) among all the Top 5 clusters.

TABLE 1. NETWORK STATISTICS OF TOP 5 CLUSTERS PRODUCED BY THE MCL ALGORITHM.

| Cluster Number | #Nodes | #Edges | Avg. Degree | Density | Avg. Clust. Coeff. | SR Avg. |
|---|---|---|---|---|---|---|
| Cluster1 | 1496 | 354939 | 474.51 | 0.317 | 0.775 | 623.7 |
| Cluster2 | 1180 | 99000 | 167.79 | 0.142 | 0.674 | 489.3 |
| Cluster3 | 634 | 106955 | 337.39 | 0.533 | 0.823 | 801.9 |
| Cluster4 | 300 | 13377 | 89.18 | 0.298 | 0.812 | 818.5 |
| Cluster5 | 255 | 13922 | 109.19 | 0.43 | 0.838 | 577.5 |

*B. Analysis of Bridge Behavior with Respect to Sufficiency Rating*

We selected two bridges from cluster5 for our analysis to look at their behavior in terms of their overall fitness ratings (i.e., SRs) as shown in Figure 8. These two bridges are highly correlated (correlation $\rho>=0.94$) with each other and hence, connected by an edge in the network. The first bridge (say Bridge1, shown in red color) has an initial SR value of 615 in the year 1992, and maintained almost the same value until the year 2013. After then, there was a sudden drop in the SR value from almost 600 to below 500, ending at a SR value of 490 in the year 2016. Similarly, the second bridge (say Bridge2, shown in green color) started with a SR value of 970 in the year 1992 and steadily maintained it until 2013. There was a sudden drop in the year 2013 to a SR value of 860 and ended at that value itself. Though the first bridge was constructed in the year 1969, and the second bridge in the year 1988, both of these bridge had almost similar SR curves from 1992 to 2016. We have also observed that the current status of the first bridge is SD, and the second bridge is structurally good.

As SR is an overall fitness rating of the bridges, and as both of these bridges had the same kind of SR curve for the last 25 years, if the first bridge is SD, the second bridge may also have a high probability of becoming SD in the near future, as both bridges are highly correlated and in the same cluster. Estimating after how many years the second bridge will become SD is not the scope of this paper. Some of the bridges' SRs comparison is given in Figure 9. In fact, all these bridges are connected to the bridge CA-B06422 (Bridge names are partially anonymized. That means the first two letters in each bridge name may indicate the state but the remaining sequence in the name does not reflect the original bridge name as it is given in [1]). This means all these bridges are adjacent bridges of the bridge CA-B06422. This figure clearly shows that the SRs pattern is almost the same for adjacent bridges as they are highly correlated. It also clearly shows that all these bridges are sooner or later going to become SD, as all bridge SRs are deteriorating. Immediate maintenance may be required for this kind of bridges. Figure 10 shows that both clusters 3 and 4 have higher SRs at the end (year 2016), while all the remaining bridges have lower averages of SRs. We can also observe that for clusters 4 and 3, there was a maintenance (in terms of reconstruction) took place in the years 1997 and 2007 respectively. Hence, these clusters have higher SRs in the year 2016 (as shown in Figure 10) and do not need immediate maintenance.

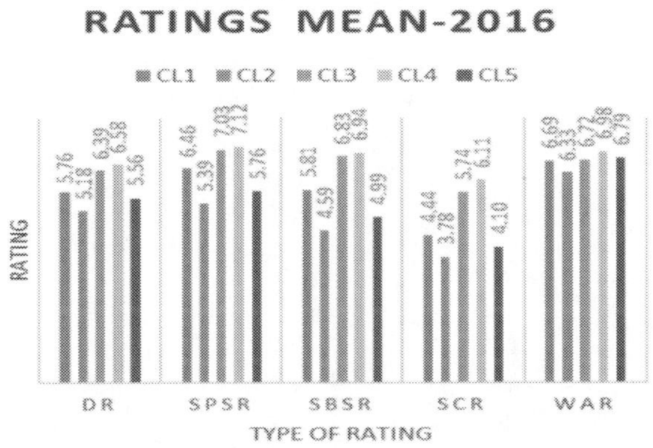


Figure 7. Ratings comparison for top 5 clusters (year 2016)

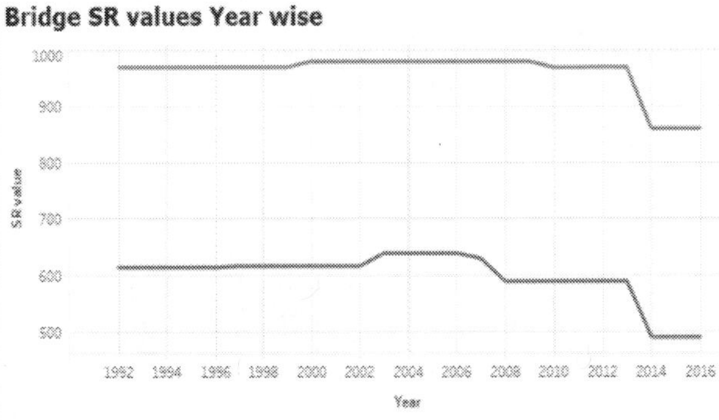


Figure 8. Comparison of SR values of two bridges from Cluster-5. (The image was generated in Tableau [25]).

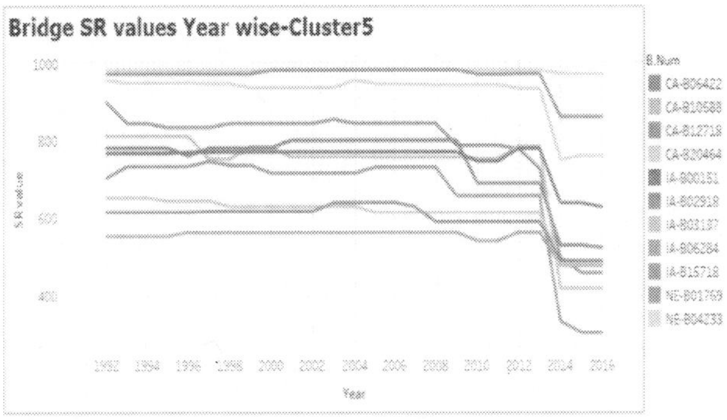


Figure 9. Ten adjacent bridges of the bridge--CA-B06422 from Cluster5 (Bridge names are partially anonymized).

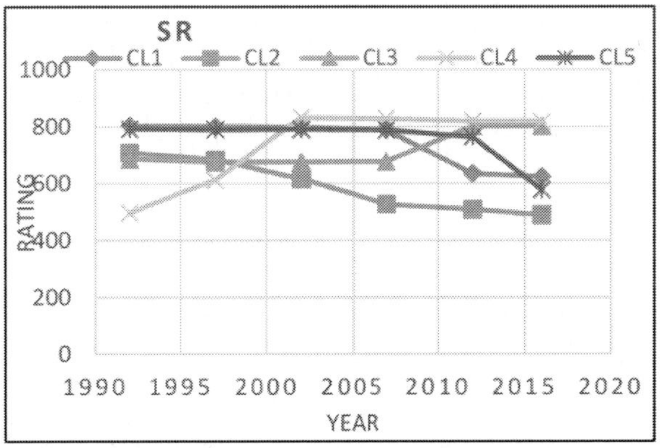


Figure 10. Comparison of Top 5 clusters' averages (dataset years 1992, 1997, 2002, 2007, 2012 and 2016) with respect to SRs.

### C. *Analysis of Top 5 clusters with respect to input rating parameters*

Various input rating parameters of output ratings, such as SR, are considered for cluster enrichment analysis. Figure 7 shows the comparison of Top 5 clusters' average input ratings, such as DR, SPSR, SBSR, WAR, and SCR of the NBI-dataset-2016. From this figure, we can see that all the ratings of both cluster 3 and cluster 4 are higher compared to all the remaining clusters. Similarly, from Figures 11 through 15, we see how different input ratings vary for all the Top 5 clusters. For example, from Figure 11, we find that both cluster 1 and cluster 2 are enriched with DR = 5. This indicates that the deck (as shown in Figure 3) is in "Fair Condition" (as specified in the FHWA coding guide [2]). If we see cluster 4 from the same Figure 11, DRs ranging from 5 through 8 are equally distributed and hence, these higher ratings led to the higher SRs as shown in Figure 16. We can also see that both cluster-3 and cluster-4 have higher input rating values as shown in Figures 11 through 15. Figure 12 shows that Cluster-2 is highly enriched with Superstructure Rating <= 5. Once these bridges' Superstructure Ratings drop from 5 to 4, then the bridges will fall into the SD bridge category. Hence, the improvement in the Superstructure Rating in terms of reducing the live load is required. This can be done by reducing Average Daily Traffic and implementing required rehabilitation services on these bridges. Cluster 2 from Figure 13 also shows that the Substructure Rating is critical, as most of the bridges' Substructure Ratings are <= 5. From Figure 14, we see that Water Adequacy Ratings are good for all the clusters and no Water Adequacy improvement measures are required for these clusters. As shown in Figure 15, most of the bridges in clusters 1, 2, and 5 are enriched with SCR value <=4, which indicates that most of the bridges in these clusters are either SD or will soon become SD. Hence, they have lower SRs as shown in Figure 16. The same can be observed from Figure 10, where the average SRs for every 5 years' interval are shown. From this graph, Clusters 1,2 and 5 are showing higher deterioration patterns as compared to Clusters 3 and 4. Hence, our decision support system recommends various bridge authorities to provide immediate attention or service to the bridges in clusters 1, 2 and 5.

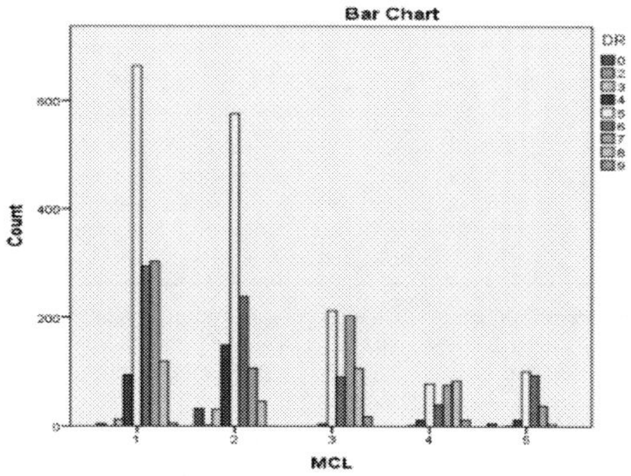


Figure 11. Comparison of Top 5 clusters with respect to Deck Rating (DR)

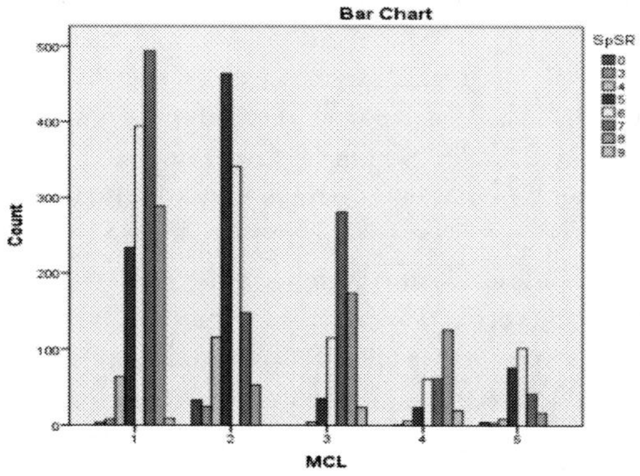


Figure 12. Comparison of Top 5 clusters with respect to Superstructure Rating (SpSR).

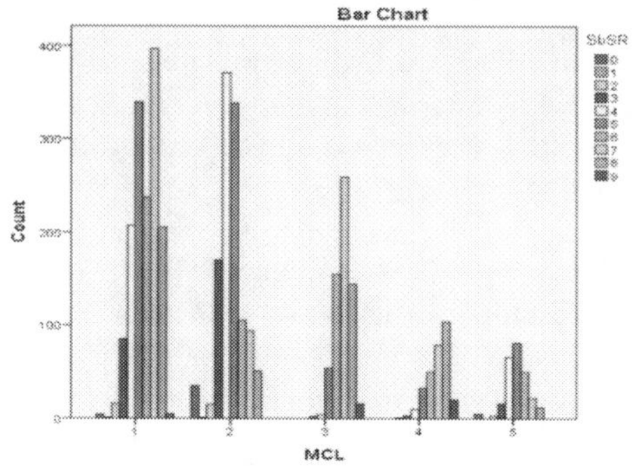


Figure 13. Comparison of Top 5 clusters with respect to Substructure Rating (SBSR).

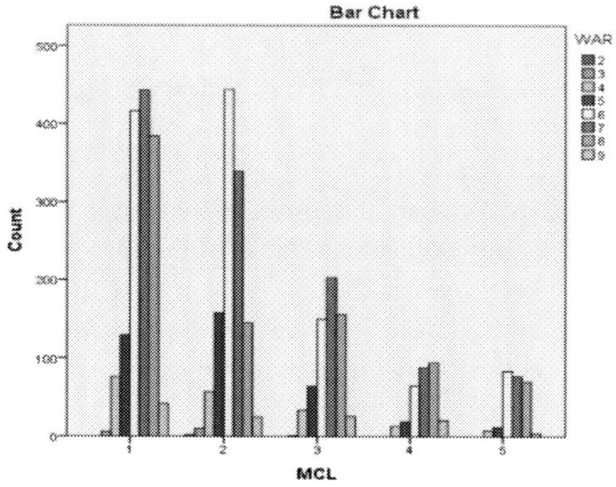


Figure 14. Comparison of Top 5 clusters with respect to Water Adequacy Rating (WAR).

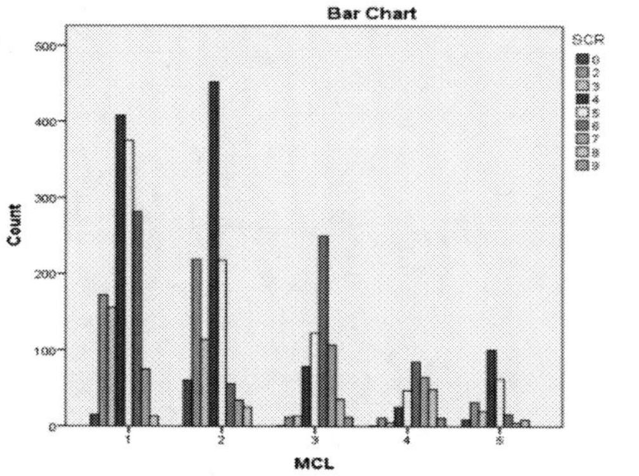


Figure 15. Comparison of Top 5 clusters with respect to Structural Condition Rating (SCR).

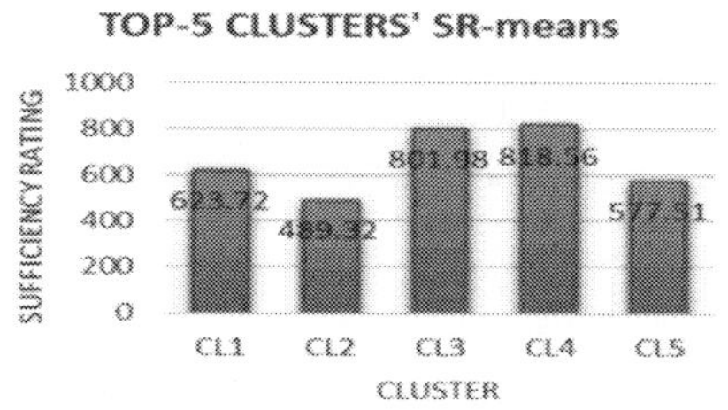


Figure 16. Averages of SRs of Top 5 clusters for the year 2016.

## VI. CONCLUSIONS

In this paper, we presented a new Correlation Network Model for analyzing civil infrastructures with a focus on the assessment of safety of bridges. We employed the network model to provide a population analysis approach to extract useful information for publicly available bridge data. The proposed method allows highly correlated bridges to be identified and form a cluster of bridges with similar safety-related characteristics, such as the overall fitness rating. The population analysis makes it possible to compare different clusters with different enrichment parameters and ratings. We conducted a pilot study with a group of bridges from three states. We were able to use the constructed correlation network to identify several groups of bridges with different safety measures. Based on the obtained classifications, we identified bridges that exhibit a higher rate of deterioration and need to receive a higher priority for receiving maintenance. With these findings, we showed that the CNM enables domain experts to categorize clusters of bridges based on their safety. CNM as a decision support system allows SHM inspectors to have a risk-based schedule for servicing bridges, and allocate funds to inspect bridges with low safety patterns. As a future step, we plan to study the effect of specific parameters, such as Average Daily Traffic, on SRs and provide a risk assessment to various groups of bridges based on their deterioration patterns.

## REFERENCES


[1] Federal Highway Administration (FHWA), retrieved on August 15, 2017 from https://www.fhwa.dot.gov/bridge/nbi/ascii.cfm

[2] Federal Highway Administration (FHWA), retrieved on August 15, 2017 from https://www.fhwa.dot.gov/bridge/mtguide.pdf

[3] C. R. Farrar, and K. Worden, "An introduction to structural health monitoring", Philosophical Transactions of the Royal Society of London A: Mathematical, Physical and Engineering Sciences 365.1851 pp. 303-315, 2007.

[4] A. Hatami, and G. Morcous, "Developing deterioration models for Nebraska bridges", No. M302, 2011.

[5] M. Radovic, O. Ghonima, and T. Schumacher, "Data Mining of Bridge Concrete Deck Parameters in the National Bridge Inventory by Two-Step Cluster Analysis," ASCE-ASME Journal of Risk and Uncertainty in Engineering Systems, Part A: Civil Engineering, Vol. 3, No. 2, F4016004, 2016.

[6] M. Nasrollahi, and G. Washer, "Estimating inspection intervals for bridges based on statistical analysis of national bridge inventory data," Journal of Bridge Engineering, Vol. 20, No. 9, 04014104, 2014.

[7] Y. Hachem, K. Zografos, and M. Soltani, "Bridge inspection strategies", Journal of Performance of Constructed Facilities, Vol. 5, No. 1, pp. 37-56, 1991.

[8] T. Karl, and W.J. Koss, "Regional and national monthly, seasonal, and annual temperature weighted by area, 1895-1983", 1984.

[9] S. Dongen, "A cluster algorithm for graphs," CWI (Centre for Mathematics and Computer Science), 2000.

[10] K. Pearson, "On the coefficient of racial likeness", Biometrika pp. 105-117, 1926.

[11] J. Benesty, et al., "Pearson correlation coefficient", Noise reduction in speech processing, Springer Berlin Heidelberg, pp. 1-4, 2009.

[12] A. Batushansky, D. Toubiana, and A. Fait, "Correlation-based network generation, visualization, and analysis as a powerful tool in biological studies: a case study in cancer cell metabolism", BioMed research international, 2016.

[13] J. Lisec, et. al., "Identification of metabolic and biomass QTL in Arabidopsis thaliana in a parallel analysis of RIL and IL populations", The Plant Journal, Vol. 53, No. 6, pp. 960-972, 2008.

[14] R.C. Meyer, et. al., "The metabolic signature related to high plant growth rate in Arabidopsis thaliana", Proceedings of the National Academy of Sciences, Vol. 104, No. 11, pp. 759-4764, 2007.

[15] H.L. Kotze, E.G. Armitage, K.J. Sharkey, J.W. Allwood, W.B. Dunn, K.J. Williams, and R. Goodacre, "A novel untargeted metabolomics correlation-based network analysis incorporating human metabolic reconstructions", BMC systems biology, Vol. 7, No. 1, pp. 107, 2013.

[16] A.K. Jain, "Data clustering: 50 years beyond K-means", Pattern recognition letters, Vol. 31, NO. 8, pp. 651-666, 2010.

[17] K. Dempsey, I. Thapa, D. Bastola, and H. Ali, "Identifying modular function via edge annotation in gene correlation networks using Gene Ontology search", Bioinformatics and Biomedicine Workshops (BIBMW), IEEE International Conference pp. 255-261, 2011

[18] A. Fuchsberger, and H. Ali, "A Correlation Network Model for Structural Health Monitoring and Analyzing Safety Issues in Civil Infrastructures", Proceedings of the 50th Hawaii International Conference on System Sciences, 2017.

[19] P. Shannon, et. al., "Cytoscape: a software environment for integrated models of biomolecular interaction networks", Genome research, Vol. 13, No. 11, pp. 2498-2504, 2003.

[20] M. Bastian, S. Heymann, and M. Jacomy, "Gephi: an open source software for exploring and manipulating networks", ICWSM, Vol. 8, pp. 361-362, 2009 ( retrieved on August 15, 2017 from https://gephi.org/)

[21] Daily Civil, retrieved on August 15, 2017 from http://www.dailycivil.com/structural-elements-bridge/

[22] Federal Highway Administration (FHWA), retrieved on August 15, 2017 from https://www.fhwa.dot.gov/bridge/britab.cfm

[23] D.J. Watts, and S.H. Strogatz, "Collective dynamics of 'small-world' networks", Nature, Vol: 393, pp. 440-442, 1998.

[24] A. Field, "Discovering statistics using IBM SPSS statistics", Sage, 2013.

[25] TABLEU Software, retrieved on August 15, 2017 from https://www.tableau.com/

[26] S. Brohee, and J. V. Helden. "Evaluation of clustering algorithms for protein-protein interaction networks." BMC bioinformatics, Vol. 7, No. 1, pp. 488, 2006.

# A Website Selection Model in Programmatic Advertising using Fuzzy Analytic Hierarchy Process and Similarity Methods

Dimitris K. Kardaras
School of Business, Dept. of Business Administration
Athens University of Economics and Business
Athens, Greece
e-mail: kardaras@aueb.gr
dkkardaras@yahoo.co.uk

Stavroula G. Barbounaki
Merchant Marine Academy of Aspropyrgos,
Aspropyrgos, Greece
e-mail: sbarbounaki@yahoo.gr

***Abstract*—The Web has already become a platform that reshapes business models, thus spawning new opportunities for growth. Furthermore, the Web constitutes an effective media rich communication channel for businesses to contact their customers, support their transactions and promote their products and service through digital marketing. This paper focuses on the applicability of fuzzy logic techniques to assessing web sites performance with respect to digital marketing objectives. This research utilizes the Fuzzy Delphi Method (FDM) the Fuzzy Analytic Hierarchy Process (FAHP) and similarity methods in order to select the web sites that mostly satisfy digital marketing targets that are set by a Communications Company (CC) in Greece. Data on a large number of digital marketing parameters is collected, representing the performance of the CC on the web over a period of time. This paper aims to identify the criteria that can be used for assessing web sites, to determine their relative importance and to rank web sites according to their contribution to CC objectives. Fuzzy logic is utilised to deal with the subjectivity inherent in setting a company's priorities. FDM is used to capture the managers' views regarding the assessment criteria and the FAHP is used for determining the criteria's weights.**

***Keywords-Fuzzy Delphi Method; Fuzzy Analytic Hierarchy Process; Similarity Methods; Web Site selection.***

## I. Introduction

Digital advertising spending is growing globally. According to [1], for countries such as the UK, China, Norway and Canada, digital advertising has already become the dominant advertising channel, which accounts for more than 50% of the total ad spending. It is also expected [1] that the global spending on digital ads will increase by 17.6% to reach $333.25 billion. As regards to the top digital ads sellers, Google is expected to outperform their competitors being the largest digital ad seller in the world in 2019, attracting 31.1% of the global ad spending, or $103.73 billion. Facebook will be No. 2, with $67.37 billion in net ad revenues, followed by China-based Alibaba, at $29.20 billion [1]. Investments in Digital Marketing (DM) are driven by companies' aims to improve cost effectiveness, as well as by changes in customer behaviour. However, DM increase is attributed to the fact that results from DM initiatives are more easily accountable for compared to those of traditional marketing [2]-[5]. Furthermore, as customers are increasingly using digital channels for their transactions with business, marketers have realized the need to track these transactions and to measure their performance [6]. In another survey [7], also discussed in [8], 65% of marketing leaders surveyed in the USA plan to increase their spending on digital advertising, due to factors that impose a continuing and consistent shift of offline media spending to digital advertising, a decline of organic social in favor of paid social and the rising importance of video, which is more expensive than other digital techniques.

For this purpose, firms have already started using Web Analytics (WA) for collecting data and assessing digital marketing performance. WA can be defined as the process of collecting, storing, analysing and reporting of Internet data aiming at understanding and optimizing Web usage and e-business performance. A recent work [2] found that digital marketing performance measurement represents a top-priority for businesses.

With the proliferation of web sites, businesses have many opportunities to showcase their brand online. Globally there are over 1.5 billion with around 200 million of them being active. The development of a DM investment plan requires the analysis of websites performance. WA provides a quite comprehensive set of websites traffic data that can be used to assess DM alternative plans. In addition, available are programmatic digital marketing platforms for automated bidding on advertising inventory in real time, that give businesses access to websites traffic data and the opportunity to show an ad to a specific customer, in a specific context.

From there, a DM agency will help businesses determine which digital channels, i.e., websites, should be used to reach their ideal buyers. DM agencies evaluate businesses' website traffic, determine the best online platforms to invest in, and continually maintain the balance between your marketing activities and the results they provide. Programmatic Advertising (PA), as a new format of online precision marketing, has sparked a new wave of explosive growth in display advertising markets [9]. In USA, the PA promotion spending reaches 32.56 billion dollars in 2017, taking up the 80% market share of the online display advertising; in the UK, programmatically traded ads account for more than 75% of online display advertising spending by the end of 2017; and in China, the PA market scale is about 11.69 billion dollars in 2017, and will grow to 29.6 billion in 2019 with the average growth rate of about 35% [9]. PA has evolved as a new model in advertising that facilitates the precise matching between advertisements and target audiences in a real-time manner, as well as it allows for the effective allocation of the limited ad resources, thus leading to the improved performance in market promotions [7]. Therefore, one critical decision that arises in the context of PA is ad inventory allocation, i.e., determining how to allocate the limited ad impressions (ad inventory) to the demanding advertisers as to optimize the publishers' various objectives [7]. Advertisement impressions allocation has been widely considered as one of the most critical decisions for publishers in PA markets [10][11].

This study suggests a methodology based on multicriteria analysis and fuzzy logic in order to identify and quantify the websites selection criteria in programmatic advertising. This paper also proposes the use of similarity methods in order to identify websites that have been overlooked, therefore they can be considered as an investment option.

This paper suggests the use of FDM in order to determine the selection criteria. The FDM is well established and used in similar studies [12]. The (FAHP) is proposed for it allows decision makers, e.g., marketing managers, to express their beliefs regarding the relative importance of selection criteria, and then it aggregates their opinions in order to produce a hierarchical model that quantifies their relative of the selection criteria. This study also utilizes similarity methods in order to identify and recommend websites for investment.

Thus, this research aims to:

- Identify the selection criteria that marketing managers adopt when allocating resource during the PA decision process.
- Propose a multi-criteria approach for identifying and assessing Websites and allocate resources in the context of PA.

The rest of the paper is structured as follows: Section II, discusses the proposed methodology and the methods utilized for the data analysis. The empirical study and the data analysis are presented in Section III. The paper concludes and indicates future research in Section IV.

## II. Methodology and Methods

This section discusses the proposed methodology and the methods used in this study.

### A. *Methodology for identifing and quantifing websites selection criteria that can be used in programmatic advertising*

This study proposes a multi-criteria approach in order to identify selection criteria upon which PA managers could evaluate the performance of websites and decide how to allocate their ad impressions and subsequently their investment budget. Data is collected from two sources. Firstly, from the management of a digital marketing agency that participated in our case study. Then data were collected from the agency's PA platform regarding multiple advertisement campaigns that have been run on behalf of a multinational telecommunication company operating in Greece. The data is analyzed by utilizing the FDM and FAHP multicriteria analysis methods. In recent years, many researchers adopted Multi-Criteria Decision Making (MCDM) approaches for solving problems such as assessing alternative solutions, selection problems, strategic analysis [13]-[18] etc. The steps of the proposed methodology adopted follow.

*Step 1*: Collect data from the management team of the digital marketing agency in Greece. The collected data refers to the management perspective of what selection criteria should be used in PA decision making. The agency manages traffic data for one its customer a big multinational telecommunication company. A group of five (5) managers, dealing with digital marketing and programmatic advertising, had agreed to participate in our study. At first, the managers were introduced to the topic of this research they were informed about procedures regarding their involvement and the methods to be used. Next, the managers were asked to review the data (variables) that were retrieved from a PA platform that the agency uses to follow the performance of advertisement campaigns. Next, they were asked to select a list of variables they would consider most important. The FDM [19]-[21] was utilized in order to prioritize and finally select managers' suggestions. The linguistic variables and corresponding Triangular Fuzzy Numbers (TFNs) that were used in FDM, for the managers to express their priorities are shown in Table I:

TABLE I. The linguistic scales and corresponding TFNs used in FDM

| Linguistic scale | Triangular fuzzy reciprocal scale |
|---|---|
| Not Important | (0,1,3) |
| Somewhat Important | (1,3,5) |
| Important | (3,5,7) |
| Very Important | (5,7,9) |
| Extremely Important | (7,9,10) |

The linguistic scale for the FDM was adopted by Sun [22]. The final list of parameters as resulted from the FDM is shown in Table II:

TABLE II. The management criteria related to the websites selection during the PA decision process

| The management team Criteria as identified from the FDM |
|---|
| Served impressions |
| Total Recordable Impressions (video msg) |
| Total Viewable Impressions |
| Unique Impressions |
| Interactions |
| Clicks |
| Unique Interacting Users |
| Unique Clicking Users |
| Unique Browsers/Users |
| Page Views |

A FAHP questionnaire was then developed and sent to five managers of the agency that participated in this case study. The questionnaire consisted of questions that referred to the relative importance of the selected criteria as perceived by the each one of the managers. The linguistic variables and corresponding (TFNs) that were used in FAHP, for the managers to express their beliefs are shown in Table III:

TABLE III. THE LINGUISTIC SCALES AND CORRESPONDING TFNS USED IN FAHP

| Linguistic scale | Triangular fuzzy scale | Triangular fuzzy reciprocal scale |
|---|---|---|
| Equally important | (1, 1, 1) | (1, 1, 1) |
| Weakly important | (2/3, 1, 3/2) | (2/3, 1, 3/2) |
| Fairly more important | (3/2, 2, 5/2) | (2/5, 1/2, 2/3) |
| Strongly more important | (5/2, 3, 7/2) | (2/7, 1/3, 2/5) |
| Extremely more important | (7/2, 4, 9/2) | (2/9, 1/ 4, 2/7) |

The linguistic scale was adopted by Kilincci et al. [23] and Lee et al. [24]. With respect to sample sizes used in AHP or FAHP, expert group sizes range from 1 in [23] to 5 in [25], 9 in [26] and 24 experts in [24]. The sample size of five is therefore adequate for applying FAHP.

*Step 2*: Apply FAHP and construct the hierarchical model for websites selection.

*Step 3*: Collect data, for to the selection criteria, from the PA platform. Data are then analyzed to assess websites performance.

*Step 4*: Assess websites performance. Examine the proposed model's validation.

*Step 5*: Apply similarity methods to identify and recommend investment opportunities in websites that currently are not considered by the agency in the advertisement portfolio of the telecommunication company.

## B. *The Fuzzy Delphi Method*

The FDM has been extensively used in many studies seeking expert consensus on MCDM problems such as developing performance appraisal indicators for mobility of the service industries [12] for logistics and supplier evaluation [27] for lubricant regenerative technology selection [19] and for developing road safety performance indicators [20]. The FDM was proposed by Murry et al. [21] as an integration of fuzzy logic with the traditional Delphi Method [28]. Expert consensus, in MCDM methods such as the FDM or the FAHP, is usually calculated using the geometric mean, which is assumed to capture expert consensus more accurately [12][20][29][30]. This paper uses TFNs with geometric means to represent expert consensus. A TFN is denoted simply as a triple ($l_{i,j}, m_{i,j}, u_{i,j}$), where:

$$l_{i,j} = \min(e_{i,j}) \ , \qquad (1)$$

represents the lowest of all experts' judgment,

$$m_{i,j} = \sqrt{\prod_{i=1}^{n} e_{i,j}} \ , \qquad (2)$$

is the geometric means of $e_{i,j}$, indicating the aggregation of all experts' judgments, and

$$u_{i,j} = \max(e_{i,j}) \ , \qquad (3)$$

represents the highest of all experts' judgment,

where i =1,…,n and j=1,…,k represent the number of experts and the number of criteria respectively, and the represents the response of the ith expert regarding the jth criterion.

## C. *The FAHP Method*

The FAHP is an extension of Analytic Hierarchy Process (AHP) introduced in [31]. Fuzzy logic is introduced to AHP by utilizing linguistic variables and fuzzy numbers in order to deal with uncertainty in judgments. FAHP prioritizes the relative importance of a list of criteria and sub-criteria through pair-wise comparisons by experts as discussed in[32]. The extent analysis method introduced in [33] is a popular method to solving MCDM problems with FAHP. Assume that $A = (a_{ij})_{nxm}$ is a fuzzy pair-wise comparison judgment matrix and $M = (l, m, u)$ is a Triangular Fuzzy Number (TFN). According to the FAHP, each object is taken and extent analysis for each goal (gi) is performed respectively. Therefore, m extent analysis values for each object can be obtained, with the following notation:

$$M_{g_i}^1, M_{g_i}^2, \ldots, M_{g_i}^m$$

where, i = 1,2,…,n (4)

and all the $M_{g_i}^j (j = 1,2,\ldots,m)$ (j=1,2,…,m) are TFNs. The steps of FAHP are shown below:

*Step 1*: The value Si of the fuzzy synthetic extent with respect to the ith object is defined as:.

$$S_i = \sum_{j=1}^{m} M_{g_i}^j \otimes \left[ \sum_{i=1}^{n} \sum_{j=1}^{m} M_{g_i}^j \right]^{-1} \qquad (5)$$

$$\text{s.t.} \ \sum_{j=1}^{m} M_{g_i}^j = \left( \sum_{j=1}^{m} l_j, \sum_{j=1}^{m} m_j, \sum_{j=1}^{m} u_j \right) \qquad (6)$$

$$\sum_{i=1}^{n} \sum_{j=1}^{m} M_{g_i}^j = \left( \sum_{i=1}^{n} l_i, \sum_{i=1}^{n} m_i, \sum_{i=1}^{n} u_i \right) \qquad (7)$$

Next, compute the inverse of the vector in Eq. (7) such that:

$$\left[ \sum_{i=1}^{n} \sum_{j=1}^{m} M_{g_i}^j \right]^{-1} = \left( \frac{1}{\sum_{i=1}^{n} u_i}, \frac{1}{\sum_{i=1}^{n} m_i}, \frac{1}{\sum_{i=1}^{n} l_i} \right) \qquad (8)$$

The TFN value of $S_i = (l_i, m_i, u_i)$ is calculated using Eqs. (5)-(8).

*Step 2*: The degree of possibility of $S_j = (l_j, m_j, u_j) \geq S_i = (l_i, m_i, u_i)$ (9) is defined as follows:

$$V(S_j \geq S_i) = \sup_{y \geq x} \left[ \min(\mu_{S_i}(x), \mu_{S_j}(y)) \right] \quad (10)$$

which can be equivalently expressed as follows:

$$V(S_j \geq S_i) = height(S_i \cap S_j) = \mu_{S_j}(d)$$

$$= \begin{cases} 1, & if\ m_j \geq m_i \\ 0, & if\ l_i \geq u_j \\ \dfrac{l_i - u_j}{(m_j - u_j) - (m_i - l_i)}, & otherwise \end{cases}$$

where d is the ordinate of the highest intersection point D between $\mu_{S_i}$ and $\mu_{S_j}$ as shown in Figure 1.

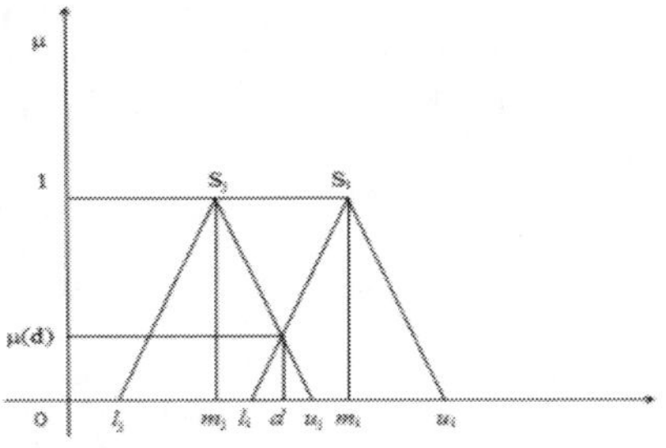


Figure 1. The intersection of $\mu_{S_i}$ and $\mu_{S_j}$.

In order to compare the Si and Sj, we need both the values of $V(S_i \geq S_j)$ and $V(S_j \geq S_i)$

*Step 3*: The minimum degree of possibility for a convex fuzzy number to be greater than k convex fuzzy numbers Si (i = 1, 2,…, k) can be defined by the following equation (11):

$$V(S \geq S_1, S_2, \ldots S_k) = V[(S \geq S_1) and (S \geq S_2) and .and (S \geq S_k)]$$

$$= \min V(S \geq S_i),\ i = 1,2,3, \ldots k.$$

Assume that

$$d'(A_i) = \min V(S_i \geq S_k), \quad for k = 1,2, \ldots, n\ and\ k \neq i$$

Then the weight vector is given by:

$$W' = (d'(A_1), d'(A_2), \ldots, d'(A_n))^T \quad (12)$$

where Ai (i=1,2,…,n) are n elements.

*Step 4*: Obtain the normalized weight vectors as follows: $W = (d(A_1), d(A_2), \ldots, d(A_n))^T$ (13)

where W is a non-fuzzy number and it represents the priority weights of one alternative over another.

*Step 5*: Calculating the Consistency Ratio (CR)

The CR is calculated by adopting the approach used in [34], who computed CR for modal values of the fuzzy numbers in the pair-wise matrices.

## III. Empirical Study and Data Analysis

After all responses from the group of the five managers were collected, the FAHP was applied (eqs. 5-13) returning the importance weights for the selection criteria. The results are shown in Table IV.

TABLE IV. THE SELECTION CRITERIA IMPORTANCE WEIGHTS

| **The management team Criteria as identified from the FDM** | **Weights resulted from FAHP** |
|---|---|
| Unique Clicking Users | 0,199881601 |
| Unique Interacting Users | 0,152037255 |
| Clicks | 0,143605756 |
| Interactions | 0,126324699 |
| Total Viewable Impressions | 0,122097554 |
| Unique Browsers/Users | 0,069015474 |
| Unique Impressions | 0,064870753 |
| Total Recordable Impressions | 0,054865414 |
| Served impressions | 0,035889417 |
| Page Views | 0,031412076 |

The results show that the agency management was concerned more about the number of users (e.g., clicks unique and interacting users) who were attracted from an ad, than other criteria, e.g., the number of impressions that have been viewed or served. Therefore, the most important key success factor for a digital ad is to firstly attract the attention of the potential customer. Next, the websites were ranked by using advertising campaigns data that were retrieved from the PA platform that the agency had access and the selection criteria weights. The campaigns data measure the performance of every website considered by the agency, in terms of the selection criteria. A sample of the ranking is shown in Table V.

TABLE V. THE WEBSITES RANKING

| Website | CR1 | CR2 | CR3 | CR4 | CR5 | CR6 | CR7 | CR8 | CR9 | CR10 | Total |
|---|---|---|---|---|---|---|---|---|---|---|---|
| WBS34 | 0,050951 | 0,040426 | 0,033822 | 0,035183 | 0,237703 | 0,027539 | 0,144043 | 0,031899 | 0,047729 | 0,091641 | 0,078343 |
| WBS1 | 0,022802 | 0,024948 | 0,03431 | 0,033572 | 0,032729 | 0,121241 | 0,083735 | 0,118752 | 0,019154 | 0,013645 | 0,066985 |
| WBS31 | 0,017084 | 0,017528 | 0,02886 | 0,023843 | 0,025443 | 0,105437 | 0,068137 | 0,107226 | 0,019135 | 0,010507 | 0,05738 |

The results indicate the overall ranking as well as the ranking for each individual criterion. So, the agency management could know how each website performed in total and for each individual criterion. Next the websites were grouped in their relevant subject categories. The FAHP was then performed to rank the websites by their category. The results are shown in Table VI.

TABLE VI. RANKING WEBSITES BY THEIR RELEVANT SUBJECT CATEGORY

| Category | CR1 | CR2 | CR3 | CR4 | CR5 | CR6 | CR7 | CR8 | CR9 | CR10 | 1 |
|---|---|---|---|---|---|---|---|---|---|---|---|
| NEWS & INFORMATION | 0,5850 | 0,5136 | 0,4891 | 0,4858 | 0,3333 | 0,3682 | 0,3141 | 0,2984 | 0,4367 | 0,4065 | 0,397939 |
| LIFESTYLE & ENTERTAINMENT | 0,1304 | 0,1671 | 0,1802 | 0,1458 | 0,0303 | 0,1280 | 0,1410 | 0,1775 | 0,1723 | 0,1114 | 0,140187 |
| PORTAL | 0,0586 | 0,0816 | 0,0901 | 0,0736 | 0,3139 | 0,0220 | 0,1254 | 0,0465 | 0,1324 | 0,1703 | 0,11583 |
| WEB TV | 0,0416 | 0,0384 | 0,0433 | 0,0400 | 0,0387 | 0,2015 | 0,1674 | 0,2235 | 0,0286 | 0,0154 | 0,102763 |
| FINANCE | 0,0562 | 0,0824 | 0,0705 | 0,0668 | 0,2096 | 0,0168 | 0,0230 | 0,0157 | 0,0378 | 0,0497 | 0,064086 |
| OTHER | 0,0327 | 0,0434 | 0,0410 | 0,0602 | 0,0155 | 0,0811 | 0,0789 | 0,1131 | 0,0089 | 0,0111 | 0,055892 |
| SPORTS | 0,0338 | 0,0291 | 0,0349 | 0,0661 | 0,0115 | 0,0604 | 0,0754 | 0,0519 | 0,0819 | 0,1135 | 0,05184 |
| FEMALE | 0,0344 | 0,0353 | 0,0376 | 0,0371 | 0,0367 | 0,0670 | 0,0555 | 0,0457 | 0,0439 | 0,0290 | 0,044316 |
| MALE | 0,0201 | 0,0054 | 0,0079 | 0,0115 | 0,0090 | 0,0476 | 0,0163 | 0,0234 | 0,0099 | 0,0029 | 0,01615 |
| PRICE ENGINE | 0,0072 | 0,0038 | 0,0051 | 0,0032 | 0,0014 | 0,0074 | 0,0030 | 0,0042 | 0,0476 | 0,0892 | 0,010998 |

The results indicate that the best performing campaigns for the telecommunication company were those ran by the agency in the *News and Information* sector, with the *Lifestyle and Entertainment* following second. However, the effectiveness of the investment in advertising depends on the budget that is spent on each website and on each sector. After normalizing the spending the ranking of each website and each sector were recalculated. The results regarding the sectors are shown in Table VII.

TABLE VII. THE COST-BENEFIT CONTRIBUTION OF EACH SECTOR

| CATEGORIES | ACTUAL TOTAL CONTRIBUTION INDEX |
|---|---|
| NEWS & INFORMATION | 0,73 |
| LIFESTYLE & ENTERTAINMENT | 1,33 |
| PORTAL | 0,86 |
| WEB TV | 2,66 |
| SPORTS | 2,64 |
| FEMALE | 1,37 |
| FINANCE | 1,04 |
| MALE | 3,11 |
| PRICE ENGINE | 4,82 |
| OTHER | 3,48 |

By taking into account the budget spent for advertising in each sector, the ranking changes. So, despite the *News and Information* sector's achievement to outperform all the other sectors, the amount of money that was spent for advertising in this sector seems to be larger than it should be being disproportioned with the sectors performance results.

The websites evaluation based on the selection criteria as well as on the advertising budget, does not highlights the best performing sites but it also reveals investment opportunities. By calculating the Chi-Square similarity method as discussed in [35], websites of similar performance but with much lower level of investments may represent a promising alternative for advertising. This study analyzed data from 123 websites. So, the resulting similarity matrix is (123x123) matrix. The values in the matrix show how much a website is similar to all the rest. The closer the value is to +1, the more similar the websites are. On contrary, values closer to -1, indicate dissimilarity. The sample of the similarity matrix shown in Table VIII indicates that WS1 Website is very much similar to WS8 with a similarity degree of 0.946.

TABLE VIII. THE SIMILARITY AMONG WEBSITES

| | WS1 | WS2 | WS3 | WS4 | WS5 | WS6 | WS7 | WS8 |
|---|---|---|---|---|---|---|---|---|
| WS1 | 1 | 0,575793 | -0,47329 | 0,492775 | 0,62571 | 0,449098 | 0,387247 | 0,946222 |
| WS2 | 0,575793 | 1 | -0,29653 | 0,357916 | 0,148567 | 0,305917 | 0,568012 | 0,647365 |
| WS3 | -0,47329 | -0,29653 | 1 | -0,28154 | -0,48859 | 0,408093 | -0,34409 | -0,44875 |

If the advertising spending on the WS1 and WS8 is far apart then an investment opportunity is worth considering. Assuming that the budget spent on WS1 is much lower that the WS8, then the WS1 is already a promising alternative for serving impressions.

## IV. CONCLUSIONS AND FUTURE WORK

Programmatic advertising and digital marketing attract a lot of attention since the focus of interacting with customers is already shifted on digital channels. Web analytics and PA platforms play an important role in assessing the effectiveness of digital marketing. Challenging decisions should be made by management teams when devising an advertising plan. There are millions of websites and other digital channels that need to be considered for serving impressions. Currently, analytics tools do not provide a comprehensive list of parameters to consider and analyze in PA related decision making. This study by utilizing multicriteria methods, such as the FDM and the FAHP, proposes a methodology to identify and analyze the relative importance of websites selection criteria and use them in developing a hierarchical model that could assist decision making in the PA. This research also suggests that similarity methods can be utilized to highlight investments opportunities in an attempt to assist PA management to revise their options. Furthermore, this research suggests that, Web analytics tools should improve their functionality by combining MCDM methods, in order to enhance their value in assessing digital marketing strategies.

Future research should focus on developing methods and tools that take into consideration time-dependent factors in a real-time manner and develop the required functionality in analyzing and managing the interactions among investment performance and customer interactions.

## REFERENCES

[1] eMarketer, "Digital Ad Spending 2019". Available from URL: "https://www.emarketer.com/content/global-digital-ad-spending-2019, last viewed 31/7/2019.

[2] J. Järvinen, and H. Karjaluoto, "The use of Web analytics for digital marketing performance measurement." Industrial Marketing Management Vol 50, pp. 117-127, 2015.

[3] T. Hennig-Thurau, et.al. "The impact of new media on customer relationships." Journal of Service Research, Vol 13, pp. 311–330, 2010.

[4] D. Pickton. "Left brain marketing planning: A Forrester Research viewpoint". Marketing Intelligence & Planning, Vol 23, pp. 537–542, 2005.

[5] R.D. Wilson. "Using clickstream data to enhance business-to-business web site performance." Journal of Business & Industrial Marketing, Vol 25, pp. 177–187, 2010.

[6] D. Chaffey, and M. Patron. "From web analytics to digital marketing optimization: Increasing the commercial value of digital analytics." Journal of Direct, Data and Digital Marketing Practice, Vol 14, pp. 30–45, 2012.

[7] Gartner, "Gartner CMO Spend Survey 2016-2017 Shows Marketing Budgets Continue to Climb." Available from URL: http://www.gartner.com/smarterwithgartner/gartner-cmo-spend-survey-2016-2017-shows-marketing-budgets-continue-to-climb/, 2016, last viewed 31/7/2019.

[8] Forbes, "US Digital Marketing Spend Will Near $120 Billion By 2021." Available from URL: https://www.forbes.com/sites/forrester/2017/01/26/us-digital-marketing-spend-will-near-120-billion-by-2021/#4aa2e6b278bb, 2017, last viewed 31/7/2019.

[9] J. Li, X. Ni, Y. Yuan, and F-Y. Wang, "A Hierarchical Framework for Ad Inventory Allocation in Programmatic Advertising Markets." Electronic Commerce Research and Applications, Vol 31, pp. 40-51, 2018.

[10] S. Muthukrishnan. "Ad Exchanges: Research Issues[C]. InternationalWorkshop on Internet and Network Economics." Springer-Verlag, pp. 1-12, 2009.

[11] M. Mostagir. "Optimal delivery in display advertising[C]. Communication, Control, and Computing." IEEE Xplore, pp. 577-583, 2010

[12] Y. Kuo, and P. Chen, "Constructing performance appraisal indicators for mobility of the service industries using Fuzzy Delphi Method." Expert Systems with Applications, Vol 35, pp. 1930-1939, 2008.

[13] E.W.T Ngai. "Selection of web sites for online advertising using AHP." Information & Management, Vol. 40, pp. 233-242, 2003.

[14] Y. C. Chen, H. Lien, G. Tzeng, and L. Yang, "Fuzzy MCDM approach for selecting the best environment-watershed plan." Applied soft computing, Vol 11, pp. 265-275, 2010.

[15] C. Lin, M. Hsieh, and G. Tzeng, "Evaluating vehicle telematics system by using a novel MCDM techniques with dependence and feedback." Expert systems with applications, Vol 37, pp. 6723-6736, 2010.

[16] J. Liou, G. Tzeng, and H. Chang, "Airline safety measurement using a hybrid model." Journal of air transport management, Vol 13, pp. 243-249, 2007.

[17] O Yang, H. Shieh, J. Leu, and G. Tzeng, "A novel hybrid MCDM model combined with DEMATEL and ANP with applications." International journal of operations research, Vol 5, pp. 160-168, 2008.

[18] G. Tzeng, C. Chiang, and C. Li, "Evaluating intertwined effects in e-learning programs: A novel hybrid MCDM model based on factor analysis and DEMATEL." Expert systems with applications, Vol 32, pp. 1028-1044, 2007.

[19] Y. Hsu, C. Lee, and V. Kreng. "The application of fuzzy Delphi method and fuzzy AHP in lubricant regenerative technology selection." Expert Systems with Applications, Vol 37, pp. 419-425, 2010.

[20] Z. Ma, C. Shao, S. Ma, and Z. Ye. "Constructing road safety performance indicators using fuzy Delphi metod and Grey Delphi method." Expert Systems with Applications, Vol 38, pp. 1509-1514, 2011.

[21] T.J. Murry, L.L. Pipino, and J.P. Gigch."A pilot study of fuzzy set modification of Delphi." Human Systems Management, Vol 5, 76-80, 1985.

[22] C.C. Sun "A performance evaluation model by integrating fuzzy AHP and fuzzy TOPSIS methods." Expert Systems with Applications, Vol 37, pp. 7745-7754, 2010.

[23] O. Kilincci, and S.A. Onal. "Fuzzy AHP approach form supplier selection in a washing machine company." Expert Systems with Application, Vol 38, pp. 9656-9664, 2011.

[24] S.K.. Lee, G. Mogi, J.W. Kim, and B.J. Gim. "A fuzzy analytic hierarchy process approach for assessing national competitiveness in the hydrogen technology sector." International Journal of Hydrogen Energy, Vol 33, pp. 6840-6848, 2008.

[25] T.J. Barker, and Z.B. Zabinsky. "A multicriteria decision making model for reverse logistics using analytical hierarchy process." Omega, Vol 39, pp. 558-573, 2011.

[26] P.F. Hsu, and B.Y. Chen. "Developing and implementing a selection model for bedding chain retail store franchisee using Delphi and Fuzzy AHP." Quality & Quantity, Vol 41, pp. 275-290, 2007.

[27] H.T. Liu, and W.K. Wang. "An integrated fuzzy approach for provider evaluation and selection in third-party logistics." Expert Systems with Applications, Vol 36, pp. 4387–4398, 2009.

[28] N.C. Dalkey, and O. Helmer. "An experimental application method to the use of experts." Management Science, Vol 9, pp. 458-467, 1963.

[29] J. Pai. "A fuzzy MCDM evaluation framework based on humanity-oriented transport for transforming scheme of major arterial space in Taipei metropolitan." Journal of Eastern Asia Society for Transportation Studies, Vol 7, pp. 1731-1744, 2007.

[30] T.H. Hsu, and T.H. Yang. "Application of fuzzy analytic hierarchy process in the selection of advertising media." Journal of management and Systems, Vol 7, pp. 19-39, 2000.

[31] T.L. Saaty. "The Analytic Hierarchy Process." New York: McGraw- Hill, 1980.

[32] H.Y. Wu, G.H., Tzeng, and Y.H. Chen. "A fuzzy MCDM approach for evaluating banking performance based on Balanced Scorecard." Expert Systems with Applications, Vol 36, pp. 10135-10147, 2009.

[33] D.Y. Chang. "Applications of the extent analysis method on fuzzy AHP." European Journal of Operational Research, Vol 95, pp. 649–655, 1996.

[34] P. Jakiel, and D. Fabianowski. "FAHP model used for assessment of highway RC bridge structural and technological arrangements." Expert Systems with Applications, Vol 42, pp. 4054-4061, 2015.

[35] N. Dessì, and B. Pes. "Similarity of feature selection methods: An empirical study across data intensive classification tasks." Expert Systems with Applications, Vol 42, pp. 4632-4642, 2015.

# Analytical Models of Firing Rate Statistics in Sensory Neuroscience Experiments

Christopher C. Pack
Montreal Neurological Institute (MNI)
McGill University
Montreal, Quebec, Canada
e-mail: christopher.pack@mcgill.ca

Charles D. Pack
Computer Science Dept.
Monmouth University
Red Bank, NJ
e-mail: cpack@monmouth.edu

*Abstract*— **Motivated by empirical results, we develop simple Taylor Series approximations (analytics) for statistics associated with neuronal response data in sensory (e.g., vision) experiments in a laboratory setting. Such responses exhibit a non-negativity constraint and additional nonlinearities, such as "normalization". These transformations also change correlations among neuronal responses, which are thought to limit the fidelity of sensory representations. Simulation studies and cases, where we have exact results, show that our models are accurate over a wide range of parameter values. Ignoring constraints, simple analytical expressions help explain how data quality, parameter values and sensitivities affect results.**

***Keywords-*** ***data; measurements; analytics; statistics; simulation; neuroscience; vision experiments.***

## I. INTRODUCTION

Many sub-disciplines within the field of brain science are concerned with the relationship between sensory (e.g., vision) stimuli and electrical activity in groups of neurons. The fidelity of this "neural code" is thought to depend on the firing rates of individual neurons and the variability or noise associated with these rates. Standard models of neural coding suggest that noise that is correlated across neurons deteriorates sensory representations in the brain [1]. Recent work has proposed that a specific transform operation, "normalization," might reduce the impact of correlated noise on neural coding. Support for this idea comes from simulations [2] and experimental observations. [3][4]. There are some analytical models for untransformed signal correlations [5][6]. Here, we develop new analytical models of pairwise correlations in neural responses to multiple replications of various sensory stimuli as well as the parametric relationship between a common nonlinear transformation and noise correlations. While we obtain some exact analytical results, degree-2 Taylor Series (T-S) approximations are particularly useful for transformed responses that require non-negativity constraints. Simulations show that our approximations are quite accurate for parameter values of interest to neuroscientists, but can be inaccurate or unstable at parameter extremes.

In Section II, we describe our neuroscience experiments, data/measurements and important statistics. In Section III, we develop some analytical models and Taylor-Series approximations. In Section IV, we provide analytical and simulation results. Section V contains a summary and important conclusions.

## II. NEUROSCIENCE EXPERIMENTS, DATA, STATISTICS

In neuroscience experiments, data come from electrophysiological recordings of two (or more) neurons, during the presentation of a sensory stimulus such as a visual image. Each neuron fire spikes, which are discrete events that we measure over some time window. The measured spike counts are generally assumed to follow a Poisson distribution. We record these responses to $N$ repetitions of the $M$ different visual stimuli. For any stimulus, $i$, we have a pair of vectors ($\hat{\lambda}_{ij1}$, $\hat{\lambda}_{ij2}$), corresponding to the measured responses of the two neurons across repetitions of the same stimulus. From those, we calculate *rnoise(i)*, the correlation between these vectors. If we then take the mean, i.e., we "smooth" the original spike counts across repetitions, $j$, we get vectors ($\hat{v}_{i1}$, $\hat{v}_{i2}$). We next calculate the correlation between $\hat{v}_{i1}$ and $\hat{v}_{i2}$ to get a measure, *rsignal(i)*, of the stimulus preferences of the two neurons. Because of limited data, neuroscientists often compute, *rsignal~*, a "pseudo-correlation" over $M$ stimuli. Finally, neuroscientists may analyze transformations of unsmoothed and smoothed responses with correlations *rnoise(i)'* and *rsignal~'*. We analyze statistics for our models of these four cases: 1. ($\hat{\lambda}_{ij1}$, $\hat{\lambda}_{ij2}$) *(rnoise(i))*; 2. ($\hat{v}_{i1}$, $\hat{v}_{i2}$) *(rsignal~)*; 3. Transformed responses ($\hat{\lambda}'_{ij1}$,$\hat{\lambda}'_{ij2}$) *(rnoise(i)')*; 4. Transformed, averaged ($\hat{v}'_{i1}$, $\hat{v}'_{i2}$) *(rsignal~')*. Cases 1-3 can be done exactly; Case 4 needs analytical approximations.

## III. ANALYTICAL MODELS

We now develop analytical models for each of the four above cases.

### A. Case 1: Original Data and rnoise(i)

For each neuron, $k = 1$ *or* $2$, there are response measurements $\hat{\lambda}_{ijk}$=$\lambda_{ik}(1+\varepsilon_{ijk})$ corresponding to stimuli $i$=$1,...,M$ and replications $j$=$1,...,N$. The $\lambda_{ik}$ and $\varepsilon_{ijk}$ are the "true" random spike counts and the independent random measurement error factors. Let $E(\lambda_{ik}) = \bar{\lambda}_{ik}$ and $var(\lambda_{ik}) = \sigma^2_{\lambda_{ik}}$. The correlation between the two neuron responses (signals) is $\rho(\lambda_{i1},\lambda_{i2}) \geq \rho(\hat{\lambda}_{ij1},\hat{\lambda}_{ij2})$. We assume $\varepsilon_{ijk}$ is $N(0,\sigma^2_{\varepsilon_k})$. It follows that $E(\hat{\lambda}_{ijk}) = \bar{\lambda}_{ik}$ and $var(\hat{\lambda}_{ijk}) = \sigma^2_{\lambda_{ik}} + \bar{\lambda}^2_{ik}\sigma^2_{\varepsilon_k} + \sigma^2_{\lambda_{ik}}\sigma^2_{\varepsilon_k}$. If measured responses are Poisson, $var(\hat{\lambda}_{ijk}) = E(\hat{\lambda}_{ijk}) = (\bar{\lambda}_{ik})$. Then, we have $cov(\hat{\lambda}_{ij1},\hat{\lambda}_{ij2}) = cov(\lambda_{i1},\lambda_{i2}) = \rho(\lambda_{i1},\lambda_{i2})\sigma^2_{\lambda_{i1}}\sigma^2_{\lambda_{i2}}$ and

$$rnoise(i) = \frac{cov(\hat{\lambda}_{ij1},\hat{\lambda}_{ij2})}{\sqrt{var(\hat{\lambda}_{ij1})var(\hat{\lambda}_{ij2})}} = \frac{\rho(\lambda_{i1},\lambda_{i2})}{\sqrt{(1+\bar{\lambda}^2_{i1}\frac{\sigma^2_{\varepsilon_1}}{\sigma^2_{\lambda_{i1}}}+\sigma^2_{\varepsilon_1})(1+\bar{\lambda}^2_{i2}\frac{\sigma^2_{\varepsilon_2}}{\sigma^2_{\lambda_{i2}}}+\sigma^2_{\varepsilon_2})}} \tag{1}$$

Note that only the denominator involves measurement uncertainty. There is one unintended impact of the product-form analytical model for Case 1 (and Case 3, below). Given the *MxNx2* measurements from a vision experiment, we might use the common variance estimator for sample variances: $\sigma^2_{\hat{\lambda}_{ijk}} = var(\hat{\lambda}_{ijk}) \approx \hat{\sigma}^2_{\hat{\lambda}_{ijk}} = \frac{\sum_{j=1}^{N}(\hat{\lambda}_{ijk}-\frac{\sum_{p=1}^{N}\hat{\lambda}_{ipk}}{N})^2}{N-1} = \frac{\sum_{j=1}^{N}(\hat{\lambda}_{ijk}-\hat{\vartheta}_{ik})^2}{N-1}$, where $\hat{\vartheta}_{ik}$ is an estimate of $E(\hat{\lambda}_{ijk})$. The problem is that $E(\hat{\sigma}^2_{\hat{\lambda}_{ijk}}) = \sigma^2_{\hat{\lambda}_{ijk}} - \sigma^2_{\lambda_{ik}} \neq \sigma^2_{\hat{\lambda}_{ijk}}$. which is *biased low* for $var(\hat{\lambda}_{ijk})$ when $\hat{\lambda}_{ijk}$ is the product of 2 random variables. We will need to correct this bias in our simulation. Similarly, if we use the standard covariance estimator for $\varsigma(i) \approx cov(\hat{\lambda}_{ij1},\hat{\lambda}_{ij2}) = cov(\lambda_{i1},\lambda_{i2})$, we get $\hat{\varsigma}(i) = \frac{\sum_{j=1}^{N}(\hat{\lambda}_{ij1}-\hat{\vartheta}_{i1})(\hat{\lambda}_{ij2}-\hat{\vartheta}_{i2})}{N-1}$, with the result that $E[\hat{\varsigma}(i)]=0$, which is *also biased low* and needs to be corrected in the simulation results.

*B. Case 2: "Smoothed" Data and rsignal(i), rsignal~*

Let $\hat{\vartheta}_{ik} = \frac{\sum_{j=1}^{N}\hat{\lambda}_{ijk}}{N} = \lambda_{ik}(1+\frac{\sum_{j=1}^{N}\varepsilon_{ijk}}{N})$ for $i=1,...,M$. Then, for all $i$, $E(\hat{\vartheta}_{ik}) = \bar{\lambda}_{ik}$, $var(\hat{\vartheta}_{ik}) = \sigma^2_{\lambda_{ik}} + \frac{\bar{\lambda}^2_{ik}\sigma^2_{\varepsilon_k}}{N} + \frac{\sigma^2_{\lambda_{ik}}\sigma^2_{\varepsilon_k}}{N}$. Further, $cov(\hat{\vartheta}_{i1},\hat{\vartheta}_{i2}) = cov(\hat{\lambda}_{ij1},\hat{\lambda}_{ij2}) = cov(\lambda_{i1},\lambda_{i2})$, and correlation $rsignal(i) = \frac{cov(\hat{\vartheta}_{i1},\hat{\vartheta}_{i2})}{\sqrt{var(\hat{\vartheta}_{i1})var(\hat{\vartheta}_{i2})}} =$

$$\frac{\rho(\lambda_{i1},\lambda_{i2})\sigma_{\lambda_{i1}}\sigma_{\lambda_{i2}}}{\sqrt{\sigma^2_{\hat{\vartheta}_{i1}}\sigma^2_{\hat{\vartheta}_{i2}}}} = \frac{\rho(\lambda_{i1},\lambda_{i2})}{\sqrt{(1+\bar{\lambda}^2_{i1}\frac{\sigma^2_{\varepsilon_1}}{N\sigma^2_{\lambda_{i1}}}+\sigma^2_{\varepsilon_1})(1+\bar{\lambda}^2_{i2}\frac{\sigma^2_{\varepsilon_2}}{N\sigma^2_{\lambda_{i2}}}+\sigma^2_{\varepsilon_2})}} \tag{2}$$

Equation (2) is quite similar to (1) except that measurement error variances are divided by *N*. Then, due in part to data limitations, neuroscientists generally use (define) *rsignal~*, a different measure of the similarity of neuronal responses to various stimuli. That is, *rsignal~*

$$= \frac{cov\sim(\hat{\vartheta}_{*1},\hat{\vartheta}_{*2})}{\sqrt{var\sim(\hat{\vartheta}_{*1})var\sim(\hat{\vartheta}_{*2})}} = \frac{E\sum_{i=1}^{M}(\hat{\vartheta}_{i1}-\hat{\vartheta}_{*1})(\hat{\vartheta}_{i2}-\hat{\vartheta}_{*2})}{\sqrt{E\sum_{i=1}^{M}(\hat{\vartheta}_{i1}-\hat{\vartheta}_{*1})^2 E\sum_{i=1}^{M}(\hat{\vartheta}_{i2}-\hat{\vartheta}_{*2})^2}} \tag{3}$$

where $\hat{\vartheta}_{*k} = \frac{\sum_{i=1}^{M}\hat{\vartheta}_{*k}}{M}$. While $cov(\hat{\vartheta}_{i1},\hat{\vartheta}_{i2}) = cov(\hat{\lambda}_{ij1},\hat{\lambda}_{ij2})$, $cov\sim(\hat{\vartheta}_{*1},\hat{\vartheta}_{*2}) \neq cov(\hat{\lambda}_{ij1},\hat{\lambda}_{ij2})$. We can compute *rsignal~*, in terms of more traditional moments, using

$$E\sum_{i=1}^{M}(\hat{\vartheta}_{i1}-\hat{\vartheta}_{*1})(\hat{\vartheta}_{i2}-\hat{\vartheta}_{*2}) = \frac{M-1}{M}\sum_{i=1}^{M}[cov(\lambda_{i1},\lambda_{i2}) + \bar{\lambda}_{i1}\bar{\lambda}_{i2}] - \frac{1}{M}\sum_{i=1}^{M}\sum_{p\neq i}^{M}[cov(\lambda_{i1},\lambda_{p2}) + \bar{\lambda}_{i1}\bar{\lambda}_{p2}], \tag{4}$$

$$E\sum_{i=1}^{M}(\hat{\vartheta}_{ik}-\hat{\vartheta}_{*k})^2 = \frac{M-1}{M}\sum_{i=1}^{M}(\sigma^2_{\varepsilon_k} + \bar{\lambda}^2_{ik}) - \frac{1}{M}\sum_{i=1}^{M}\sum_{p\neq i}^{M}[cov(\lambda_{ik},\lambda_{pk}) + \bar{\lambda}_{ik}\bar{\lambda}_{pk}]. \tag{5}$$

Assume inter-stimuli covariances in (4), (5) are negligible.

*C. Cases 3 and 4: Transformed Responses*

First, we define the normalization transformation that we use in this report:

$$\begin{aligned}\hat{\lambda}'_{ijk} &= f(\lambda_{ik},\lambda_{ik-},\varepsilon_{ijk},\varepsilon_{ijk-}) \\ &= \max\left(0, \frac{\hat{\lambda}^2_{ijk}}{s\hat{\lambda}^2_{ijk}+c} - r\frac{\hat{\lambda}^2_{ijk-}}{s\hat{\lambda}^2_{ijk-}+c}\right) \\ &= \max\left(0, g(\lambda_{ik},\lambda_{ik-},\varepsilon_{ijk},\varepsilon_{ijk-})\right)\end{aligned}$$

$$= \max\left(0, \frac{[\lambda_{ik}(1+\varepsilon_{ijk})]^2}{s[\lambda_{ik}(1+\varepsilon_{ijk})]^2+c} - \frac{r[\lambda_{ik-}(1+\varepsilon_{ijk-})]^2}{s[\lambda_{ik-}(1+\varepsilon_{ijk-})]^2+c}\right) \tag{6}$$

where *s, c, r* are non-negative constants and *k-* is the opposite neuron index from *k*. The first term in expanded (6) corresponds to the standard form of normalization used in neuroscience [7]; the terms in the denominator can be thought of as corresponding to pools of neurons that are correlated (first term) or uncorrelated (second term) with the neuron in the numerator. The second term in the equation allows for the possibility of opponent processing, a common neural operation that is hypothesized to influence noise correlations [8]. The max function captures the fact that neural firing rates cannot, by definition, be negative. We will see that the transformations in Cases 3 and 4 increase complexity because they:

- Are highly non-linear and may need to be *constrained* to be non-negative
- Add many parameters to the model
- Reduce the non-negative magnitude of the (transformed) responses, $\hat{\lambda}'_{ijk}$, to near 0
- Cause correlation statistics, such as *rnoise(i)'* and *rsignal~'*, to become very sensitive to important system parameters, e.g., as $\hat{\lambda}'_{ijk}$ approaches 0.

In our simulation of Case 3, i.e., smoothed transformed data and *rnoise(i)'*, we have to correct biases in the *classic* variance and covariance estimators, $\hat{\sigma}^2_{\hat{\lambda}'_{ijk}}$ and $\hat{c}(\hat{\lambda}'_{ij1},\hat{\lambda}'_{ij2})$, for $var(\hat{\lambda}'_{ijk})$ and $cov(\hat{\lambda}'_{ij1},\hat{\lambda}'_{ij2})$. That is, for $j \neq p$:

$$E\left(\hat{\sigma}^2_{\hat{\lambda}'_{ijk}}\right) = var(\hat{\lambda}'_{ijk}) + E^2(\hat{\lambda}'_{ijk}) - E(\hat{\lambda}'_{ijk}\hat{\lambda}'_{ipk}) \tag{7}$$

and

$$E\left(\hat{c}(\hat{\lambda}'_{ij1},\hat{\lambda}'_{ij2})\right) = cov(\hat{\lambda}'_{ij1},\hat{\lambda}'_{ij2}) + E(\hat{\lambda}'_{ij1})E(\hat{\lambda}'_{ij2}) - E(\hat{\lambda}'_{ij1}\hat{\lambda}'_{ip2}). \quad (8)$$

We also developed exact and T-S analytical models for Case 3. Our exact approach conditions on $\lambda_{ijk}$ and $\lambda_{ijk-}$ in (6), then assumes a joint distribution for them and integrates out to obtain expected values, variances and covariances for $\hat{\lambda}'_{ijk}$. The limits on the integrals reflect the non-negativity constraint. Our analytical approximations focus on degree-2 Taylor Series (TS-2) models (extensive empirical analyses show that the much more complex higher degree models "overfit" the data), with a differentiable approximation of the non-negativity constraint for $\hat{\lambda}'_{ijk}$ in (6). We use Taylor Series models because they often provide very good approximations and reveal critical statistical relationships between input parameters and results. We have not quantified the very small approximation errors. Important TS-2 moments, including correlations, are linear combination of input variances/ covariances, with weights being algebraic expressions of input parameters. Of special interest is the Simplified TS-2 (STS-2) version of the model that is valid when the non-negativity constraint is "non-binding". To develop the TS-2 Model, we replace the non-negativity constraint in the $f$ form of (6) with

$$\hat{\lambda}'_{ijk} = f(\lambda_{ik},\lambda_{ik-},\varepsilon_{ijk},\varepsilon_{ijk-})$$

$$\approx \frac{g(\lambda_{ik},\lambda_{ik-},\varepsilon_{ijk},\varepsilon_{ijk-})+\sqrt{g(\lambda_{ik},\lambda_{ik-},\varepsilon_{ijk},\varepsilon_{ijk-})^2+\delta}}{2} \quad (9)$$

where $\delta$, which is required for differentiability, is a very small positive number. Then, the Taylor Series fit to $f$, as given by (9), is around the "point" $(\bar{\lambda}_{ik},\bar{\lambda}_{ik-},\bar{\varepsilon}_{ijk},\bar{\varepsilon}_{ijk-})$. We assume that the $\lambda$'s have a bivariate Normal distribution with means $(\bar{\lambda}_{ik},\bar{\lambda}_{ik-})$, variances $(\sigma^2_{\lambda_{ik}},\sigma^2_{\lambda_{ik-}})$ and correlation $\rho(\lambda_{ik},\lambda_{ik-})$. The $\varepsilon$'s are each (independently) normally distributed with 0 means and variances $\sigma^2_{\varepsilon_k}$ *and* $\sigma^2_{\varepsilon_{k-}}$, respectively. Accuracy is usually best when variances $(\sigma^2_{\lambda_{ik}},\sigma^2_{\lambda_{ik-}},\sigma^2_{\varepsilon_k},\sigma^2_{\varepsilon_{k-}})$ are small. To get the simpler STS-2 model results, we ignore the non-negativity constraint, i.e., $f\equiv g$. With limited space, we present some results. First, the TS-2 expression for the mean is:

$$E(\hat{\lambda}'_{ijk}) \approx f + \frac{1}{2}\left[f_{\varepsilon_{ijk}\varepsilon_{ijk}}\sigma^2_{\varepsilon_k} + f_{\varepsilon_{ijk-}\varepsilon_{ijk-}}\sigma^2_{\varepsilon_{k-}} + f_{\lambda_{ik}\lambda_{ik}}\sigma^2_{\lambda_{ik}} + f_{\lambda_{ik-}\lambda_{ik-}}\sigma^2_{\lambda_{ik-}}\right] + f_{\lambda_{i1}\lambda_{i2}}cov(\lambda_{i1},\lambda_{i2}) \quad (10)$$

In (10), the subscripts on $f$ and $g$ represent partial derivatives and all expressions in $f$ and $g$ are evaluated at the mean point $(\bar{\lambda}_{ik},\bar{\lambda}_{ik-},0,0)$. Also, all of the partials, $f_{xy}$, are of the form:

$$f_{xy} = \frac{1}{2}\left[g_x g_y \frac{\delta}{(g^2+\delta)^{1.5}} + \left(1+\frac{g}{\sqrt{g^2+\delta}}\right)g_{xy}\right] \quad (11)$$

with the following pairs for (x,y), with corresponding $g$ partials (evaluated at mean):

- $(\varepsilon_{ijk},\varepsilon_{ijk})$: $g_{\varepsilon_{ijk}} = \frac{2c\bar{\lambda}^2_{ik}}{[s\bar{\lambda}^2_{ik}+c)^2}$, $g_{\varepsilon_{ijk}\varepsilon_{ijk}} = \frac{2c\bar{\lambda}^2_{ik}(c-3s\bar{\lambda}^2_{ik})}{[s\bar{\lambda}^2_{ik}+c)^3}$ (12A)
- $(\varepsilon_{ijk-},\varepsilon_{ijk-})$: $g_{\varepsilon_{ijk-}} = \frac{-2rc\bar{\lambda}^2_{ik-}}{[s\bar{\lambda}^2_{ik-}+c)^2}$, $g_{\varepsilon_{ijk-}\varepsilon_{ijk-}} \frac{-2rc\bar{\lambda}^2_{ik-}(c-3s\bar{\lambda}^2_{ik-})}{[s\bar{\lambda}^2_{ik-}+c)^3}$ (12B)
- $(\lambda_{ik},\lambda_{ik})$: $g_{\lambda_{ik}} = \frac{2c\bar{\lambda}_{ik}}{[s\bar{\lambda}^2_{ik}+c)^2}$, $g_{\lambda_{ik}\lambda_{ik}} = \frac{2c(c-3s\bar{\lambda}^2_{ik})}{[s\bar{\lambda}^2_{ik}+c)^3}$ (12C)
- $(\lambda_{ik-},\lambda_{ik-})$: $g_{\lambda_{ik-}} = \frac{-2rc\bar{\lambda}_{ik-}}{[s\bar{\lambda}^2_{ik-}+c)^2}$, $g_{\lambda_{ik-}\lambda_{ik-}} = \frac{-2rc(c-3s\bar{\lambda}^2_{ik-})}{[s\bar{\lambda}^2_{ik-}+c)^3}$ (12D)
- $g_{\lambda_{i1}\lambda_{i2}} = 0$ (12E)

The TS-2 approximation for the variance, $var(\hat{\lambda}'_{ijk})$, is:

$$var(\hat{\lambda}'_{ijk}) \approx f^2_{\varepsilon_{ijk}}\sigma^2_{\varepsilon_k} + f^2_{\varepsilon_{ijk-}}\sigma^2_{\varepsilon_{k-}} + f^2_{\lambda_{ik}}\sigma^2_{\lambda_{ik}} + f^2_{\lambda_{ik-}}\sigma^2_{\lambda_{ik-}} + 2f_{\lambda_{i1}\lambda_{i2}}cov(\lambda_{i1},\lambda_{i2}), \quad (13)$$

where $f_{\lambda_{i1}\lambda_{i2}}$ is given in (11), the weights $f_x$ are

$$f_x = \frac{1}{2}g_x\left(1+\frac{g}{\sqrt{g^2+\delta}}\right), \quad (14)$$

and the various cases for the partials, $g_x$, are in (12A)-(12E).

The TS-2 approximation for the covariance, $cov(\hat{\lambda}'_{ij1},\hat{\lambda}'_{ij2})$, is complicated by the fact that it involves two (transformed) random responses: $\hat{\lambda}'_{ij1}$ and $\hat{\lambda}'_{ij2}$:

$$cov(\hat{\lambda}'_{ij1},\hat{\lambda}'_{ij2}) \approx f_{\varepsilon_{ij1}}\overleftarrow{f}_{\varepsilon_{ij1}}\sigma^2_{\varepsilon_1} + f_{\varepsilon_{ij2}}\overleftarrow{f}_{\varepsilon_{ij2}}\sigma^2_{\varepsilon_2} + f_{\lambda_{i1}}\overleftarrow{f}_{\lambda_{i1}}\sigma^2_{\lambda_{i1}} + f_{\lambda_{i2}}\overleftarrow{f}_{\lambda_{i2}}\sigma^2_{\lambda_{i2}} + (f_{\lambda_{i1}}\overleftarrow{f}_{\lambda_{i2}} + f_{\lambda_{i2}}\overleftarrow{f}_{\lambda_{i1}})cov(\lambda_{i1},\lambda_{i2}) \quad (15)$$

where all of the partials of the form, $f_x$, are given in (14). However, the term, $\overleftarrow{f}_x$, requires some explanation. Because of the symmetries of the graded transformation (6), $\hat{\lambda}'_{ijk} = f(\lambda_{ik},\lambda_{ik-},\varepsilon_{ijk},\varepsilon_{ijk-})$ and $\hat{\lambda}'_{ijk-} = f(\lambda_{ik-},\lambda_{ik},\varepsilon_{ijk-},\varepsilon_{ijk})$, i.e., $\hat{\lambda}'_{ijk}$ is $\hat{\lambda}'_{ijk-}$ but with $k$ and $k$- arguments reversed. This symmetry suggests that partials on the "reverse $f$", call it $\overleftarrow{f}$, can be calculated as partials on $f$ if we reverse $k$ and $k$- everywhere. For example, we use 2 steps to compute $\overleftarrow{f}_{\varepsilon_{ij1}}$ in the TS-2 expression (15): (1) Find the partial, $f_{\varepsilon_{ij2}}$ and then (2) Evaluate it at the reverse (mean) argument $(\bar{\lambda}_{i2},\bar{\lambda}_{i1},0,0)$. All expressions needed for $f_x$ are given in (14). We can compute the TS-2 or STS-2 versions of *rnoise(i)'*. For STS-2

$$rnoise(i)' \approx \frac{-r\bar{\lambda}^2_{i1}\sigma^2_{\hat{\lambda}_{ij1}} - rR^4\bar{\lambda}^2_{i2}\sigma^2_{\hat{\lambda}_{ij2}} + R^2\bar{\lambda}_{i1}\bar{\lambda}_{i2}(1+r^2)cov(\lambda_{i1},\lambda_{i2})}{\sqrt{\left(\bar{\lambda}^2_{i1}\sigma^2_{\hat{\lambda}_{ij1}} + r^2R^4\bar{\lambda}^2_{i2}\sigma^2_{\hat{\lambda}_{ij2}}\right)\left(r^2\bar{\lambda}^2_{i1}\sigma^2_{\hat{\lambda}_{ij1}} + R^4\bar{\lambda}^2_{i2}\sigma^2_{\hat{\lambda}_{ij2}}\right)}} \quad (16)$$

where $R = \frac{\bar{\lambda}_{i1}^2 + c/s}{\bar{\lambda}_{i2}^2 + c/s}$ captures all the effects of *s* and *c*. Equation (16) simplifies at *r=0* to be *rnoise(i)'* ≈ *rnoise(i)*, i.e., the transform has (approximately) no effect; this applies to TS-2 and STS-2 since the constraint is not needed.

For Case 4, i.e., the smoothed transformed data (and *rsignal~'*), exact solutions are impractical because they require conditioning on at least 6 partially-dependent random variables with integrations over a complicated region of feasibility. Now, let $\hat{v}'_{ik} = \frac{\sum_{j=1}^{N} \hat{\lambda}'_{ijk}}{N}$ and $\hat{v}'_{*k} = \frac{\sum_{i=1}^{M} \hat{v}'_{ik}}{M}$. Then, we can provide expressions for the TS-2 and STS-2 components of *rsignal~'*. That is, the expressions for $E(\hat{v}'_{ik})$, $var(\hat{v}'_{ik})$ and $cov(\hat{v}'_{i1}, \hat{v}'_{i2})$ are the corresponding versions of the untransformed responses, but in TS-2 the measurement-error variances, $\sigma^2_{\varepsilon_k}$ and $\sigma^2_{\varepsilon_k-}$ are divided by *N* and in STS-2, $\sigma^2_{\hat{\lambda}_{ijk}}$ and $\sigma^2_{\hat{\lambda}_{ijk-}}$ are replaced by $\sigma^2_{\hat{v}_{ik}}$ *and* $\sigma^2_{\hat{v}_{ik-}}$. If we used the classical correlation, $rsignal(i)' = \frac{cov(\hat{v}'_{i1}, \hat{v}'_{i2})}{\sqrt{var(\hat{v}'_{i1}) var(\hat{v}'_{i2})}}$, we would have all we need for TS-2 and STS-2. The STS-2 expression for *rsignal(i)'* would be (16) with $\sigma^2_{\hat{\lambda}_{ijk}}$ replaced by $\hat{v}'_{ik}$ for *k=1, 2*. Moreover, for TS-2 and STS-2, we would find that when *r=0*, *rsignal(i)'*≈ *rsignal(i)*, i.e., that transform does not affect correlation (as for *rnoise(i)'*). However, the "pseudo-correlation",

$$rsignal\sim' = \frac{E\sum_{i=1}^{M}(\hat{v}'_{i1} - \hat{v}'_{*1})(\hat{v}'_{i2} - \hat{v}'_{*2})}{\sqrt{E\sum_{i=1}^{M}(\hat{v}'_{i1} - \hat{v}'_{*1})^2 E\sum_{i=1}^{M}(\hat{v}'_{i2} - \hat{v}'_{*2})^2}}, \quad (17)$$

$$E\sum_{i=1}^{M}(\hat{v}'_{ik} - \hat{v}'_{*k})^2 = \frac{M-1}{M}\sum_{i=1}^{M}[var(\hat{v}'_{ik}) + E^2(\hat{v}'_{ik})] - \frac{1}{M}\sum_{i=1}^{M}\sum_{m \neq i}[cov(\hat{v}'_{ik}, \hat{v}'_{mk}) + E(\hat{v}'_{ik})E(\hat{v}'_{mk})], \quad (18)$$

$$E\sum_{i=1}^{M}(\hat{v}'_{i1} - \hat{v}'_{*1})(\hat{v}'_{i2} - \hat{v}'_{*2}) = \frac{M-1}{M}\sum_{i=1}^{M}[cov(\hat{v}'_{i1}, \hat{v}'_{i2}) + E(\hat{v}'_{i1})E(\hat{v}'_{i2})]] - \frac{1}{M}\sum_{i=1}^{M}\sum_{m \neq i}[cov(\hat{v}'_{i1}, \hat{v}'_{m2}) + E(\hat{v}'_{i1})E(\hat{v}'_{m2})] \quad (19)$$

where we usually assume $cov(\hat{v}'_{ik}, \hat{v}'_{mk})$ and $cov(\hat{v}'_{i1}, \hat{v}'_{m2})$ are neglibile for $i \neq m$.

## IV. Analytical and Simulation Results

Before we discuss results, let us overview our simulation. Our simulation generates random measured responses $(\hat{\lambda}_{ijk})$ to various stimuli in visual neuroscience experiments. While $\hat{\lambda}_{ijk}$ are often modeled as Poisson, we assume that they are Bi-Normal with $BN\left(\bar{\lambda}_{i1}, \sigma^2_{\hat{\lambda}_{ij1}}; \bar{\lambda}_{i2}, \sigma^2_{\hat{\lambda}_{ij2}}; \rho(\hat{\lambda}_{ij1}, \hat{\lambda}_{ij2})\right)$. For each simulation sample, we generate *2xNxM* random responses. We consider various pairs of values for the mean responses ($\bar{\lambda}_{i1}, \bar{\lambda}_{i2}$), each on [25,50]. In assigning key parameter values, we prescribe response correlation to be $\rho(\lambda_{i1}, \lambda_{i2}) = 0.7$ for all stimuli, *i* and let the coefficient of variation for $\lambda_{ik}$ be 5%, i.e., $var(\lambda_{ik}) = (0.05E(\lambda_{ik}))^2$. Next, we *derive* values for the (Poisson) measurement error variances, $var(\varepsilon_{ijk})$. Finally, we compute the statistics required for Cases 1-4 and contrast them to those obtained analytically. To assure the statistical validity, we generate up to ***S****=500* experiment "samples" and we correct biases, for Cases 1, 3 variance and covariance estimates, as in Sections III-B and III-C.

In Section IV-A, we provide only brief comments on Cases 1 and 2, the untransformed responses, because our analytical models are "exact". In Section IV-B, we look at simulation and T-S analytical results for the transformed responses; we focus on Case 3 statistics, $var(\hat{\lambda}'_{6j1})$ and *rnoise(6)'*, because Case 4 observations do not change significantly as we vary key parameters. This similarity of empirical results is quite consistent with the striking similarity of the approximate analytical results in Section III-C.

### A. Cases 1 and 2: Untransformed Responses

For *classical* means and covariances, the true, measured and smoothed analytical results are the same. However, the unsmoothed and smoothed *classical* variances may differ significantly because averaging reduces the variance of measured responses. The key challenge for these Cases is to make sure the simulation yields accurate estimates of the associated transformed results for Cases 3 and 4. In that regard, we note the following:

- The simulation biases for variances and covariances, are corrected as in Section III-B.
- "Pseudo variances and covariances" seem to differ only slightly from the classical ones.
- Correlation statistics, *rnoise(i)* and *rsignal~*, are difficult to estimate, may be unstable, using simulation (or experimental data) because they are ratios of other statistics.

### B. Cases 3 and 4: Transformed Responses

Using our simulation, we studied extensively the accuracy of TS-2 and STS-2 for the moments of transformed response statistics. The transformed cases are difficult to analyze:

- The transformation, as in (6), introduces many additional parameters.
- Transformations are nonlinear, further complicated by the non-negativity constraint.
- Transformed responses are quite small, on the order of $10^{-3}$ to $10^{-4}$ for Case 4, and approaching *0* for parameter extremes, e.g., large values for *s*, *c*, or *r*.

In addition, variances and covariances are much more challenging than means to estimate, at parameter extremes, and correlations depend strongly on variance and covariance accuracy. We also know that STS-2 will (TS-2 may not) have accuracy problems where the non-negativity constraints are needed. We will see that, despite these difficulties, TS-2 and STS-2 are accurate and fast over important parameter ranges.

Neuroscientists restrict *r* to be on [0,1], and often in the "neighborhood" of 0.5. However, in our analyses, we extend the domain to [0,1.5] to better understand the properties of the transforms and our models. We use the ratio *c/s* in our examples because, in our studies, we found that individual values of *s* and *c* matter only at extremes (e.g., *s=0, c=0,* or *r>> 0.5*). For example, the STS-2 expression for *rnoise(i)'* (16) only depends on *c/s*. We assume arbitrarily *i=6, k=1*.

*1) Accuracy of Analytical Models for Variances.* In Figure 1, below, we look at the accuracy of TS-2 and STS-2 (vs. simulation) of $var(\hat{\lambda}'_{6j1})$ as we vary r, c/s and $(\bar{\lambda}_{61}, \bar{\lambda}_{62})$. The rows of graphs correspond to different values of c/s and columns to ratios $\frac{\bar{\lambda}_{62}}{\bar{\lambda}_{61}}$ . For each graph, the y-axis is $var(\hat{\lambda}'_{6j1})$ and the x-axis is $0 \le r \le 1.5$. Some observations:

- For these data, the analytical and simulation results match well except for STS-2 when *r>>0.5* or $\frac{\bar{\lambda}_{62}}{\bar{\lambda}_{61}} >> 1$. The analytical model "errors" are usually small in absolute value.
- The $var(\hat{\lambda}'_{6j1})$ graph is a unimodal non-negative function of *c/s*, starting at *0* when *c/s=0*, becoming positive and then approaching *0* again for large *c/s*. While not shown here, all three models do a good job of exhibiting this property.
- Because of the non-negativity constraint in (6), $var(\hat{\lambda}'_{6j1}) \rightarrow 0$ for large *r*. We see that TS-2 generally provides accurate estimates for large *r*, while STS-2 does not. However, neuroscientists see little practical application in their models for *r>>0.5*.
- TS-2 estimates of $var(\hat{\lambda}'_{6j1})$ are somewhat inaccurate when $\frac{\bar{\lambda}_{62}}{\bar{\lambda}_{61}} >> 1$ because the non-negativity constraint is needed. It would be much less important to $var(\hat{\lambda}'_{6j1})$ if $\frac{\bar{\lambda}_{61}}{\bar{\lambda}_{62}} >> 1$.

*2) Accuracy and Stability of Correlation Statistics.* Figure 2 (see the y-axes), below, helps us gain insights into the accuracy and stability of our *rnoise(i)'* models. Some observations:

- The analytical models are accurate (match the simulation well) if $r \le 0.75$; $\frac{\bar{\lambda}_{62}}{\bar{\lambda}_{61}} \le \frac{4}{3}$, i.e., ≈ 1 due to symmetries.
- The trajectory of *rnoise(6)'* vs. *r* is inherently volatile but necessarily within [-1,1]. It starts near *0* for *r=0*, decreases sharply as *r* increases and, when the non-negativity constraint "kicks in", turns up towards *0* again. TS-2 tracks the upturn pretty well, but (of course) STS-2 does not.
- The TS-2 model shows some apparent numerical instability, relative to the simulation, for large *r*. This is because, as the numerator $cov(\hat{\lambda}'_{6j1}, \hat{\lambda}'_{6j2})$, and denominator, $var(\hat{\lambda}'_{6j1})var(\hat{\lambda}'_{6j2})$, each approach *0*, estimates of *rnoise (6)'* approach 0/0 and are sensitive to the rates of convergence of the ratio components.
- Recall (Section III-C), that at *r=0*, *rnoise(i)' ≈ rnoise(i)*, i.e., the transform is insensitive to *c/s* and $\frac{\bar{\lambda}_{62}}{\bar{\lambda}_{61}}$. This *c/s* insensitivity for *rnoise(6)'* extends to $r \le 0.75$, $\frac{\bar{\lambda}_{62}}{\bar{\lambda}_{61}} \approx 1$.

## V. Summary and Conclusions

We conclude, based on our example analytical and simulation results, that TS-2 and STS-2 are accurate for a wide range of parameter values. Because the STS-2 models omit non-negativity constraints, their accuracy is best when $r \le 0.75$; $\frac{\bar{\lambda}_{i2}}{\bar{\lambda}_{i1}} \le \frac{4}{3}$ for $var(\hat{\lambda}'_{ij1})$ and $\frac{\bar{\lambda}_{i2}}{\bar{\lambda}_{i1}} \approx 1$ for correlation, *rnoise(i)'*. In addition, their simple expressions help us better understand relationships between model parameters and results. Our approximations are extremely fast, linear combinations of input parameters, with algebraic expressions for the weights. Two key conclusions for neural coding are:

- Transformations, such as normalization, can influence noise correlations, but the relationship between these two factors, *rnoise(i)* and *rnoise(i)'* (or between *rsignal' and rsignal)*, is highly sensitive to parameter choices, and hence unlikely to be robust in real neural networks.
- Opponent processing, i.e., the combining of response data from multiple neurons, has a profound influence on noise correlations.

## References


[1] E. Zohary, M. Shadler, and W. Newsome, "Correlated Neuronal Discharge Rate amd Its Implication for Pshycophysical Performance," vol. 370, pp. 140-143, 1994.

[2] B. Tripp, "Decorrelation of Spiking Variability and Improved Information Transfer Through Feedforward Divisive Noralization," Neural Computation, vol. 24, No. 4, pp. 867-894, April 2012.

[3] D. Ruff, J. Alberts, and M. Cohen, "Relating Normalization to Neuronal Populations Across Cortical Areas," Neurophysiology, vol. 116, Issue 3, pp. 1375-1386, September 2016.

[4] L. Liu, R. Haefner, and C. Pack, "A "Neural Basis for the Spatial Suppression of Visual Motion Perception," eLife 2016; 5:e16167 doi: 10.7554/eLife.16167, May 2016.

[5] D. Lyamzin, J. Macke, and N. Lesica, "Modeling Population Spike Trains with Specified Time-Varying Spike Rates, Trial-to-Trial Variability, Pairwise Signal and Noise Correlations," Front. Comp. Neuro., *4:144, doi:10.3389/fncom.2010.00144, pmid:21152346,* November 2010.

[6] Y. Hu, J. Zylerberg, and E.Shea-Brown, "The Sign Rule and Beyond: Boundary Effects, Flexibility, and Noise Correlations in Neural Population Codes," PLoS Computational Biology, vol. 10, *e1003469. doi:10.1371/journal.pcbi.1003469,* 2014.

[7] D. Heeger, "Normalization of Cell Respomses in Cat Striate Cortex," Visual Neuroscience, vol. 9, Issue 2, pp. 181-197, August 1992.

[8] Y. Chen Y, W. Geisler, and E. Seidemann, "Optimal Decoding of Correlated Neural Population Responses in the Primate Visual Cortex," Nat Neurosci., vol. 9, pp. 1412–1420, 2006.

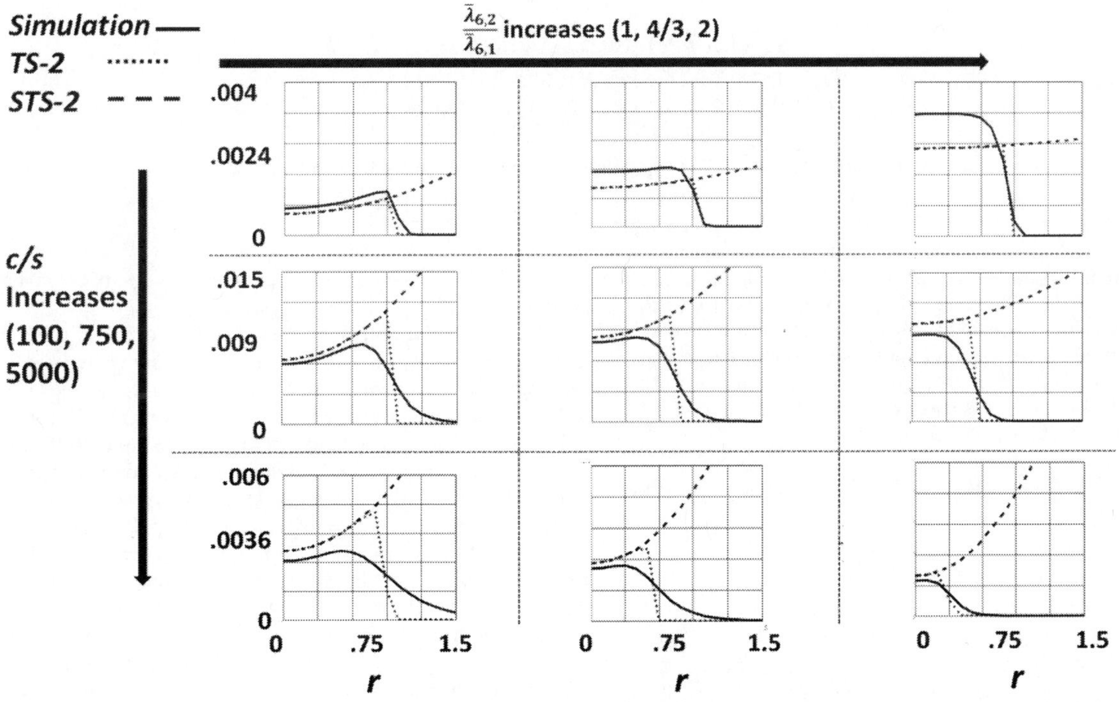


Figure 1. Transformed Variances, $var(\hat{\lambda}'_{6j1})$, vs. $r$

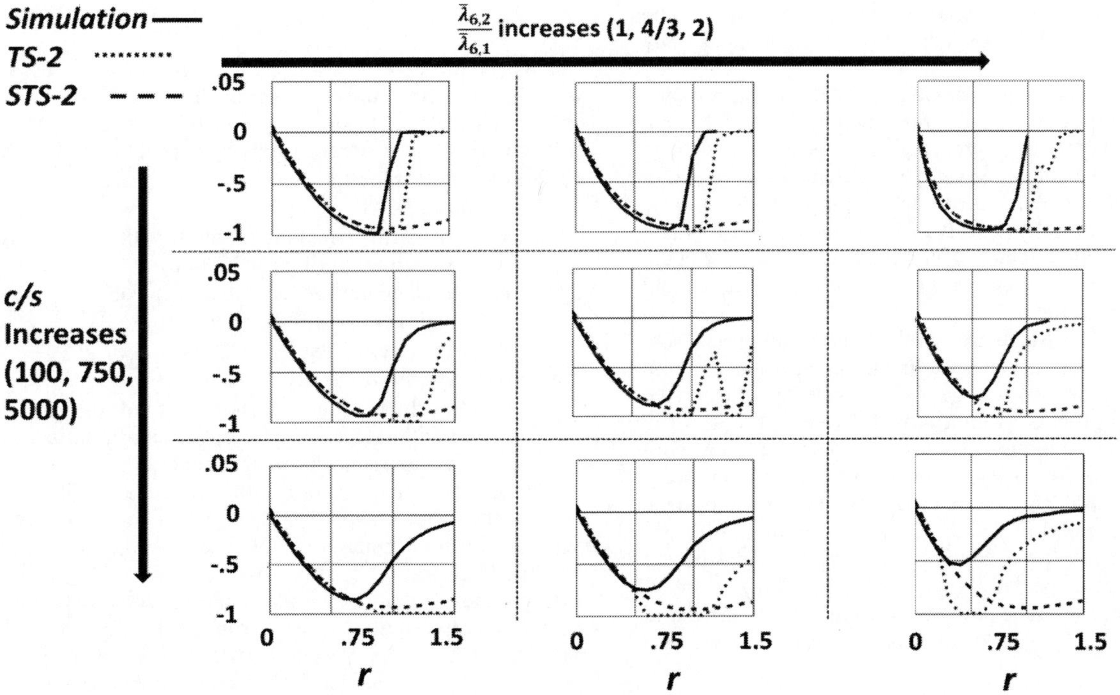


Figure 2. Correlation Statistics, *rnoise(6)'*, vs. $r$

# Architecture of a Big Data Platform for a Semiconductor Company

Daniel Müller, Stephan Trahasch
Institute for Machine Learning and Analytics
Offenburg University of Applied Sciences
Offenburg, Germany
e-mail: daniel.mueller@hs-offenburg.de, stephan.trahasch@hs-offenburg.de

***Abstract*—Apache Hadoop is a well-known open-source framework for storing and processing huge amounts of data. This paper shows the usage of the framework within a project of the university in cooperation with a semiconductor company. The goal of this project was to supplement the existing data landscape by the facilities of storing and analyzing the data on a new Apache Hadoop based platform.**

***Keywords—Big Data Analytics; Big Data Storage; Apache Hadoop; Metrics***

## I. Introduction

Over the past few years, the world of data changed. More and more data-driven processes are coming up. They can be used to monitor or even improve existing processes. Especially the industry benefits from this new know-how that can be retrieved from analyzing Big Data where Big Data refers to the large volumes of structured, semi-structured, or unstructured data, acquired from a variety of heterogeneous sources. On the other hand, new devices and techniques need to be applied to enable such potential of Big Data. This often leads to high costs for the acquisition of new hard- and software, and even the knowledge how to implement a Big Data solution.

The semiconductor industry is one of the most complex manufacturing processes, and large amount of data retrieved during the manufacturing process has to be stored in huge databases [1]. The automatic analyses of that data may lead to reduction in the manufacturing cost. This is true for basic analyses, but especially for advanced analyses like anomaly detection and quality control. Insights can be gained about the production process if those data can be stored, retrieved and analyzed in an easy way.

The Institute for Machine Learning and Analytics (IMLA) [2] together with a semiconductor manufacturer from Germany examines how large data - collected during the manufacturing process - can be stored and analyzed in a Big Data system. The company has widened their machines with sensor technology, to be able to track their production process in large part. This led to a mass of new data, that must be stored and processed in an adequate duration of time, to be able to handle all this data and react as fast as possible on different events (especially in case of a problem). Another challenge comes with the previous analyses, which are based on different datasets – a lot of this data was collected and joined manually by some employees, which meant a huge overhead and delay on the analyses.

The goals of the project are to build a cost-effective and scalable database for storing and processing the sensor-generated data, to accelerate the search and analysis of data and to implement advanced analyses with machine learning. In this paper we focus on the first two goals: the architecture and implementation of a scalable data base and the integration in the IT environment to support the analysis process. The approach is based on the Apache Hadoop [3] and Apache Spark [4] framework, very popular platforms for subjects concerning Big Data handling. The next step of the project is the implementation of machine learning algorithms.

The structure of this paper is organized as follows: Section II provides background information about the data base, while Section III shows the basic information about the Apache Hadoop cluster that was used to implement the project. Section IV of this paper discusses various ways to store the data and shows ways to import and analyze this data. Section V provides first benchmarks on the imported data, and Section VI concludes the paper with a brief summary.

## II. Background

This section describes the data and the database used so far. The company uses different database systems and Network-based File Systems (NFS) to store the data that accrues during the different production processes. The data consists of various types:

*1) Structured Data*

- Lot history (tracking of the steps that were passed by each lot during production)
- Machine data (events that occur on the different machines, lot independent)
- Many more smaller datasets

*2) Semi-structured Data*

- Results of quality tests (results of tests that run after production, e.g., power consumption, heat development, mechanical checks)

The structured data comes with a fix schema, like every entry has the same amount and datatypes of columns. Typical examples for this format are CSV files, which represent data in a table-like form.

In contrast to that comes the semi-structured data, which can have a very different schema from file to file. The quality test results are of this schema-less format, so every file (or even every entry) can have different number of columns and/or datatypes. Due to the various families of semiconductors there are also different test cases for each. This data diversity has also a second reason: In the course of time, the sensors for checking the products and the software changed, which also led to different test cases (which are reflected in the different schemas) within the same product families. Saving these differing data sets inside the same storage pool was also a big challenge on the project.

Altogether these information sets filled up (amongst others) an Oracle database with approximately 13 TB of data. Since this system run into capacity limits, one of the main goals of the project was to source older data out into another file storage, e.g., the Hadoop Distributed File System (HDFS), which is part of the Apache Hadoop ecosystem. More about the task of data moving in the "Solution" section.

As already mentioned in the introduction section, there were a lot of analyses that took a long time or even overloaded the system, that ran on capacity limits. In addition to this issue, many analyses needed some manually gathered and filtered data as input. These issues are pain points because a lot of time is wasted on getting and processing the desired data. Realtime results (or even getting any results at all) were not possible for these kinds of analyses. By using the parallelism of the Apache Hadoop platform, we wanted to be able to automate the information gathering and bring up new ways for faster analyses.

## III. The Apache Hadoop Cluster

The IMLA runs an in-house Apache Hadoop cluster, which is based on the Hortonworks Data Platform [5]. This platform is a combination of different tools that can be used for storing and analyzing huge datasets [6]. Figure 1 shows the main structure of the cluster components:

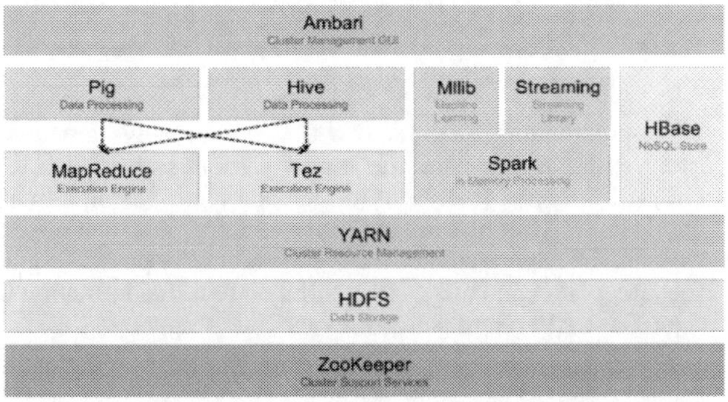


Figure 1. The coarse structure of the components in the Hadoop cluster

Since the Hadoop ecosystem is a collection of different tools for storing and analyzing datasets, it is applicable for most tasks all around working with Big Data. Some important tools that were used in the project are the following:

- **HDFS**: Distributed data storage inside a cluster.
- **Apache Hive**: SQL-like interface to structured data stored inside HDFS.
- **Apache HBase**: Distributed NoSQL database, using HDFS as background data storage.
- **Apache Spark**: In-memory processing engine with interfaces to various datastores, like HDFS, Hive, HBase and many more.

Stand May 2019 the Hadoop cluster of the university has the following setup: We use eight nodes, two of which are set up as name nodes (high availability) and the other six as data nodes. The name nodes are responsible for the administration of the metadata of the HDFS and the requests of the different services running inside the cluster and coordinate the incoming tasks submitted by the users. The data nodes hold the datasets in themselves and execute the processes, which in turn work with this data.

These are the actual components of the cluster:

- 2 x NameNode
  - CPU: 2 x Intel Xeon E5-2630v4 @ 2.2 GHz (10 cores, 20 threads)
  - RAM: 256 GB (DDR4, ECC-reg.)
  - SSD: 2 x 480 GB (RAID-1)
  - OS: CentOS 7
- 6 x DataNode
  - CPU: 2 x Intel Xeon E5-2630v2 @ 2.6 GHz (6 cores, 12 threads)
  - RAM: 64 GB (DDR3, ECC-reg.)
  - HDD (System): 1 x 1 TB
  - HDD (HDFS): 4 x 3 TB
  - OS: CentOS 7

We use the Hortonworks Data Platform 2.6.5, which is a free Hadoop distribution from Hortonworks that is based on the Hadoop 2.7 stack. As operating system we use CentOS 7. In the future, the cluster will be upgraded to Hadoop 3 and equipped with graphics cards to enable also GPU computing.

## IV. Solution

This section covers the realization of the project, which consists of the four thematic areas data import, storage of structured data, storage of semistructured data, and the data processing. For a better understanding of the other topics, first the storage of the data is treated, before continuing with the import of the data into the cluster.

### A. *Storing the structured data*

First, the Hadoop framework contains a distributed file system that can be used to store all types of data. The user has access to appropriate interfaces for writing and reading this storage. Even other tools used in a Hadoop platform usually store their data on the filesystem called HDFS.

The basic Hadoop framework can be extended with a data warehousing software called Apache Hive that is based on HDFS [7]. Hive is an interface for working with structured data (that is stored in HDFS) using an SQL-like syntax called HiveQL. It brings also new interfaces (e.g., command line tool, JDBC driver and REST-based webservice) and supports the common data types like numeric, date/time, string, misc (boolean, binary) and complex (array, maps, structs).

There are also multiple file formats that can be read and written by Hive. One of the best-known formats in storing structured data in Hadoop is the Apache Optimized Row Columnar (ORC) [8] format, which is also supported by Hive and used in this project for storing the structured data. ORC is a memory-optimized and column-based data format with helpful features like ACID support, built-in indexes and support of complex types. It is optimized for Big Data workloads, especially for parallel readings from HDFS. It allows filtering close to the data, by passing the filter criteria to the data store, thus selecting and returning only the desired data at a lower level. This feature is called "predicate pushdown" and accelerates queries many times over, because it significantly reduces the network load and therefore the size of data, that must be processed in further steps. ORC also supports zlib and Snappy compression to reduce data size in addition to the default column-based compression.

There are different ways to bring any Hive-readable format into the ORC format and vice versa. This is very helpful, especially to bring data from external systems into this optimized format (e.g., if the external system can not work with ORC files but can export data as CSV). For example, to put CSV-based data into an ORC-based table, a user could go one of the following ways:

- Create an external hive table to reference the newly imported data (e.g., in CSV format) in HDFS. Then add an internal hive table that contains the same column definitions but uses the ORC format for storing [9]. After that, the ORC table can be filled using a simple "INSERT INTO ... SELECT ... FROM ..." command. This generates the corresponding ORC files on HDFS in background [10].
- Using a Spark job to read in the original files (e.g., in CSV format), optionally transform the data and write it to Hive (or HDFS) in ORC-based format.

### *B. Storing the semistructured data*

As explained in the introduction section, the data base of the project partner also consists of semistructured data created during the quality tests after production (different schema from file to file, depending on test type, and software version). Since this data makes up a large part of the data base, the outsourcing of these files was also examined.

#### *1) Composition of the semistructured data*

The quality test results don not have this well-known CSV structure, as they contain some metadata at the beginning of each file, and every file can have another bunch of columns, that contain the test results. Figure 2 is an illustration of the coarse structure of such a test result file:

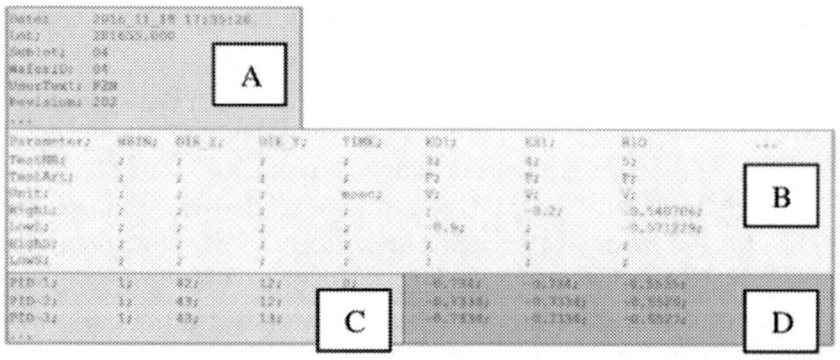


Figure 2. Schema of a test result file

The header rows (A) have always the same structure and can help to identify a single test file within all the files. Also, the first columns (C) are always the same in every file, they identify the rows inside a test file. Area (B) contains meta information about the following rows, like column names, min / max values, and units. Its width depends on the amount of test columns. The test columns (D) contain the results of the test cases and can be different in each file (but are the same within one file, containing null values if necessary).

#### *2) Storing the semistructured data in HBase*

Since these files have different schemas, the default bulk-load mechanisms can not be used for importing this data. That is why we have decided to process the data with Apache Spark, because it has an extensive API and can handle almost any kind of data. Spark also has interfaces to almost all datastores that exist for Hadoop, e.g., HDFS, Hive and HBase. We examined two different approaches for storing these test data files, that follow in the next sections.

##### *a) Spark-Job that writes an HBase table*

The first approach of storing the data was a combination between Spark and Apache HBase. We decided to use Spark to read in and transform the data into key-value pairs, that could be written into the NoSQL database HBase afterwards. Since HBase stores data in form of key-value pairs this is an interesting opportunity for storing un- or semi-structured data. To do so, we had to split the regarding rows that contained the test results into a combination of row key and key-value pairs. The row key is used to identify a row globally within the entire data base (i.e., across all files). To get a unique key, we had to combine the information of the header rows (file identification) and the base columns, which identify the rows inside a single file. So, the key consists of the following parts:

$id_{File}$ = <Lot>_<Sublot>_<WaferID>_<Date>_<Revision>_<UserText>
$key_{Row}$ = <$id_{File}$>_<PID>_<HBIN>_<DIE_X>_<DIE_Y>

Figure 3. Composition of the row key. DIE_X and DIE_Y are the x and y coordinates of the die on the wafer.

In combination with the row key, a list of key-value pairs (that represent the test name and its value) can be added to a HBase Put object to be sent to the database by using a Spark application. After reading the different CSV files (test results) from HDFS, Spark creates these Put objects by processing the files in parallel and afterwards calling a bulk-load function on the HBase API. Here is the relevant code snippet:

```
// This is inside the Spark Job
JavaRDD<HBaseRowEntry> rowsRDD = ...
hbaseContext = new JavaHBaseContext(sc, baseConf);
hbaseContext.bulkPut(rowsRDD, name, new PutFunction());

public class PutFunction
 implements Function<HBaseRowEntry, Put> {
  @Override
  public Put call(HBaseRowEntry entry) throws Exception {
    Put put = new Put(entry.getKey().getBytes());
    for(MyKeyValue kv: entry.getKeyValues()) {
      put.addColumn(kv.getCF, kv.getCQ(), kv.getValue());
    }
    return put;
}}
```

Figure 4. Writing to HBase using the Java API

We were able to try this approach in a test phase and we successfully imported more than 100 GB of test result files into HBase by running this Spark Job. The problem is that additional skills would be needed to launch and administrate the HBase infrastructure.

*b) Spark-Job that writes an Hive table*

After evaluating the first approach, we took a closer look at the data and found out that it was possible to bring this semistructured data into a structured form. That was possible, because we learned from the company's employees that they will always read at least one entire column of the test result files for analysis purposes. With this new knowledge, we were able to plan a new data structure, which then enabled to have a fix schema over all files. Figure 5 shows the transformation that brings the data into a globally identical schema:

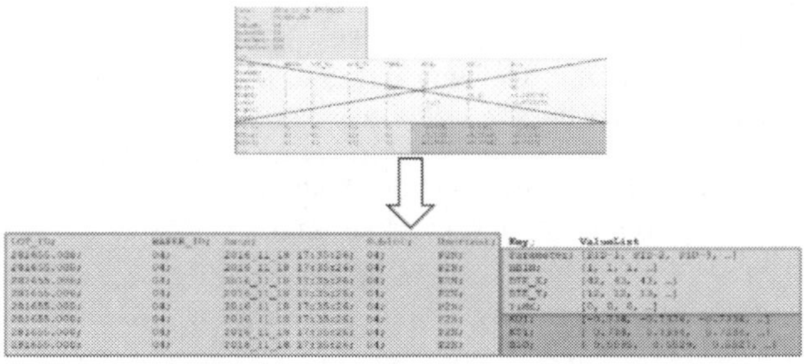

Figure 5. Transforming the test result file

As shown in the figure, the headers that identify a file have been moved into the test rows below. They are still used to be able to find a specific file. The main difference is the transformation of the test columns, as they have been converted to row-based key-value pairs. The new "Key" column contains the test names, while the test results can be found in an array of values under the new column "ValueList". This means, that the array of the ValueList column has as much elements as the test result file had test rows before. Also, there will be generated as much rows for a test result file as the original file had columns. This schema can be used to store the contents of all test result files in a common, structured table together. As already mentioned, this only works performant under the condition that the smallest unit read out is an entire (former) test column, which means the reading of a complete ValueList array in the new format. Reading smaller units could cause performance issues, as the array has to be iterated to find the correct item (then the key-value approach with HBase would be a better solution). But since the company wants to read complete test columns this is a better solution, as we could use Apache Hive to save this data. As Hive is already chosen in the company for storing the structured data, they don nott need to administrate and learn a new tool. Spark also has native connectors to the Hive warehouse and can write this data to it in parallel, after bringing the test results into the new format.

### C. Realizing the data import process

Now that it has been determined, how and where the data will be stored, the import process could be planned. An SAP system acts as the data supplier, while the HDFS and Apache Hive serve as data sink. We also decided to use Apache Spark for data import, as it is flexible and can operate natively with these Hadoop components, and this also avoids the introduction of another tool. The idea now was to upload the relevant data files into HDFS and then read them via Spark, transform (if necessary) and finally write them into the corresponding Hive tables. A basic scheme of the import process is shown in Figure 6.

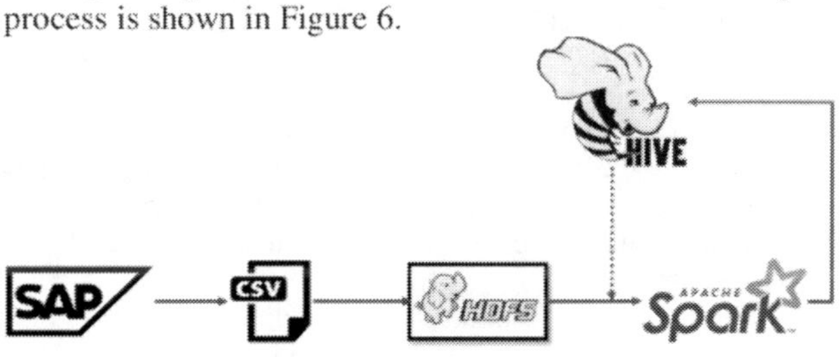


Figure 6. Import Process steps

The following steps are performed in the import process:

- SAP: Exporting the data as CSV files and uploading them into HDFS.
- Spark: Read the files from HDFS and read in the corresponding Hive table into datasets (in-memory).
- Update the dataset by combining the CSV file(s) with the Hive table content.
- Writing the final dataset content back to Hive table (overwrite).

The CSV file that is exported from SAP system must have a separate column that contains information, whether the corresponding row shall be added or removed – updates are realized by a deletion, followed by an insert. Figure 7 is an example of such an import file:

Figure 7. Example of an import file

As explained before, Spark first reads in the complete Hive table, where the updates should be run against. The table content is held in-memory during Spark job execution. In the next step, the update file is read from HDFS and split into delete and insert rows. Then the delete rows are used to remove the corresponding rows from the table content (null values are treated as wildcards). Afterwards the rows containing the inserts are appended to the table content. Finally, the dataset containing the updated content is written back into the Hive table. The complete Hive table is overwritten in this step.

To trigger the explained Spark import job, we use Apache Livy. Livy is a REST based interface that enables to submit Spark jobs from everywhere, also from outside the cluster. This is helpful since the company needs to start the import job from their SAP system, after writing the update files into HDFS. In the final status (May 2019), the data is gathered inside the SAP system at night and written to HDFS, before the Spark import job is triggered by a Livy call.

### *D. Data processing*

The data processing is also done by using Apache Spark jobs. Since Spark has connectors to data stores like Hive and HBase, it is possible to read and write them from a native Spark application. There is also another tool that is particularly suitable for prototyping new Spark jobs. Apache Zeppelin is a web-based notebook, with interfaces to Hive (via JDBC), HBase (via Phoenix) and Spark. The respective tools are connected to Zeppelin via so-called interpreters. A user gets access to a Spark session, that is created automatically on starting the corresponding interpreter. In these notebooks, for example, Spark program code can be tried out in a direct and uncomplicated way, without the effort of creating Spark sessions, application packaging and publishing in the phase of prototyping.

The partner company also decided to use Zeppelin notebooks to introduce and try out new application logic. After a successful test phase, the logic is moved into a separate, stand-alone application, that is created, compiled and packaged in an appropriate IDE. Since the Spark interpreter for Zeppelin works with Scala (alternatively also with Python), we use a Scala IDE to export the final application logic as JAR files. These files are moved into the HDFS and can be executed by using the spark-submit script or by making a corresponding Livy call from outside the cluster. Second is the standard procedure, since a large part of the applications are started from the external SAP system or from user's client computers. Since the results of these data processing applications can be very big, storing these datasets in HDFS or Hive tables is a better approach than sending results back to the client, which could lead to local memory problems. After finishing a job, the user can preview (or download) the results by exploring the data in HDFS or querying the corresponding Hive tables.

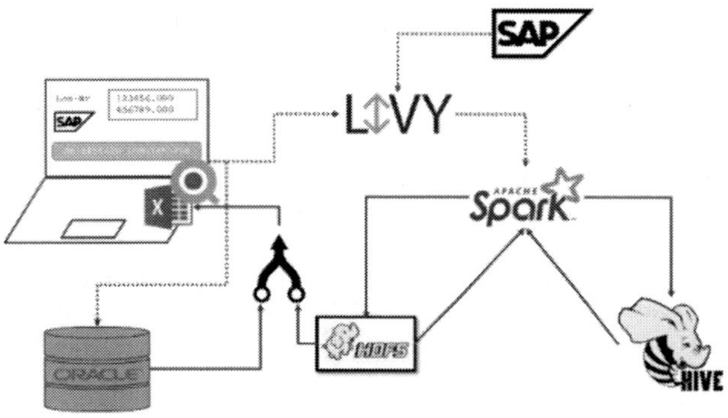


Figure 8. Data processing overview

Figure 8 shows the tools that are used for data processing with Spark (SAP and Oracle DB are external components that are used in the company).

## V. BENCHMARKS

In order to show and compare the performance of the new Hadoop system, first benchmarks were carried out. For a better comparability, the queries were executed on the old and afterwards on the new system.

### *A. Comparison of the data size*

The graph below shows the various amounts of data required to store the "HistStep" table, which contains the operations performed on the lots during production. The data has the following characteristics:

- approx. 275 mio. rows
- 17 columns (String, VarChar[1-20])

In Oracle database, this table required about 34.9 GB of disk space, plus optional (for performance reasons) index information of around 29.9 GB. So, the table thus required a total of 64.8 GB. In contrast, the ORC-based Hive table only requires about 5.2 GB in HDFS (partitioned, but without bloom filters and without replication). Using bloom filters would increase the storage space by a small amount, but these are not needed for current performance. So, the Hive tables reduced the disk space requirements by factor 6.7 (without Oracle table index) or even by factor 12.5 (with Oracle table index) (see Figure 9).

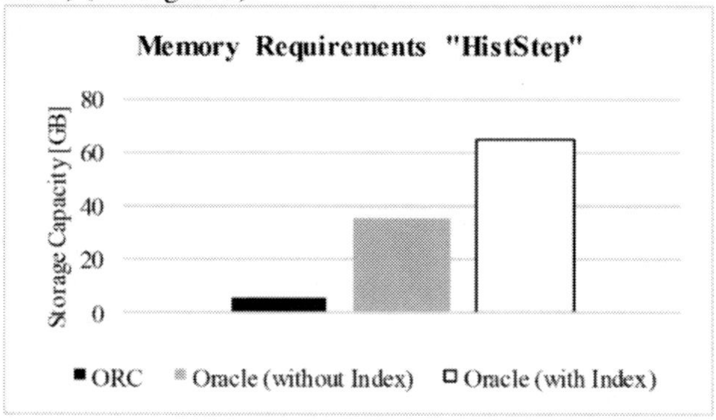


Figure 9. Storage requirements for table "HistStep"

The comparison of space needed to save the results of the product quality tests shows similar results. Saving this data takes around 13 TB in the Oracle database while Hive table only needs about 1.6 TB of HDFS storage without replication (see Figure 10).

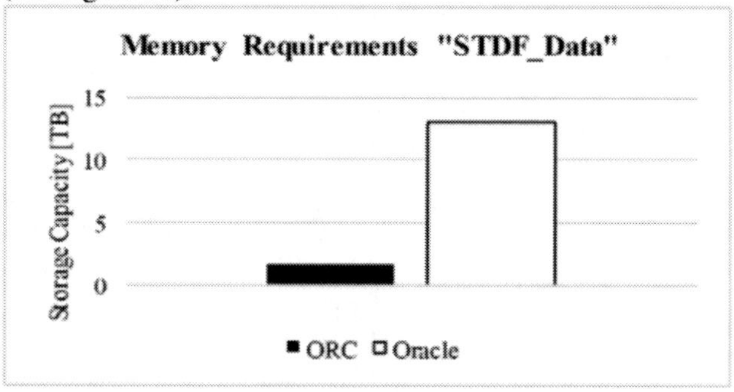


Figure 10. Storage requirements for table "STDF_Data"

We have also received first performance benchmarks from our project partner. The results show the runtimes of lot-based queries, executed on the "HistStep" table, showed in the first benchmark. On small queries, where only a few lots are selected, Oracle is much faster than Hive. But even with queries for a few hundred lots, Hive takes less time to select, process and return the data. Since lot-based analyses must include thousands of lots, the result on the far right of the diagram is the most interesting for the company. The difference in performance can be clearly seen in Figure 11.

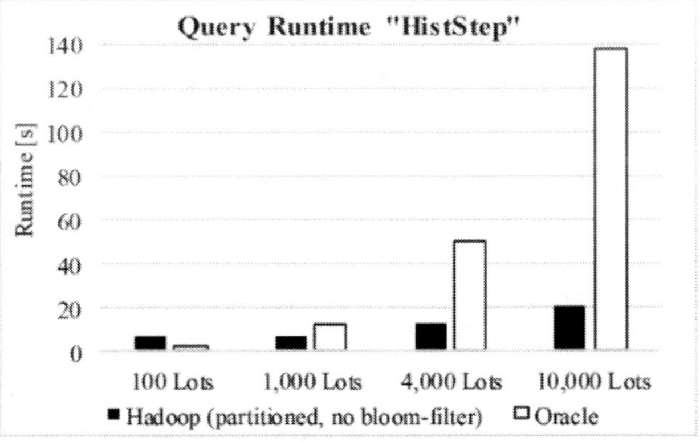


Figure 11. Query Runtime for table "HistStep"

While Oracle scales rather linearly, Hive's runtime increases only minimally. In this scenario, Hive also offers a major performance advantage over the previous system.

## VI. CONCLUSION

This project examined the applicability of a Hadoop-based platform for the storage and processing of company-relevant data. Alternative ways to import, store and process different types of data were demonstrated on practical examples. Depending on the problem, the Apache Hadoop framework offers various components to implement the different tasks. In this project, a Hadoop-based cluster was successfully introduced to a company's existing data platform to store and analyze data over a longer time. Helpful tools are especially the basic Hadoop components like the HDFS, the SQL interface Apache Hive, the NoSQL database HBase, as well as the processing engine Apache Spark. This project confirms by means of an industrial project that Hadoop can be used to build such a data-driven platform. Hadoop comes with special storage formats and engines that can be used for efficient storage and high-performance analyses.

## REFERENCES

[1] Y. Zhu and J. Xiong, „Modern Big Data Analytics for 'Old-fashioned' Semiconductor Industry Applications," Piscataway, NJ, USA, IEEE Press, 2015, p. 776–780.

[2] Institute for Machine Learning and Analytics - IMLA. [Online]. Available: https://imla.hs-offenburg.de. [retrieved: May, 2019].

[3] „The Apache Hadoop project," [Online]. Available: https://hadoop.apache.org. [retrieved: May, 2019].

[4] „The Apache Spark project," [Online]. Available: https://spark.apache.org/. [retrieved: May, 2019].

[5] „Hortonworks Data Platform," [Online]. Available: https://de.hortonworks.com/products/data-platforms/hdp/. [retrieved: May, 2019].

[6] A. Oussous, F.-Z. Benjelloun, A. Ait Lahcen, and S. Belfkih, „Big Data technologies: A survey," *Journal of King Saud University - Computer and Information Sciences*, Bd. 30, Nr. 4, p. 431–448, 2018.

[7] A. Ismail, H.-L. Truong, and W. Kastner, „Manufacturing process data analysis pipelines: a requirements analysis and survey," *Journal of Big Data*, Bd. 6, Nr. 1, p. 1, 2019.

[8] „Apache ORC," [Online]. Available: https://orc.apache.org/. [retrieved: May, 2019].

[9] „Apache ORC - Hive DDL," [Online]. Available: https://orc.apache.org/docs/hive-ddl.html. [retrieved: May, 2019].

[10] „Convert an HDFS file to ORC," [Online]. Available: https://docs.hortonworks.com/HDPDocuments/HDP3/HDP-3.1.0/migrating-data/content/hive_convert_an_hdfs_file_to _orc.html. [retrieved: May, 2019].

# A Multi-source Experimental Data Fusion Evaluation Method Based on Bayesian Method and Evidence Theory

Huan Zhang, Wei Li, Ping Ma, Ming Yang
Control and Simulation Center
Harbin Institute of Technology, Harbin, Heilongjiang, China
e-mail: zhanghuan_1996@163.com, fleehit@163.com, pingma@hit.edu.cn, myang@hit.edu.cn

*Abstract*—**The experimental data used for system performance evaluation have many sources and multiple granularity. Thus, it is necessary to fuse multi-source experimental data for evaluation. Aiming at multi-source experimental data fusion problem, a multi-source experimental data fusion evaluation method based on Bayesian and evidence theory is proposed. According to the size of the data sample size, the large sample data are fused by the classical frequency method, while the small sample data are fused by Bayesian method. Then the parameter information is updated by the Bayesian method and data fusion result is obtained. The experimental data of different scenarios are fused by evidence theory. The evidence combination method is used to fuse the data when the evidence bodies do not conflict, while the weighted average correction method is used for data fusion when there is conflict between the evidence bodies. The result of the multi-source experimental data fusion is obtained based on Bayesian method and evidence theory.**

***Keywords- data fusion; performance evaluation; Bayesian method; evidence theory***

## I. INTRODUCTION

As the complexity of the system increases, the performance evaluation of the system becomes more and more important [1]. The performance evaluation of the system is based on experimental data. However, only a small amount of measured data can be obtained because the cost of system real experiments is more and more expensive due to the use of high technology [2]. Besides, experimental data can be obtained through semi-physical simulation and digital simulation experiments. Therefore, the experimental data of performance evaluation have the characteristics of multi-source, multi-capacity, multi-granularity and multi-type, etc., and it is necessary to fuse multi-source data and then conduct comprehensive evaluation. The concept of data fusion originated in the 1970s, first used in the military field [3], and later gradually applied to various non-military fields [4]. There is no uniform definition of data fusion, and researchers have given multiple definitions from different aspects. The typical definition is: data fusion is a multi-level and multi-faceted data processing process that automatically detects, correlates, estimates and combines data from multiple sources [5].

Data fusion is applied to various theoretical knowledge and cutting-edge technologies, but no uniform algorithm is suitable for all scenarios due to its wide range of applications [6][7]. Data fusion method can be mainly divided into three categories: signal processing and estimation theory method, statistical inference theory method, and information theory method. The commonly used data fusion methods mainly include weighted average, classical reasoning, Bayesian fusion [8] and fuzzy theory. Aiming at the multi-source experimental data of performance evaluation, Bayesian method, as a commonly used method [9], can process data in the form of static probabilities and has good validity; evidence theory, second only to Bayesian method, has no requirement for data sample size and has good data fusion effect; classical reasoning method is also suitable for processing large sample size data and also has good validity; other commonly used data fusion methods, such as fuzzy theory, are applicable to processing experimental data.

Aiming at multi-source experimental data, a data fusion method is proposed. In section 2, we analyze the characteristics of experimental data and the applicable conditions of Bayesian method and evidence theory. Then we propose a data fusion evaluation scheme based on the characteristics of experimental data. In section 3, data fusion method is introduced in detail. According to the sample data, multi-type Bayesian fusion can be divided in two cases and evidence theory fusion is also related to whether the evidence bodies are in conflict. In section 4, we present the conclusion of experimental data fusion method in system performance evaluation and the future work in next step.

## II. MULTI-SOURCE EXPERIMENTAL DATA FUSION SCHEME

Experimental data used for system performance evaluation can be divided into measured data, semi-physical simulation data, digital simulation data, etc. The measured data and semi-physical simulation data are obtained through real experiments and semi-physical simulation respectively, while the digital simulation data are obtained by running the digital simulation system. Therefore, there are multiple types of data in the experimental data. Otherwise, the experimental data can also come from different experimental scenarios. The experimental scenario defines the scope and constrains of the problems studied in the system, variables, activities and interactive relations related to the experimental objects, etc., and it includes the setting and organization of all kinds of data in the system [10]. Thus, multi-source experimental data fusion problem can be divided into two aspects: one is the multi-type data fusion problem, and another is different experimental scenarios' data fusion problem.

Bayesian fusion method can process the data in the form of static probability and has no requirement on sample size, which is also the most efficient fusion method. Therefore, Bayesian method is considered for using to fuse multi-type data. For data fusion problem of different experimental scenarios, Bayesian fusion method is also considered for data fusion in order to ensure the validity of fusion results and the uniformity of methods. Because the experimental data are from different types of data under different scenarios, the posterior density $\pi(\theta,\lambda|X)$ is considered in Bayesian fusion, where parameter $\lambda$ and parameter $\theta$ characterize the mean of the variables and different experimental scenarios respectively and $X$ is observation sample. However, $\theta$'s posterior density $\pi(\theta|X)$ is focused on generally. The calculation of $\pi(\theta|X)$ needs the information about $\pi(\lambda)$ and $\pi(\theta|\lambda)$ . $\pi(\lambda)$ is the parameter distribution of different experimental scenarios, which is easily to obtain, while $\pi(\theta|\lambda)$ is conditional probability which is hard to obtain directly in the actual engineering application. Therefore, Bayesian method is not suitable for data fusion of different experimental scenarios. Evidence theory also has great advantages in data fusion and can process data of different types or different sample sizes. Thus, evidence theory is used to fuse data from different scenarios.

Above all, Bayesian fusion method is suitable for multi-type data fusion while evidence theory is suitable for fusing sample data from different scenarios. Thereout, the multi-source experimental data fusion scheme based on Bayesian method and evidence theory is obtained (see Figure 1). That is, classify the multi-source experimental data firstly, fuse the multi-type data of the same experimental scenario using Bayesian data fusion method and then fuse the single data from different scenarios using evidence theory fusion method. Considering multi-type data mainly from simulation data, semi-physical simulation data and measured data, it is necessary to classify data before data fusion, perform data preprocessing for each type of data, and then fuse data. The simulation data have a large amount of data and low authenticity, and the classical frequency estimation method is used for data fusion. However, the semi-physical simulation data and the measured data have a small number of data, and Bayesian method is used. Then, regarding large sample frequency data fusion result and small sample Bayesian data fusion result as prior information and observation sample data, respectively, the Bayesian method is used to update the prior information parameters to obtain the multi-type data fusion results under the same scenario. After obtaining the multi-type data fusion results of each scenario, the evidence theory method is used to fuse data of different experimental scenarios. Firstly, model the sample data of each scenario and describe it as a form of evidence body. When the evidence bodies do not conflict, the conventional evidence body fusion method is used for processing; when the evidence bodies are in conflict, process using the weighting method and preprocess the conflict evidence before the evidence combination. Finally, multi-source experimental data fusion results are obtained.

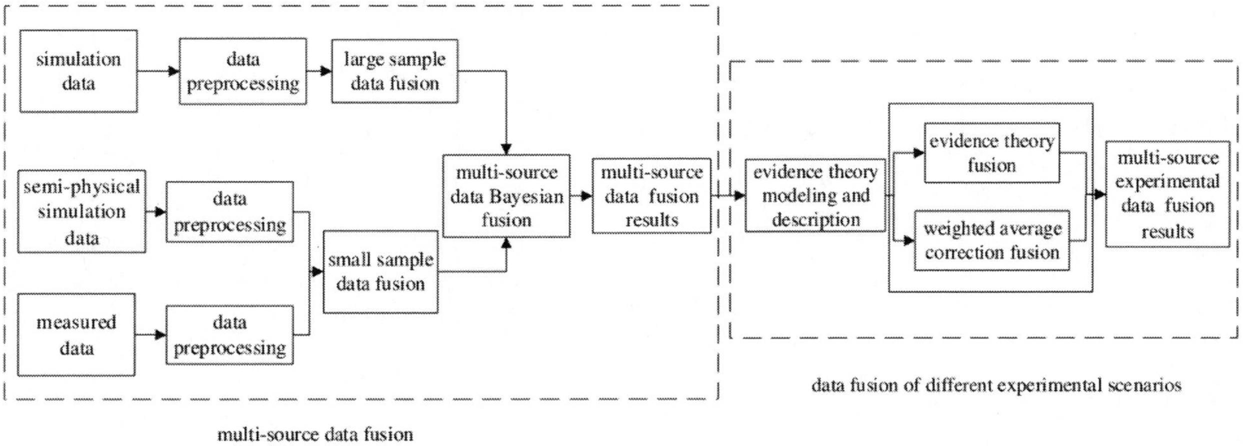


Figure 1. Multi-source experimental data fusion scheme

## III. MULTI-SOURCE DATA FUSION METHOD BASED ON BAYESIAN AND EVIDENCE THEORY

According to the multi-source experimental data fusion scheme described above, multi-source experimental data fusion mainly uses multi-type data Bayesian fusion method and evidence theory fusion method of different experimental scenarios. The description of these two data fusion methods is given.

### A. *Multi-type Bayesian Fusion*

The multi-type data Bayesian fusion method mainly uses the Bayesian method to update the prior information parameters, and the obtained result is the data fusion result.

The principle of the Bayesian update method is described as follows. Assuming that parameter $\theta$ is the mean of a variable, $X$ is observation sample and $\pi(\theta)$ is the prior density of parameter $\theta$. Then, the posterior density $\pi(\theta|X)$ of $\theta$ according to Bayesian formula is

$$\pi(\theta|X)=\frac{f(X|\theta)\pi(\theta)}{\int_{\Theta} f(X|\theta)\pi(\theta)d\theta} \tag{1}$$

where $\Theta$ is the parameter space and $f(X|\theta)$ is the likelihood function of $X$ given by $\theta$. From (1), we can see that the observation sample and the prior density of $\theta$ are used to calculate the posterior density. In system performance evaluation, the measured data and the semi-physical simulation data generally have small sample sizes, but the degree of authenticity is high, which can be used as the observation sample; the digital simulation data generally have large sample size, but the degree of authenticity is low, from which can obtain the prior density of $\theta$. Thus, digital simulation data, semi-physical simulation data and measured data need to be fused before Bayesian fusion.

*1) Classical frequency fusion of large sample data*

Generally, digital simulation data are large sample data and classical frequency parameter estimation is widely used in data fusion under large sample conditions. Therefore, the large sample data are fused by the classical frequency method. Firstly, assume that there are $n$ independent sample data sets in the simulation data. Their estimated value of the same distribution parameter $\theta$ is $\{\theta_1,\theta_2,...,\theta_n\}$. And the observation for each sample data set is $\theta_i=\theta+\xi_i, i=1,2,...,n$, where $\xi_i$ is a random error and independent of each other and $\xi_i$ also obeys normal distribution. The estimated value $\hat{\theta}$ of $\xi_i$ is described as arithmetic mean of observations, i.e., $\hat{\theta}=\frac{1}{n}\sum_{i=1}^{n}\theta_i$ and the mean variance of $\hat{\theta}$ is $\hat{\sigma}^2=\frac{1}{n(n-1)}\sum_{i=1}^{n}\left(\theta_i-\bar{\theta}\right)^2$.

For ease of processing data, $n$ observations are divided into $k$ batches, where the $j$ th batch is described as $\left\{\theta_{j1},\theta_{j2},...,\theta_{jn_j},n_j\geq 2, j=1,2,...,k\right\}, \sum_{j=1}^{k}n_j=n$. The mean of the $j$ th batch is $\bar{\theta}_j=\frac{1}{n_j}\sum_{i=1}^{n_j}x_{ji}, j=1,2,...,k$ and its variance is $\hat{\sigma}_j^2=\frac{1}{n_j(n_j-1)}\sum_{i=1}^{n_j}\left(\theta_{ji}-\bar{\theta}_j\right)^2, j=1,2,...,k$. When $\left\{\bar{\theta}_1,\bar{\theta}_2,...,\bar{\theta}_k\right\}$ is seen as $k$ unequal precision observations or observations from $k$ different sample sets of distribution parameter $\theta$, each $\bar{\theta}_j$ can be expressed as $\bar{\theta}_j=\theta+\xi_j', j=1,2,...,k$, where $\xi_j'$ is a random error and independent of each other and $\xi_j' : N\left(0,\hat{\sigma}_j^2\right)$. The likelihood function of $\left\{\bar{\theta}_1,\bar{\theta}_2,...,\bar{\theta}_k\right\}$ is obtained and it is

$$L=\prod_{j=1}^{k} f\left(\bar{\theta}_j,\hat{\sigma}_j^2,\theta\right) \tag{2}$$

where $f\left(\bar{\theta}_j,\hat{\sigma}_j^2,\theta\right)=\frac{1}{\sqrt{2\pi}\hat{\sigma}_j}\exp\left[-\frac{\left(\bar{\theta}_j-\bar{\theta}\right)^2}{2\hat{\sigma}_j^2}\right]$.

Then, the estimated value of parameter $\theta$ is obtained by maximum likelihood estimation. The estimated value is $\hat{\theta}=\bar{\theta}=\left(\sum_{j=1}^{k}\frac{1}{\hat{\sigma}_j^2}\bar{\theta}_j\right)\left(\sum_{j=1}^{k}\frac{1}{\hat{\sigma}_j^2}\right)^{-1}$ and the mean variance is $\hat{\sigma}^2=\left(\sum_{j=1}^{k}\frac{1}{\hat{\sigma}_j^2}\right)^{-1}$. Thus, the prior information of parameter $\theta$ is obtained by fusing digital simulation data through classical frequency fusion method.

*2) Bayesian fusion of small sample data*

The measured data and the semi-physical simulation data may be small sample data, and Bayesian method is used to fuse small sample data. Assume that there are $n$ sets of the same type of prior information before the small sample data, which is compatible with small samples. The prior density $\pi_i(\theta)$ of the distribution parameter $\theta$ can be obtained from each set of prior samples, whose weight is $b_i$, $(i=1,2,\mathrm{K},n)$. The prior distribution density of parameter $\theta$ is

$$\pi(\theta)=\sum w_i\pi_i(\theta) \tag{3}$$

where $w_i=b_i/\sum b_i$, $(i=1,2,\mathrm{K},n)$. Then, the posterior density of the distribution parameter $\theta$ is obtained by Bayesian formula, which is

$$\pi(\theta|X)=\frac{f(X|\theta)\pi(\theta)}{\int_{\Theta} f(X|\theta)\pi(\theta)d\theta} \tag{4}$$

where $\Theta$ is parameter space and $X$ is the sample obtained in the field test. $f(X|\theta)$ is the distribution density of subsample $X$ when given $\theta$. Thus, the posterior density of $\theta$ is

$$\pi(\theta|X)=\frac{1}{m(X|\pi)}\sum_{i=1}^{n}w_i\pi_i(\theta)f(X|\theta) \quad (5)$$

where $m(X|\pi)=\int_{\Theta}f(X|\theta)\pi(\theta)d\theta$, which is the edge density of $X$.

For easy to calculation, an expression of posterior density when $n=2$ is given. In this case, there are two prior information, i.e.,

$$\pi(\theta|X)=\frac{1}{m(X|\pi)}\sum_{i=1}^{2}w_i\pi_i(\theta)f(X|\theta) \quad (6)$$

Where

$$\pi_i(\theta|X)=\frac{\pi_i(\theta)f(X|\theta)}{m(X|\pi_i)},i=1,2 \quad (7)$$

Then, we can get

$$\pi(\theta|X)=\frac{\sum_{i=1}^{2}w_i m(X|\pi_i)\pi_i(\theta|X)}{m(X|\pi)} \quad (8)$$

Assume that

$$\lambda_1=\frac{w_1 m(X|\pi_1)}{m(X|\pi)},\lambda_2=\frac{w_2 m(X|\pi_2)}{m(X|\pi)} \quad (9)$$

Finally, we obtain that

$$\pi(\theta|X)=\lambda_1(X)\pi_1(\theta|X)+\lambda_2(X)\pi_2(\theta|X) \quad (10)$$

Using similar mathematical derivation like above, when $n$ kinds of prior information exist in general, there is

$$\pi(\theta|X)=\sum_{i=1}^{N}\lambda_i(X)\pi_i(\theta|X) \quad (11)$$

where $\lambda_i(X)=\frac{w_i m(X|\pi_i(\theta))}{m(X|\pi(\theta))},(i=1,2,\text{K},n)$ .From the above we can see, the posterior distribution of $\theta$ is fused by multiple posterior distributions when there is a variety of prior information and the weighted average of these posterior distributions is fusion posterior distribution. Then, the Bayesian fusion result of small sample data can be obtained.

Finally, the large sample data fusion result and the small sample data fusion result are regarded as prior information and observation sample data, respectively. The Bayesian method is used to update the prior information parameters, and the obtained result is the multi-type data fusion result under the same experimental scenario. Furthermore, multi-type data fusion results under different scenarios can be obtained.

### *B. Evidence Theory Fusion*

The experimental data used in performance evaluation mostly come from different experimental scenarios, which evidence theory fusion method is used to fuse. After obtaining multi-type data fusion results of different experimental scenarios, the sample data of each scenario are described as evidence body using evidence theory. The evidence combination method is adopted when the evidence bodies do not conflict, while the weighted average correction fusion method is adopted when the evidence bodies conflict. Then, the data fusion results of different experimental scenarios are obtained.

#### *1) Evidence combination*

The evidence theory fusion criterion is used to synthesize the nonconflicting evidence bodies. This combination method is a strict AND operation method. The basic probability distribution of common focal elements of multiple belief functions is proportional to the respective basic probability distribution. Therefore, the evidence method has a focusing effect. This effect will strengthen support for common goals and weaken the impact of divergent goals. The principle of evidence combination is: if $Bel_1,Bel_2,...,Bel_n$ is the $n$ belief functions on the same identification frame; $m_1,m_2,...,m_n$ is the corresponding basic probability assignment functions; $A_i,A_j,A_k,...$ is the corresponding focal elements. Assume that

$$K=\sum_{A_i\cap A_j\cap A_k\cap\text{L}=\varnothing}m_1(A_i)m_2(A_j)m_3(A_k)\text{L}<1 \quad (12)$$

Belief function $Bel_D$ synthesized by $Bel_1,Bel_2,...,Bel_n$ is determined by the basic probability assignment function $m_D$ given below:

$$m_D(A)=\begin{cases}\frac{1}{1-K}\sum_{\cap A_i=A}\prod_{1\le i\le N}m_i(A_i) & A\ne\varnothing\\ 0 & A=\varnothing\end{cases} \quad (13)$$

Belief function $Bel_D$ given by $m_D$ is called the direct sum of $Bel_1,Bel_2,...,Bel_n$, i.e.,

$$Bel_D=Bel_1\oplus Bel_2\oplus\text{L}\oplus Bel_n \quad (14)$$

According to (14), the core of the belief function $Bel_D$ is equal to the intersection of the cores of $Bel_1,Bel_2,...,Bel_n$. If the cores of $Bel_1,Bel_2,...,Bel_n$ do not intersect, $Bel_1,Bel_2,...,Bel_n$ could not be synthesized, i.e., the evidence they correspond to supports completely different propositions. When $Bel_1, Bel_2, ..., Bel_n$ represents multiple batches of completely different evidence, it is the completely conflict evidence and cannot be synthesized by the evidence combination method.

*2) Weighted average correction fusion*

When evidence bodies are in high conflict, the result of combination is contrary to the common sense. The solutions to this problem can be mainly summarized into two categories: one is to modify the data fusion rules, and the other is to modify the data model and pre-process the conflict evidence before evidence combination. Because modifying the data fusion rules can lead to the destruction of the commutative law and associative law of Dempster's combination rule, the second solution conforms to the theoretical framework of the evidence theory method [11]. Weighted average correction method can reduce evidence conflict and guarantee the focusing effect of fusion to some extent. Thus, weighted average correction fusion method is used to deal with the contradictory evidence bodies.

The principle of weighted average correction is as follows:

$$m(A) = \frac{1}{n}\sum_{1}^{n} w_i m_i(A) \qquad (15)$$

where $w_i$ is the weight of each evidence and $\sum_{i=1}^{n} w_i = 1$. Weighted average correction method can achieve the suppression of evidence conflict through using different weighting methods and comprehensively consider the information of multiple conflicting evidence bodies. Furthermore, this method reduces the evidence conflicts by weighting, which has been widely used in the fusion of conflicting evidence bodies.

## IV. Conclusion

In the performance evaluation, the experimental data need to be fused since it comes from digital simulation experiments, semi-physical simulation experiments and real experiments, etc., and it also comes from different experimental scenarios in some cases. The multi-source experimental data fusion problem is decomposed into multi-type data fusion problem and data fusion problem under different experimental scenarios, where multi-type data fusion adopts Bayesian method and data fusion of different scenarios uses evidence theory method. In the case of multi-type data fusion, the results obtained by the fusion of large sample data with the classical frequency method and the results obtained by the fusion of small sample data with the Bayesian method are respectively taken as prior information and observation sample data, and the Bayesian method is used to obtain the multi-type data fusion result. In the case of data fusion of different scenarios, each sample is described as the form of evidence body, and different data processing methods are adopted according to the relationship between the evidence bodies. The final result of multi-source experimental data fusion/is obtained through the proposed method.

The proposed data fusion method is suitable for processing static data. In the next step, we will select the appropriate data using the proposed method and other existing methods to do experiments. Then, according to the experimental results, compare fusion results to verify the effectiveness of this method.

## References


[1] Z. Xiaoge and M. Sankaran. Aircraft re-routing optimization and performance assessment under uncertainty. Decision Support Systems, vol. 96, pp. 67-82, Apr. 2017, DOI:10.1016/j.dss.2017.02.005.

[2] C. Fei and W. Xin. Application of Data Fusion in Anti-jamming Performance Evaluation of Missile Weapon Equipment System. Aerospace Electronic Warfare, vol. 30, no. 3, pp. 1-4, Jun. 2017.

[3] D. L. Hall and J. Llinas, "An introduction to multisensor data fusion," in Proceedings of the IEEE, vol. 85, no. 1, pp. 6-23, Jan. 1997.

[4] G. Li, C. Tiejun, W. Yuhai, and L. Chenyan. Study For Multi-resources Geospatial Data Integration. Geomatics World, no. 1, pp. 62-66, Feb. 2007.

[5] C. Kewen, Z. Zuping, and L. Jun. Multisource Information Fusion: Key Issues, Research Progress and New Trends. Computer Science, vol. 40, no. 8, pp. 6-13, Aug. 2013.

[6] R. R. Yager. Set Measure Directed Multi-Source Information Fusion. in IEEE Transactions on Fuzzy Systems, vol. 19, no. 6, pp. 1031-1039, Dec. 2011.

[7] Q. Youjie and W. Qi. Review of Multi-source Data Fusion Algorithm. Aerospace Electronic Warfare, vol. 33, no. 6, pp. 37-41, Dec. 2017.

[8] H. Jiang and S. Youchao. Application Study of Multi-sourced Reliability Data Fusion Method Based on Bayes Theory. Aircraft Design, vol. 32, no. 6, pp. 52-55, Dec. 2012.

[9] L. Qingmin, W. Hongwei, and L. Jun. Small sample Bayesian analyses in assessment of weapon performance. in Journal of Systems Engineering and Electronics, vol. 18, no. 3, pp. 545-550, Sept. 2007.

[10] Z. Ying, L. Jiangtao, and Z. Meng. Operational Experiment Scenario Design Based on UML. Command Control & Simulation, vol. 37, no. 2, pp. 86-91, Apr. 2015.

[11] Q. Xiaochao. Research on Simulation Model Validation and Calibration Methods Under Uncertainty. Harbin Institute of Technology, 2016.

# Automated Extraction of Domain-Specific Information from Scientific Publications

Philipp Kief*, Clarissa Marquardt†, Katja Nau†, Steffen Scholz†, and Andreas Schmidt*†
* Department of Computer Science and Business Information Systems,
Karlsruhe University of Applied Sciences
Karlsruhe, Germany
Email: philipp.kief@gmx.de, andreas.schmidt@hs-karlsruhe.de
† Institute for Automation and Applied Informatics
Karlsruhe Institute of Technology
Karlsruhe, Germany
Email: clarissa.marquardt@kit.edu, nau@kit.edu, scholz@kit.edu, schmidt@kit.edu

***Abstract*—As the number of scientific publications in many subject areas continues to increase, it is becoming more and more important to support researchers in filtering out relevant information from papers and to identify relevant papers as well. In the present work, the field of nanotoxicology is used to investigate how dictionary-based disambiguation and extraction of entities of the domain can be implemented and how information on entire scientific papers can be extracted. By developing an analysis tool, it can be shown that the automated analysis of scientific publications in the field of nanotoxicology can be realized in basic terms. The analysis tool is based on the General Architecture for Text Engineering (GATE), D3.js and additional Node.js services, as well as Angular.js and represents an application that can be controlled intuitively by the scientists and provides a suitable user interface to visualize the extracted information in an aggregated way.**

***Keywords*–*Named entities; Domain specific entities; Entity cooccurrence; Visualization.***

## I. Introduction

The number of potentially relevant publications in the field of nanotoxicology is increasing at a rate that is difficult to manage even for experts in the respective fields. As a consequence, more time is needed to extract certain information from different sources. Here, mostly local document collections or public platforms like PubMed or ResearchGate can be mentioned. This trend will certainly continue due to the distribution possibilities on the Internet and in particular due to the great research potential at least in the field of nanotoxicology. Therefore, approaches that automatically attempt to extract semantic information from scientific work are becoming increasingly important for researchers to keep track of other research in their field.

A common difficulty is that ambiguities (example "Paris": city, ship, band, hotel, biological term for a plant genus, etc.) must be resolved. This process is called Named Entity Disambiguation (NED). Entities are words or phrases that represent a real object (e.g., persons, organizations, places, etc.). These objects do not necessarily have to exist physically, but can also be abstract, such as a year or date. These entities are commonly referred to as *Named Entities*, where here the proper name of an entity is meant (e.g., the name of a person, where the person is an entity) [1]. In this paper, we will investigate exemplarily how an automatic extraction of the entities from the field of nanotoxicology can be carried out. Therefor, it is important to recognize the relevant entities in the respective domain. In the case of nanotoxicology these are, for example, chemical substances, diseases and medical terms.

In the context of this work, a concept is to be developed, with which entities relevant for the nanotoxic domain can be extracted from text. For this purpose, existing knowledge databases such as eNanoMapper [2], Medical Subject Headings (MeSH) [3], etc. will be used. Based on these results, various analyses, such as cooccurrences, analysis of temporal trends, clustering of similar documents, etc., are to be carried out by means of suitable visualization.

### A. Information Extraction

Information Extraction (IE) is a sub-area of Natural Language Processing (NLP) and is used to extract information from a large amount of unstructured data. After extraction, the resulting data is presented in structured form. Based on this structured data it is possible to conclude further knowledge afterwards. IE is mainly used in areas where a very large amount of text, from which information needs to be extracted in a very short time, are available. An example for IE is the extraction of entities from over 500 different news feeds [4]. In this case the relationship between different entities are to be determined (e.g., how often appear the entities "Donald Trump" and "Angela Merkel" together in the collection of news articles).

The first phase of the IE process contains domain-independent tasks. These include *sentence splitting*, *tokenization*, *morphological analysis* and *Part-Of-Speech* (POS) tagging [5], which are only dependent on the language but not on the domain. Since a sentence represents a semantically closed unit and the words within a sentence have a strong relation to each other, it is necessary to perform a sentence splitting as one of the first steps within IE. In addition, tokenization transforms all words and punctuation marks into so-called tokens. A token represents the smallest text element of a text and is the basis for further IE steps. In a further morphological analysis, the properties of a token are determined. Properties are the POS and the lemma of a word. Lemma is the basic form of a word under which it can also be found in a dictionary. The POS is the type of word (e.g., noun, adjective, verb, preposition, etc.). In the subsequent second phase, domain-specific components such as NED or the identification of related entities are located.

### B. Named Entity Recognition

Named Entity Recognition (NER) can be seen as a subcategory of IE. NER aims to identify the entities in a text that are relevant to a subject area. In biomedical text, the names of persons, addresses, telephone numbers as well as symptoms, diseases, medications or anatomical features are of importance [6]. Nevertheless, it depends on the concrete application of an analysis tool which entities have to be extracted from a text corpus. The extraction of the entities is therefore important, since they contain a large part of the information about the content of a document.

### C. State of the Art

There exist already many different tools and frameworks that can extract information from documents. For example, the National Library of Medicine (NLM) has developed a program called MetaMap [7] to extract biomedical sections of a text to match them to the concepts of the UMLS (Unified Medical Language System). UMLS is a terminology that comprises over 2 million names on 900,000 biomedical concepts and is freely available for research purposes [8]. Another tool is PolySearch2 [9], which is a web-based tool that can extract the relations between biomedical entities. It is mainly designed to formulate queries according to the scheme "Given X, find all associated Ys". An example query can look like this: "Find all diseases associated with Bisphenol A". The results of the queries are based on data from MEDLINE [10], PubMed [11] and 14 other biological databases such as UniProt [12], Drug-Bank [13] and Human Metabolome Database [14].

### D. Contribution of the paper

The main contributions of this paper are the following: (1) Extraction of all relevant information from large document collections in the domain of nanotoxicology. (2) Further processing of the extracted data such as the recognition of relationships between entities or temporal dependencies as well as the calculation of the relevance of an entity to a document. (3) Implementation of a generic analysis tool into which a corpus of documents can be loaded and analyzed. Results of the analysis are made available by means of visually descriptive visualizations. Although this is shown by the example of nanotoxicology, the procedure can be regarded as a blueprint for any domain, since only the steps for the extraction of the entities have to be adapted.

## II. Conception

This section shows how a document corpus can be read and analyzed, so that the collected information can later be displayed graphically via suitable visualizations.

### A. Preprocessing

Preprocessing is the part of the application that is responsible for extracting all the necessary data from the documents and storing it in a structured data format. The extracted data must be available in such a form that it forms a suitable basis for later calculations and analyses. This process is executed once for each document and the data will be stored in a database.

The first step is the importing of the documents into the tool. Since the documents are available in different formats such as PDF, Word documents or images, they must be converted into a uniform, processable format. The aim is to have the text of the documents as raw text, i.e., without markup elements or other syntax that is responsible for the layout. Many documents contain additional information in the form of metadata, which is also stored in the document. Metadata includes, e.g., the name of the author, the creation date, the date of the last modification, various keywords, the title or a short description of the content. For example, keywords provide very precise information about the content of a document and the creation date can be used to classify the document by year.

Finally, the potential retrieval of documents from Open Access sources should also be mentioned. Some of them have potentially useful Application Programming Interfaces (APIs), so that publications on a particular topic can be automatically retrieved via the analysis tool and then analyzed. The results of this analysis can be sent to the user by e-mail. Such a scenario can save the user a lot of time, as the tool can search for potential publications and trigger the analysis fully automatically without further manual steps.

### B. Extraction of Named Entities

Once a document has been loaded and the content has been converted to the appropriate format, the next step is to extract the relevant entities. In order to recognize entities, a comparison with different dictionaries is necessary. The dictionaries typically contain a number of terms per entity. For example, for the geographical area, there are dictionaries that list the names of the cities of the world. If a word or phrase from the text is found in such a dictionary, it can be marked as a city-entity. By the information which entity a word is, further information can be obtained in the following steps. Important entities in the context of this work are names of persons, places, organizations, dates, addresses as well as domain-specific technical terms of the nanotoxicology domain. A separate dictionary was compiled for the latter by collecting 855,237 entries from different databases such as MeSH [3], eNanoMapper [2], Nanoparticle Ontology [15], Springer Nature (SN) SciGraph and the DaNa Glossary.

If entities are recognized in the text, further information about this entity is also stored. As a result, the positions at which the entity occurs in a document are recorded. A position contains the information about the document, the index of the surrounding sentence and the position of the word within the sentence. Since an entity usually occurs more than once in a document, a list of item information is assigned to this entity.

### C. Text Normalization

Different methods can be used to find terms with similar meaning. Based on the lemmatization algorithm [16], two words, which differ from each other only for grammatical reasons, can be adapted. In lemmatization, a word is reset to its basic form, which is also called Lemma [16]. Thus, for the words "studies" and "studying" the lemma "study" can be determined. In this case, both words can be summarized under the term "study". An alternative to lemmatization is the stemming algorithm. A stemmer or stemming is generally understood as the truncation of the suffix of a word [17]. With the same word base and different suffix, many words usually have the same meaning (e.g., "connect", "connected", "connecting" or "connection") [17]. Both methods are similar and both can be used to summarize terms. Since the words are more consistently reduced to one form by stemming than by lemmatization, this paper will focus on stemming. As only a comparison between the words is made here, the shortened words do not necessarily have to be readable, as is the case with lemmatization. In the medical field, many abbreviations are used in scientific documents. In this case, the abbreviations should also be combined with the spellings written out as they can be referred to the same entity.

### D. Relations between Entities

The situation that two entities occur close to each other is known as cooccurrence. The concept of this work is based on the assumption, that entities that often appear together (coocurrence) have a potentially strong relationship. In order to be able to measure this relationship, we must quantify the dependency, based on the cooccurences of two or more entities. Beside the frequency of this coccurence, also the distance between the entities, which form the cooccurence, must be considered. The smaller the distance between two entities, the stronger is their cooccurrence.

The concept envisions that as a preprocessing step for all existing entities located in a defined proximity, the respective distance to all other entities is calculated. A threshold-value must be defined for the maximum distance between two entities. The larger the value, the longer the calculations take, since the distance between more entities must be calculated. The maximum distance thus represents a compromise between the duration of the calculation and the coverage of all relationships. However, since widely spread entities have a minimal relationship to each other, a calculation does not have to be performed for all occurrences. For this work the limit value was set to 20 words, because the strong relationships between entities could be determined and the calculation speed is still acceptable high.

To measure the strength of the distance between two entities ($E_1$ and $E_2$), we developed a formula, that includes several factors. If the two entities are in the same sentence, only the distance between the words is calculated. The distance is given by subtracting the index of $E_1$ from $E_2$. If the entities can be found in different sentences ($S_1$ and $S_2$), the distance of the sentences to each other is additionally calculated here, i.e., how many sentences lie between entity $E_1$ and entity $E_2$. Finally, the distance of entities contained in different paragraphs ($P_1$ and $P_2$) will also be added to the formula. Each distance can be weighted differently with an exponent (here $\alpha$, $\beta$ and $\gamma$). The exponents are weighted in descending order because the distance between the entities has a strong influence on the strength, the distances between the sentences and the paragraphs should have a weaker influence. Finally, an inverse value is calculated from the sum of the differences, so that large distances lead to a lower strength and vice versa.

$$strength = \frac{1}{(E_2 - E_1)^\alpha + (S_2 - S_1)^\beta + (P_2 - P_1)^\gamma}$$

### E. Identification of Relevant Documents

The relevance of a document to an entity should not only be based on the number of occurrences of the entity in a document, but should be calculated from a combination of several factors. If only the number of occurrences of an entity were taken into account when calculating relevance, this could result in the name or year of an author appearing very frequently in the bibliography at the end of a document and not reflecting the entire content of a document. From a frequently appearing name of a person in the bibliography, one can only conclude the fact that the author of the document has often used that person's literature. This does not mean that the document has anything to do with this person. Similar to Information Retrieval (IR) procedures, various factors should be taken into account, such as how often an entity appears in the text, whether it is part of the document title, where it appears in the document, how widely it spreads throughout the document, and whether it is listed in the keywords of a document. If an entity is part of the title or the keywords, the relevance for this document increases considerably. Title and keywords usually describe a document very concisely and contain essential entities to describe the content.

In addition, it is also conceivable to include the entities that are part of an abstract more strongly in the calculation of the relevance of a document. An abstract usually describes the content of a document in a few concise sentences. An entity extracted from it can thus have an important meaning for the content of the according document.

Another possibility that can be considered for the relevance of a document is the temporal frequency of an entity. Thus, for example, it can be determined in which years there was a certain trend in the use of a term. Documents, which in this case are no longer in the period of the trend, should be weighted less strongly, because they, for example, only report retrospectively on the trend and do not supply any more new knowledge.

### F. Frequency History

There are always periods in which certain entities are used particularly frequently by authors in literature. Time trends can be determined from the frequency, with which an entity appears over several years in different documents. Researchers at Harvard University, for example, found that the term "slavery" was very widely used in the early 1860s during the civil war and the civil rights movement from 1955 to 1968, by analyzing over 5 million books from the 16th to the 20th century [18].

The investigation of the frequency of entities over a certain period of time allows the identification of trends and a temporal classification. When searching for specific entities, the user can find out in which years many documents deal with the entity or when the entity first appeared. In the periods when entities occur more frequently than average or rarely, further analyses can be carried out by the researchers in order to search for the cause.

### G. Architecture

The architecture for an automated document analysis tool essentially consists of three components. Before the preprocessing can take place, the documents must be uploaded. Afterwards, the entities with their position information are extracted from the text and stored in a database. The processing service in turn retrieves the data from the database and sends it to the client to display it visually. The client can use a search to decide for which entity he wants to receive additional information and for which entity relevant documents should be displayed. An autocompletion helps the user find the right entities and the search can also be limited by search criteria such as entity type or number of related entities. A rough overview about the architecture is given in Figure 1.

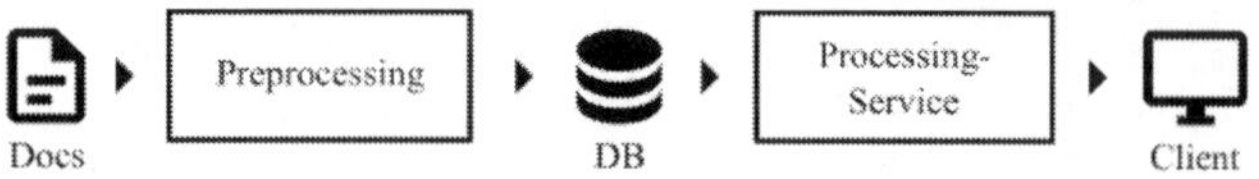


Figure 1. Components of the tool

The preprocessing step can be started automatically after the documents have been successfully uploaded into the tool. Depending on the number of documents, it may take some time to process the individual steps. During processing, the client should be shown a status, which document is currently being preprocessed and how long it will take. Since preprocessing consists of several smaller sub-processes such as tokenization, sentence separation, POS, comparison with dictionaries, calculation of relations, determination of the relevance of documents, extraction of metadata, recognition of abbreviations, stemming as well as the assignment of terms to an entity, these must be brought together to form a pipeline. Within the pipeline, the subprocesses are executed one after the other, since some of them also depend on previous ones.

The only component that is actually dependent on a specific domain is the comparison with the dictionaries. In order to be able to recognize technical terms in documents, it is necessary to create certain terminologies that can be used for comparison. Such an approach is, on the other hand, very generic, since for another domain only the dictionary has to be exchanged in order to identify the relevant entities from the documents. Thus, the analysis tool could also be used very well in other fields than nanotoxicology.

## III. Implementation

The implementation of a prototypical analysis tool will be used to demonstrate how the analysis of scientific documents in the field of nanotoxicology can be realized. The application can be controlled centrally via the client, which is a web application based on the web framework Angular. A web application was chosen, because the client only has to make requests to the implemented services and displays the data on the user interface at the end. A web application does not need to be natively installed on a computer and is lightweight and fast. All preprocessing steps and calculations are handled by the backend. The backend in turn consists of a Node.js server, which answers the client's requests and initiates the necessary analysis steps of the documents. Since the stored information about the extracted entities from the documents partly have different attributes, the NoSQL database MongoDB was used. This database makes it easy to store data records as JSON objects, regardless of which keys are contained in the JSON object. The dataformat used is JSON because JSON is a very lightweight format for storing data and can be easily processed with Node.js. Also JSON is the native dataformat in MongoDB and very well suited for transmission via REST interfaces, which have also been implemented here.

### A. Apache Tika

The toolkit Apache Tika [19] was used for the conversion of the PDFs, because it can not only extract the text but also recognize the metadata of a PDF file. A big advantage of this toolkit is the output in HTML format via the option "–html". In HTML output, paragraphs are syntactically marked with a <p> tag, so that in a next step in the pipeline, the paragraphs can be saved as entity information as well. Occasionally, words whose syllables were separated with a hyphen at the end of the line by a line break could no longer be correctly combined with Tika. Consequently, a regular expression is used to search for exactly these occurrences and the line breaks are removed by a script.

### B. GATE - General Architecture for Text Engineering

A large part of the further steps of the preprocessing is realized by a Java-based tool called GATE [20]. It offers a variety of plugins that can be combined to a pipeline. A plugin can be individually added to a pipeline via a plugin manager. Since many plugins are already included by default, only a few plugins have to be added manually for the prototype. By default it includes tools for tokenization, gazetteers, sentence splitting or POS tagging. Each plugin can create annotations in the text and add additional information to them. An annotation represents a marking of a certain place in the text and enhances this with additional information. These can be very diverse and depend on the plugin that can add, change and remove new information in the form of properties (so-called "features").

Which plugins are used for the implementation of the tool can be seen in Table I. The Document Normalizer plugin normalizes various special characters in the texts, then the ANNIE English Tokenizer splits the words into tokens and the sentences are annotated by the RegEx Sentence Splitter. The ANNIE Gazetteer compares the tokens with basic dictionaries such as city names, addresses, people names, etc. and annotates recognized words as corresponding entities. The ANNIE POS Tagger applies POS-Tagging to all tokens and with the help of the ANNIE NE Transducer several so-called JAPE (Java Annotation Pattern Engine) rules are applied to the annotations. These rules ensure that some properties of the annotations are renamed (e.g., "minorType" to "gender") for better semantics. With the Transfer Original Markups plugin mainly the paragraph tags from the HTML output of Tika are converted into paragraph annotations. The Morphological analyzer plugin calculates the word root for each word and adds this information to the annotation. To recognize the annotations an Abbreviation Extraction plugin was developed, which implements the algorithm of S. Schwarz and M. Hearst [21] which is mainly designed for the recognition of abbreviations in biomedical text. This plugin also detects how an abbreviation is written out and adds this information to the according annotation. Abbreviations also need to be stemmed by an Abbreviation Stemmer plugin so that they can be more easily combined later. The last plugins in the pipeline are all those that are domain-specific for nanotoxicology, which is why they are marked with the prefix "NANO". These plugins perform the same tasks as the previous plugins only that they are directly designed for annotations that can be assigned to nanotoxicology. This is because, for example, specially designed dictionaries are used, which only contain technical terms from the domain or special JAPE rules, which have to adapt these annotations in order to obtain a better data structure later.

As a result of the execution of the GATE pipeline, a separate JSON document exists for each document in which all annotations are contained as objects. Based on several Node.js scripts, these JSON documents are combined into a single data set. The annotation objects are compared with each other on

TABLE I. PLUGINS OF THE GATE PIPELINE

| # | Plugin | Functionality |
|---|---|---|
| 1 | Document Normalizer | Replace special characters |
| 2 | ANNIE English Tokenizer | Split words into tokens |
| 3 | RegEx Sentence Splitter | Annotate sentences |
| 4 | ANNIE Gazetteer | Detect entities from GATE |
| 5 | ANNIE POS Tagger | Recognize POS of word |
| 6 | ANNIE NE Transducer | Customizing annotations |
| 7 | Transfer original markups | Annotate HTML tags |
| 8 | Morphological analyzer | Recognize root word |
| 9 | Abbreviation Extraction | Extract abbreviations |
| 10 | Abbreviation Stemmer | Stemming of abbreviations |
| 11 | NANO Gazetteer | Extracting NANO entities |
| 12 | NANO Abbreviation Gazetteer | Extracting NANO abbreviations |
| 13 | NANO Transducer | Adapting NANO annotations |
| 14 | NANO Stemmer | Stemming NANO entities |

the basis of their stemmed value and merged as appropriate. Based on these data sets, the relations between the annotations are calculated as already described in the conceptual part of this paper. As a result, for each annotation it is stored to which other annotations a very strong relation exists. The same is done for the calculation of relevant documents as well as for the calculation of the temporal classification of an entity. The calculated data is stored in a MongoDB in the form of JSON data records.

### C. Orchestration of the processing tasks

To be able to start GATE directly by a request comming from the Node.js server, the Java API (GATE Embedded) is called. Thereby a configuration file is specified at the start of GATE, in which all plugins of the pipeline are defined. Since Tika and various Node.js scripts are executed in addition to GATE, a higher-level pipeline of process calls must be defined. This is realized via a Makefile. In the Makefile, the individual processes are configured as targets whose order is clearly defined when the Makefile is called.

### D. Web application

The web application is based on the Angular.js web framework. A file upload was realized, with which the PDF documents can be uploaded. The PDF documents must always be part of a document collection. A document collection is created in the database after the upload. Furthermore, it is possible to edit the dictionaries via the web application or to create new dictionaries with new technical terms. This enables researchers to keep the identification of relevant terms up to date in the future. After a document collection has been created, the analysis can be triggered for it. The Web application triggers this with a request to the processing service. During the processing of the individual steps of the original processing, a status dialog is displayed in the Web application that shows which step is currently being prepared. This was realized by transferring the standard output of the process pipeline in the console to the Web application via a Web socket connection. The web application then interprets the logs in such a way that a process bar is generated out of it.

When the analysis of the document collection is finished, the user has the possibility to search the data set from the database for certain terms. The user is supported by an autocompletion function (see Figure 2). The number behind a search suggestion indicates how often this term occurs in the document collection.

Figure 2. Autocompletion

After the user has clicked on one of the search suggestions, a new page will opened, displaying all available information about the selected entity (see Figure 3). The relationships of the selected entity to other entities are visualized in the form of a graph. The strength of the lines corresponds to the strength of the relationship between the entities. The nodes in the dark blue color represent direct relationships, while the nodes in the light blue color represent the most relevant entities of the dark blue nodes. This attempts to contextualize the entities within the graph. If required, additional information about the selected entity can be displayed in a panel next to the graph. This includes, for example, information about existing abbreviations as well as a descending list of the most relevant documents for this entity. The documents can also be opened or downloaded directly from this view.

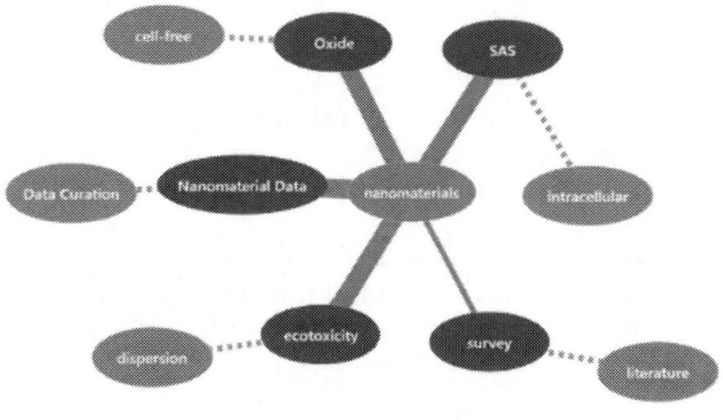


Figure 3. Visualization of entity relationships

Another visualization is to compare the most common entities of two document collections. A graph visualization is also generated, which displays the entities from both document collections in two different colors. In a third color, which represents a mix color tone of the other two colors, the intersection is displayed (see Figure 4). The intersection includes those entities that occur very frequently in both document collections. From this it can be concluded that the two document collections have a certain thematic intersection concerning these entities.

## IV. Evaluation

The prototypical implementation of a tool for the automated analysis of scientific documents showed that common concepts of information extraction can be combined to extract information from unstructured texts and to transform them

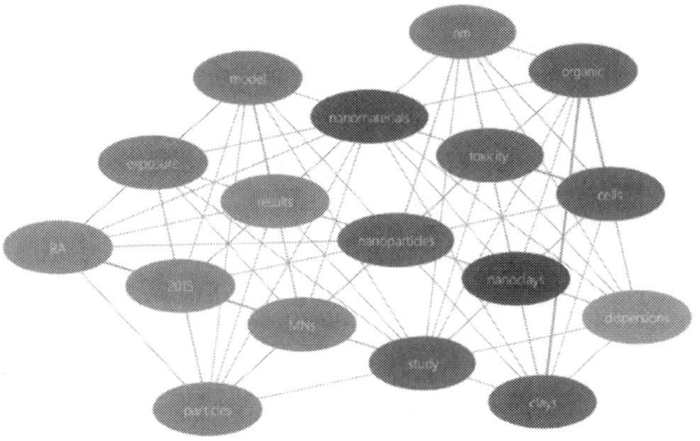


Figure 4. Comparison of document collections

into a structured, machine-processable data model. However, this concept is very much based on the quality of the dictionaries. If, for example, the terminology used in a particular department is not as good as in nanotoxicology, the quality of the results will also suffer. A good selection of dictionaries and terminologies is therefore crucial. The advantage of the implementation is the concept of the web application and the decoupled services in the backend, so that there are no hurdles during the installation of the software at the end user. The loose coupling of services and process steps in the pipeline makes it easy to add new components or replace existing ones in the future.

## V. Conclusion and Further Work

The paper reported on an automated analysis of scientific publications on nanotoxicology. It was shown, with which concepts a solution can be implemented, which can facilitate the daily work of scientists when searching through large document collections. Several tools and technologies were presented, with which a prototypical software was developed. In addition, it was shown which possibilities are available to visualize large amounts of collected information in a suitable way.

As a further step towards automated document analysis, it can be explored whether the presented solution can also connect to online databases to automatically download and analyze new documents and information. The concept could even go to the point where the researcher is informed by e-mail that a new document is available after the analysis has been carried out. Certain filter rules could also define that the researcher is only notified if the document is relevant to him and his current research. In this way, further manual steps in literature research could be automated, making it easier for researchers to find relevant publications for their research.

## Acknowledgements

The work presented in this paper was partly funded under the DaNa2.0 project funded by the German Federal Ministry of Education and Research (FKZ 03X0131).

## References

[1] A. Siu, "Knowledge-driven entity recognition and disambiguation in biomedical text," Ph.D. dissertation, 2017.

[2] J. Hastings, N. Jeliazkova, G. Owen, G. Tsiliki, C. R. Munteanu, C. Steinbeck et al., "eNanoMapper: harnessing ontologies to enable data integration for nanomaterial risk assessment," J Biomed Semantics, vol. 6, 2015, p. 10, ISSN: 2041-1480.

[3] "Medical Subject Headings - The NLM's curated medical vocabulary resource," 2019, URL: https://www.nlm.nih.gov/mesh/meshhome.html [retrieved: 2019-07-21].

[4] A. Schmidt and S. Scholz, "Quantitative considerations about the semantic relationship of entities in a document corpus," in Proceedings of the 51st Hawaii International Conference on System Sciences, Hilton Waikoloa Village, Hawaii, January 2-6, 2018, 2018, pp. 933–942, URL: http://hdl.handle.net/10125/50003 [retrieved: 2019-07-21].

[5] M. Rodrigues, "Advanced applications of natural language processing for performing information extraction," Cham, 2015, URL: https://doi.org/10.1007/978-3-319-15563-0 [retrieved: 2019-07-21].

[6] H. Dalianis, "Clinical text mining : Secondary use of electronic patient records," Cham, 2018, URL: https://doi.org/10.1007/978-3-319-78503-5 [retrieved: 2019-07-21].

[7] A. R. Aronson, "Effective mapping of biomedical text to the umls metathesaurus: the metamap program." in Proceedings of the AMIA Symposium. American Medical Informatics Association, 2001, p. 17.

[8] O. Bodenreider, "The unified medical language system (umls): integrating biomedical terminology," Nucleic Acids Research, vol. 32, 2004, URL: http://dx.doi.org/10.1093/nar/gkh061 [retrieved: 2019-07-21].

[9] Y. Liu, Y. Liang, and D. Wishart, "Polysearch2: a significantly improved text-mining system for discovering associations between human diseases, genes, drugs, metabolites, toxins and more," Nucleic Acids Research, vol. 43, 2015, URL: http://dx.doi.org/10.1093/nar/gkv383 [retrieved: 2019-07-21].

[10] "MEDLINE," 2019, URL: https://www.nlm.nih.gov/bsd/medline.html [retrieved: 2019-07-21].

[11] "PubMed," 2019, URL: https://www.ncbi.nlm.nih.gov/pubmed/ [retrieved: 2019-07-21].

[12] "UniProt," 2019, URL: https://www.uniprot.org/ [retrieved: 2019-07-21].

[13] "DrugBank," 2019, URL: https://www.drugbank.ca/ [retrieved: 2019-07-21].

[14] "HMDB," 2019, URL: http://www.hmdb.ca/ [retrieved: 2019-07-21].

[15] D. G. Thomas, R. V. Pappu, and N. A. Baker, "Nanoparticle ontology for cancer nanotechnology research," Journal of Biomedical Informatics, vol. 44, no. 1, 2011, pp. 59–74, ontologies for Clinical and Translational Research, URL: http://www.sciencedirect.com/science/article/pii/S1532046410000341 [retrieved: 2019-07-21].

[16] C. Manning, P. Raghavan, and H. Schütze, Introduction to Information Retrieval. Cambridge University Press, 2008, URL: http://www.informationretrieval.org [retrieved: 2019-07-21].

[17] M.F.Porter, "An algorithm for suffix stripping," 1980, URL: https://tartarus.org/martin/PorterStemmer/def.txt [retrieved: 2019-07-21].

[18] J.-B. Michel, Y. K. Shen, A. P. Aiden, A. Veres, M. K. Gray, J. P. Pickett et al., "Quantitative analysis of culture using millions of digitized books," Science, vol. 331, no. 6014, 2011, pp. 176–182, URL: http://science.sciencemag.org/content/331/6014/176 [retrieved: 2019-07-21].

[19] C. A. Mattmann and J. L. Zitting, Tika in Action. Manning, 2011.

[20] H. Cunningham, D. Maynard, K. Bontcheva, V. Tablan, M. Dimitrov, M. Dowman et al., Developing Language Processing Components with GATE Version 8. University of Sheffield Department of Computer Science., 2018, URL: https://gate.ac.uk/sale/tao/tao.pdf [retrieved: 2019-07-21].

[21] A. S. Schwartz and M. Hearst, "A simple algorithm for identifying abbreviation definitions in biomedical text," University of California, Berkeley, 2003, URL: http://biotext.berkeley.edu/papers/psb03.pdf [retrieved: 2019-07-21].

# Leveraging Statistical Methods for an Analysis of Demographic Factors of Opioid Overdose Deaths

Amna Alalawi[1], Daniel Fooks[2], Les Sztandera[3], and Sean Zakrzewski[4]

[1]DMgmt in Strategic Leadership Program, Thomas Jefferson University, Philadelphia, PA, USA
Email: Amna.Alalawi@Jefferson.edu

[2]School of Business, Thomas Jefferson University, Philadelphia, PA, USA
Email: Daniel.Fooks@Jefferson.edu

[3]Kanbar College of Design, Engineering, and Commerce, Thomas Jefferson University, Philadelphia, PA, USA
Email: Les.Sztandera@Jefferson.edu

[4]School of Business, Thomas Jefferson University, Philadelphia, PA, USA
Email: Sean.Zakrzewski@Jefferson.edu

**Abstract - Deaths from drug overdose including opioid overdose have been increasing at an alarming rate, and authorities still find tackling this problem an acute challenge. This paper applies Artificial Intelligence and statistical techniques to big data to identify the demographic and socio-economic factors that have led to the increasing number of drug overdose deaths in Allegheny County, Pennsylvania, United States. Using Artificial Intelligence software, we analyzed a dataset of over 3,500 patients alongside demographic and socio-economic variables to gain detailed insights into the issue, insights that we can generalize to craft solutions to this problem in both domestic and global communities. Our findings revealed patterns ranging from possible psychological and behavioral factors and drug use on weekends, as well as a direct market supply effect on the number of deaths. These findings imply the need for authorities to offer educational workshops to individuals and their families about the dangers of the current drug epidemic and to design an effective policy for the oversight of drug market supply that includes taking firm action against violators.**

***Keywords – data analytics; big data; opioids; drug overdose***

## I. INTRODUCTION

Deaths caused by the opioid crisis have reached epidemic levels in the US, with more people dying from opioid overdose than by either motor vehicle incidents, gun violence, or HIV [2]. In 2016, more than 42,000 Americans lost their lives as the result of a drug overdose, including 613 Allegheny County residents, a rise in deaths of over 44 percent. This has largely been attributed to the presence of newer, stronger drugs such as fentanyl in US communities [7]. Local health officials have found it difficult to keep pace with the new drugs being introduced into common usage, especially the presence of fentanyl in most of the heroin sold on the streets. Fentanyl is extremely potent and can cause a fatal overdose on the first try for some users [7]. Today, drug abuse is indeed a major problem in the US. A study by the Center for Disease Control (CDC) clearly evidences the existence of this crisis, stating that in 2017, more than 47,000 people died of a drug overdose in the country [6]. It was found that more than 2,000,000 Americans live with drug addiction, such as opioid addiction [9].

This study uses Artificial Intelligence (AI) and machine learning techniques to explore a dataset containing information on 3,551 fatal incidents of opioid overdose in Allegheny County, Pennsylvania, with the aim of finding ways to minimize the consequences of the opioid crisis in communities in the US and globally.

Opioid overdose has become an epidemic in the US as well as Allegheny County [13]. In 2015, the country experienced more than 400 deaths, and from then, the trend continued to increase. Data showed that individuals affected were within the age range of 25 to 54 years old. It was found that there are plenty of opportunities that have not been taken full advantage of in terms of intervention for opioid users [13]. The authors recommended that screening for opioid and other drugs among adults involved in child welfare should be improved. Further, enhancing the ability of the direct care staff to identify opioid use and risk of overdose, as well as access to expert consultants should be increased to improve the effectiveness of the care mechanism.

In Section 2 of this paper, we discuss and highlight different statistical tools and methods used to carry out the investigation to study several demographic factors of those affected in Allegheny County. While Section 3 focuses on providing a thorough analysis of the data collected through various sources, Section 4 highlights key findings of the study as well as trends in relation to the subject matter. Section 5 provides conclusion and recommendations pertaining to drug overdose in the community that can be used for prevention intervention.

## II. METHODOLOGY

To gain greater insight into the social and economic factors that have increased the risk of fatal opioid overdose in Allegheny County, PA, we used multiple approaches utilizing AI and statistical software and programming languages, including IBM SPSS Analytics, IBM Watson Analytics, Microsoft Power BI, and Python, to explore the dataset, which contained information on 3,551 fatal incidents of opioid overdose in Allegheny County.

The dataset, which covers opioid overdose deaths from the year 2008 to 2017, includes fatal accidental overdoses in the country and contains information on the date of death, the time of death, the manner of death, the age, gender, and race of the decedent, the seven most prevalent drugs found in overdose victims, the zip code of the overdose incident, and the zip code of the decedent's residence [1]. To look further into this issue, we searched for other variables that may have a relationship with opioid overdose rates. These other variables can be divided into two general categories: climate and economic.

The climate variables we examined were: monthly average temperature and temperature departure from mean levels for the 2008-2017 base period. This data was retrieved using the National Oceanic and Atmospheric Administration "Climate at a Glance" tool.

The economic indicators we examined were: county unemployment rate and income inequality in the county (measured as a ratio of the mean income of the highest quintile of earners divided by the mean income of the lowest quintile of earners in the county). These two datasets were collected from the FRED Economic Data service of the St. Louis Federal Reserve Bank. The final variable examined in this category was the uninsured rate, data on which was sourced using the U.S. Census Bureau's Small Area Health Insurance Estimates program [12].

## III. ANALYSIS

It has proven valuable to first observe the overdose dataset by itself to get a full understanding of the situation and to provide a baseline against which to compare the climate and economic variables examined.

The timespan of this dataset is from 01/03/08 to 12/31/17, a total of 9 years, 11 months and 28 days. The most surprising and saddening takeaway from the data is the age range of those affected by fatal drug overdose, which is an astonishing 1 to 91. The n for this dataset is 3,460.

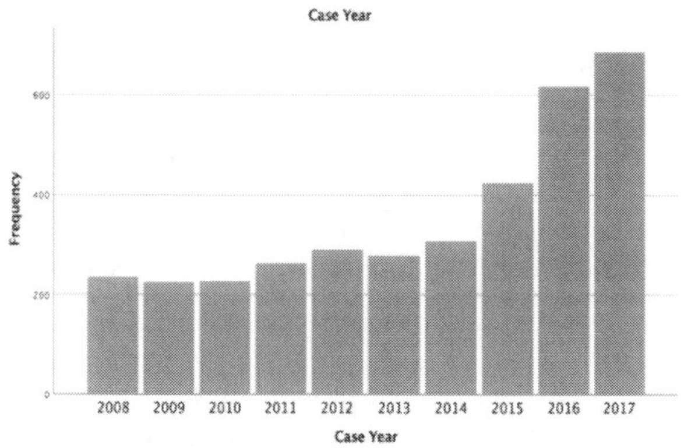


Figure 1. Overdose deaths in Allegheny Country, PA (2008-2017)

Figure 1 indicates overdose deaths over the past several years have been increasing at an exponential rate. This cannot be explained simply by an increase in population as the population of Allegheny County has fluctuated over the past decade and has, in fact, not grown at all. The graph uses data from 2010 (the earliest year in which reliable data was collected) to 2017, to illustrate the rising trend in overdose deaths.

Across all ten years covered by the dataset, it becomes clear that the crisis appears to have two distinct peaks in terms of age: one among those in their 20s and 30s and another among those in their 50s. The most common age for someone in the county to die of an overdose is 51, indicating that there is a slight skew toward the older of the two age peaks. Moreover, the standard deviation is 12.5, showing that most deaths occur within an approximately 24-year timeframe in mid-life.

It is interesting to observe how age distribution across drug overdose deaths changes over time. The double peaks are not initially pronounced, but develop over time until 2017, when they seem to disappear. It is also interesting to see how age range widens over the years as well, and how age distribution starts to skew toward younger people. Nonetheless, the opioid epidemic is more prevalent among men than women given that women accounted for a comparably low 31 percent of fatal drug overdoses in this timeframe.

It is also clear that the overdose deaths in this county occur overwhelmingly among Caucasians. However, it is worth looking at the demographics of the county overall to identify any major disparities. In Table 1, we compare overdose deaths with county population data that closely aligns with U.S. Census data. While there may be some disparities in the total percentages due to non-matching categories, for the purposes of a "sanity check" on the proportions of overdose deaths in the dataset, the table serves its purpose.

TABLE I. PERCENTAGE OVERDOSE DEATHS BY RACE WITH COUNTY POPULATION DATA

| Race | Percent of County Population | Percent of Overdose Deaths | Difference |
|---|---|---|---|
| Asian | 4.0 | .2 | 3.8% |
| Black or African American | 13.4 | 14 | -.06% |
| Hispanic | 2.1 | .2 | 1.9% |
| White | 78.6 | 85.5 | -6.9% |

It appears that Asian and Hispanic ethnic groups are comparatively less affected by overdose deaths to a small degree and African Americans are more affected, again by a small amount. Meanwhile, Caucasian people are overrepresented as victims of overdose deaths by a larger difference than any other, although still not by a significant degree.

It is interesting to note that April and August are the most common months for overdose deaths to occur. The reasons for this are not obvious and warrant further investigation. However, other than August, there is a decline in deaths during the summer months, which may suggest a possible seasonal element in overdose deaths.

Figure 2 shows the number of deaths by day of the week, the results collected here are perhaps unsurprising. Friday, Saturday, and Sunday see the highest number of overdose deaths. People are less likely to be working on these days and will thus have more leisure time. These days are also when people are most social, which, depending on the person, can involve alcohol or recreational drug use.

The spike in overdose deaths that occurs at around 5 pm is also of interest. This is when many people get out of work and there may be a connection here. The fact that most overdose deaths occur in the middle of the day is interesting as well, particularly the spike observed at 1 pm.

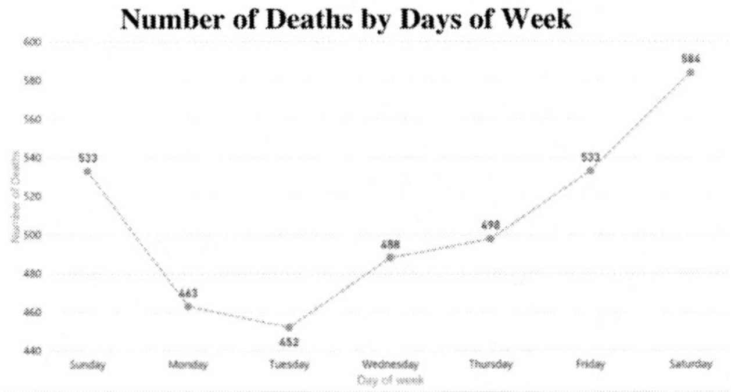


Figure 2. Number of deaths due to drug overdose by day of week

| | | Frequency |
|---|---|---|
| Valid | Total | 3522 |
| | 15210 | 184 |
| | 15212 | 165 |
| | 15136 | 112 |
| | 15216 | 108 |
| | 15132 | 93 |

Figure 3. Top five zip codes for the locations of overdose deaths in the county during the period examined

Figure 3 shows the top five zip codes for the locations of overdose deaths in the county during the period examined. They account for a substantial proportion of all overdose deaths, but overall distribution remains quite wide and dispersed.

| | | Frequency |
|---|---|---|
| Valid | Total | 3493 |
| | 15210 | 171 |
| | 15212 | 154 |
| | 15136 | 114 |
| | 15216 | 97 |
| | 15132 | 94 |

Figure 4. Top five zip codes for the residences of people who suffered a fatal drug overdose in Allegheny County during the period examined

Figure 4 shows the top five zip codes for the residences of people who suffered a fatal drug overdose in Allegheny County during the period examined. They are the same as the zip codes identified as the top five locations of fatal overdoses. This overlap indicates that people tend to overdose in the zip code in which they live, which seems reasonable. Nonetheless, there are some differences in frequency and a far larger range of zip codes cover the residences of the decedents. So, some people do travel and then overdose, including from as far away as West Virginia and even Minnesota.

## IV. FINDINGS AND TRENDS

This section highlights key findings of the study, as well as trends in relation to the subject matter as per the demographic variables tested.

### *A. Temperature and Overdose Deaths*

The graph in Figure 5 charts temperatures and uninsured rates and reveals a higher death rate for uninsured people in the warmer months. In contrast, in the graph above, a higher death rate is observed to occur in the colder months. This is both fascinating and difficult to explain. It is possible that uninsured people are less motived to go to the hospital in the warmer months, believing that whatever ailment they may have will pass on its own since they don't have the cold weather working against them. Moreover, illnesses, such as flu and pneumonia, tend to arise in the colder months, and this again suggests people are less concerned about illness in the warmer months. Therefore, there is no significant dependence on temperature in relation to drug overdose deaths.

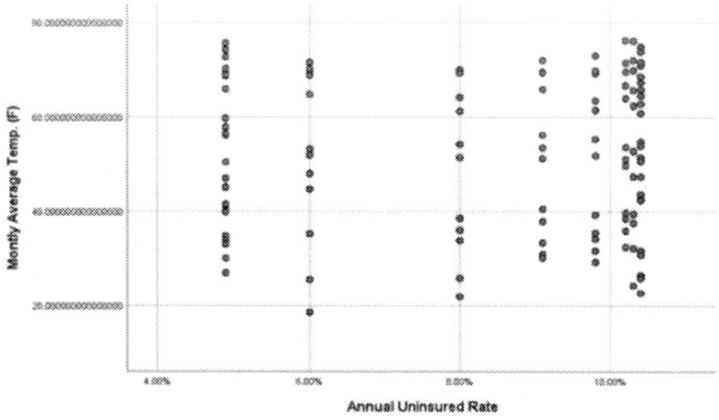


Figure 5. A chart showing how the monthly average temperature and annual uninsured rate influenced the death rate

Figure 6 analyzes the distribution between male and female in overdose deaths in Allegheny County. The study revalidates that overdose deaths are more amongst men, which make up around 69 percent of the total deaths. Women account for 31 percent of the total deaths.

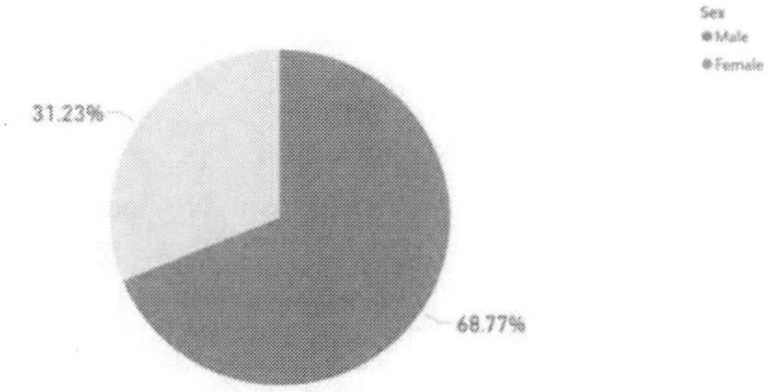


Figure 6. A chart showing the number of deaths by sex in Allegheny County, PA

Figure 7 identifies the number of deaths by race. It is seen that Whites represent the highest segment of the population that is affected among drug users and number of fatalities due to the opioid crisis.

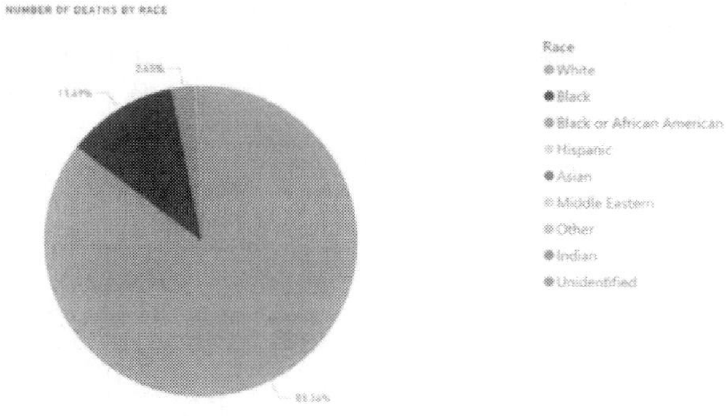


Figure 7. A pie chart showing number of deaths by race in Allegheny County, PA

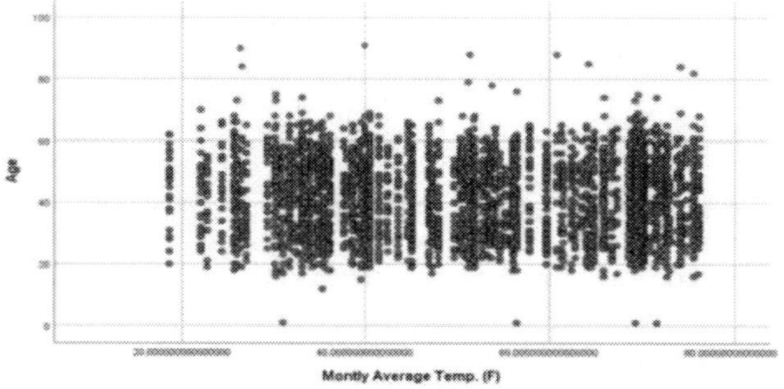


Figure 8. Shows how the rate of overdose deaths is determined by age and the monthly average temperatures

The graph in Figure 8 plots average monthly temperatures against the age of the decedents. The graph shows that there are strong clusters and then gaps around certain temperatures as compared with age, which shows a distinct range. It is interesting to observe certain gaps around temperatures at which no overdose deaths appear to have occurred versus clusters where many overdose deaths occurred. Again, this graph further supports our finding that there is no significant dependence on temperature in relation to drug overdose deaths.

### *B. Month to Month Fluctuations*

Looking at every year separately on IBM Watson, a cloud system for data analytics, another pattern emerges whereby months with abnormally high death counts are followed by months with abnormally low death counts, and vice versa. This may be related to the availability of drugs in the market, reflecting the high level of addiction to drugs containing fentanyl and heroin specifically. The authorities have successfully taken down various platforms that were previously used to sell and buy drugs, but not a lot of information has been gathered in terms of the effects of such an action [4].

**Number of Deaths in Year 2017**

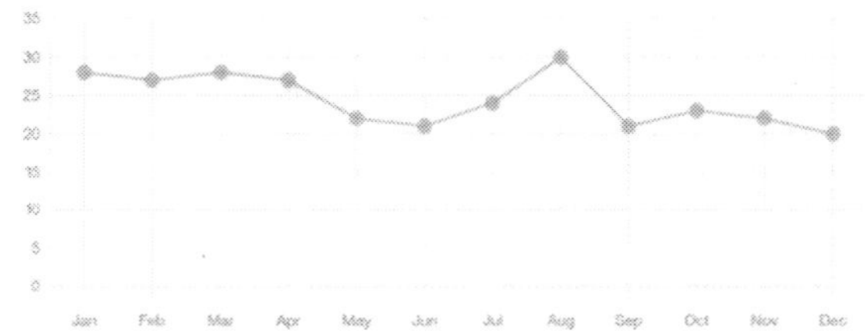


Figure 9. A visualization of the death rates of each month of the year 2017

In 2017, the aforementioned pattern was most visible in the months of August and September. August saw a high number of deaths and was followed by September, a month with lower deaths, which is the pattern we recognized through IBM Watson which we concluded that this could be related to market supply. When one particular month has a high death number, the following month is much lower, suggesting that the supply is lower in the market. The year ended with relatively low death rates in comparison with previous months.

**Number of Deaths in Year 2013**

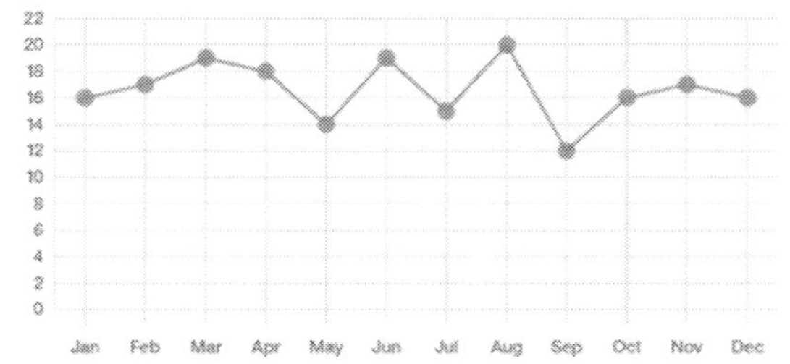


Figure 10. A visualization of the death rates of each month of the year 2013

As per the visualization in Figure 10, the year 2013 is a very good example of the potential oscillating trend, in which months with very high fatal drug overdose rates are followed by months with significantly lower overdose death rates.

**Number of Deaths by Month (2008-2017)**

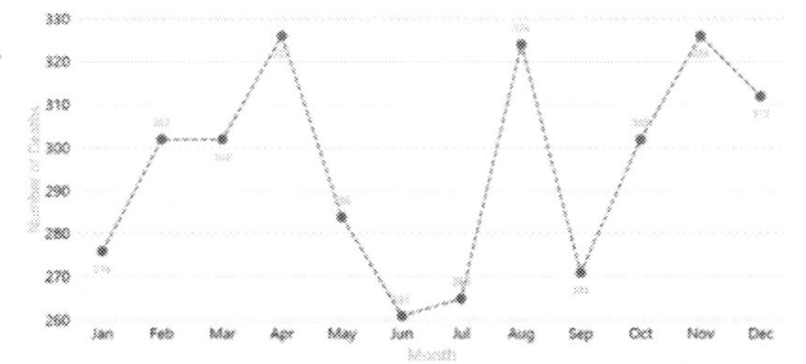


Figure 11. A visualization of the number of deaths for each month of all the years of observation

Looking at all the years examined together in Figure 11, we can confirm the pattern that shows that it may be due to the supply of drugs in the market which causes fluctuation in deaths by months. Looking at August for example, we see a peak in deaths, of which then September shows much lower deaths. As previously mentioned, and can be seen from Figures 9 and 10, this was also apparent when we studied each year separately on IBM Watson. There was a high indication that after a month of high deaths, the following month sees much lower deaths. The visualization in Figure 11 was generated using Microsoft Power BI.

## V. CONCLUSION AND RECOMMENDATIONS

This data analytics study provides an expanded exploration of the problem of opioid drug overdoses in Allegheny County. Applying several statistical techniques, including pattern recognition, and generating other data visualizations, we were able to validate previously identified findings about overdose deaths, such as the age range and general demographics of affected populations [7]. We found the tools we used to be very useful in helping us to gain a better understanding of our sample set and to generate informative and understandable visuals.

Data Analytics also allowed us to find new information about our sample, particularly when combined with the additional variables added to the base dataset. We were able to generate highly practical visuals and illustrate clear trends from a large dataset with many variables, indicating that there is a possible relationship between drug addiction and lower temperatures and between psychological and behavioral factors and weekend drug use as well as a direct market supply effect on the number of deaths. These findings imply the need for authorities to offer educational workshops to individuals and their families, as well as health practitioners, about the dangers of the current drug epidemic and to design an effective policy for the oversight of drug market supply that includes taking firm action against violators.

We recommend that the authorities spend more time and funds on advertisements to educate individuals and families about the problem as well as investing in approaches to oversee market supply to drug users.

The issue of drug overdose deaths is so pressing that more research by data and population scientists is needed to gain further insight into this epidemic, so that impactful solutions can be found to reduce its harmful effects on communities both in the United States and around the globe.

Results of the current study supported results of the past studies. Thus, the limitation of this research was that there were no new findings obtained. The tools used in this study helped in enabling us to recognize patterns through data visualizations, and we encourage future researchers to leverage the use of multi-dimensional data to find factors that could possibly correlate to the drug addiction epidemic to explore new findings within regional and global communities. It is the hope that this information will be used in enhancing understanding of readers regarding the subject matter.

## REFERENCES


[1] Allegheny County Fatal Accidental Overdoses. (2018, April 11). Retrieved April, 2019, from https://catalog.data.gov/dataset/allegheny-county-fatal-accidental-overdoses

[2] D. Ciccarone, "Fentanyl in the US heroin supply: a rapidly changing risk environment", The International journal on drug policy, vol. 46, pp. 107-111, 2017.

[3] Climate at a Glance. (n.d.). Retrieved April, 2019, from http://www.ncdc.noaa.gov/cag/county/time-series/PA-003/tavg/all/1/2008-2017?base_prd=true&firstbaseyear=2008&lastbaseyear=2017&trend=true&trend_base=10&firsttrendyear=1895&lasttrendyear=2019

[4] B. R. Edlin, "Access to treatment for hepatitis C virus infection: Time to put patients first", The Lancet Infectious Diseases, vol. 16(9). doi:10.1016/s1473-3099(16)30005-6, 2016.

[5] Income Inequality in Allegheny County, PA. (2018, December 7). Retrieved April, 2019, from https://fred.stlouisfed.org/series/2020RATIO042003

[6] Lopez, G. (2019, February 26). A new study shows America's drug overdose crisis is by far the worst among wealthy countries. Retrieved May 20, 2019, from https://www.vox.com/science-and-health/2019/2/26/18234863/drug-overdose-death-america-international-study

[7] Lord, R. (2017, April 06). Allegheny County drug overdose deaths surge to 613 in 2016, breaking record. Retrieved May, 2019, from http://www.post-gazette.com/news/overdosed/2017/04/06/Allegheny-County-drug-overdoses-610-deaths-break-record/stories/201704060199.

[8] Percent Without Health Insurance Data for Allegheny County, PA. (n.d.). Retrieved May, 2019, from http://www.opendatanetwork.com/entity/0500000US42003/Allegheny_County_PA/health.health_insurance.pctui?year=2014&age=18 to 64&race=All races & sex=Both sexes & income=All income levels

[9] B. Saloner, "A public health strategy for the opioid crisis", Public Health Reports, vol. 133, pp. 24S-34S, 2018.

[10] Sederer, L. (2016, February 1). Take Action Against Addiction. Retrieved May 20, 2019, from https://www.usnews.com/opinion/blogs/policy-dose/articles/2016-02-01/10-ways-to-combat-americas-drug-abuse-problem

[11] Unemployment Rate in Allegheny County, PA. (2019, May 31). Retrieved May, 2019, from https://fred.stlouisfed.org/seri

[12] U.S. Census Bureau's Small Area Health Insurance Estimates Program. (N.d.). Retrieved April 2019, from https://www.opendatanetwork.com/entity/0500000US42003/Allegheny_County_PA/health.health_insurance.nui?ref=entityquestion&year=2014&age=18%20to%2064&race=All%20races&sex=Both%20sexes&income=All%20income%20levels

[13] E. Hulsey, and et. al., Opiate-Related Overdose Deaths in Allegheny County – Risks and Opportunities. (2016, July). Retrieved August, 2019, from https://alleghenycounty.us/uploadedFiles/Allegheny_Home/Health_Department/Programs/Special_Initiatives/Overdose_Prevention/Opiate-Related_Overdose_Deaths_in_Allegheny_County.pdf

# Effects of New Media on Eviction Rates

Regina Ruane, Ph.D.
Yulia Vorotyntseva, Ph.D.
Subodha Kumar, Ph.D.
Edoardo M. Airoldi, Ph.D
*Data Science Institute*
*Temple University*
*Philadelphia, PA USA*
*e-mail: regina.ruane@temple.edu*

*Abstract*— **Social media has impacted society in many unexpected ways, including the real estate and housing markets. Particularly, in these markets, social media can affect the structure of the communities, landlord-tenant relationships and, subsequently, the eviction problem. With the growing availability of search data from online sources, there is increasing interest in how individuals' choices reveal submarkets in domains, especially those that have a social component, i.e. online reviews and connection to social media among others. To demonstrate the structural components of the subnetworks that develop via the rental market that cause eviction and the market outcomes that result, we will use network analysis. This research aims to combine online review and social media data with eviction data to explore the range of effects of new media on the eviction rates.**

**Keywords-*big data; social network analysis; data analytics; data visualization; eviction.***

## I. Introduction

The eviction crisis in the united states has recently drawn a plethora of public attention – much of which is due to the efforts of dr. Matthew desmond who authored the pulitzer-prize winning book *evicted: poverty and profit in the american city,* which was published in 2016. Drawing on social science research, including his own, desmond (2016) has made a compelling argument that evictions are not only the result of poverty, but are a major source of poverty perpetuation and exacerbation.

Philadelphia, like other cities, is currently facing an eviction crisis with over 240,000 evictions filings in 2017 alone. To address this problem, the Mayor's Task Force on Eviction Prevention and Response has been established. Temple University's Data Science Institute aims to contribute to the City of Philadelphia's and the nationwide effort to combat the eviction crisis. The research outlined in this proposal aims to yield findings that will aid existing programs and inform the development of new programs and policies.

The proposed project is concerned with the effects of new media, such as social media and shared economy platforms, on eviction rates and housing scene in general. In the next section, we outline the questions that we will address within the scope of the proposed project.

## II. Research Questions

In this section, we provide and elaborate on the research questions that we will address within the scope of the proposed project.

A. *How does advertising targeting affect the eviction problem, and more generally, the housing situation?* Targeted online advertising can help municipal and national programs reach out to vulnerable populations and inform them about their rights and government assistance programs. For example, New York City runs a Propel app that helps people manage SNAP benefits and relies heavily on Facebook advertising. On the other hand, it has been argued that advertising targeting can be used for discrimination purposes: for instance, housing advertising may exclude protected categories of potential tenants. As a response to those concerns, Facebook recently agreed to restrict targeting options for housing, employment and credit ads. However, it is not clear how widespread is the abuse of advertising targeting and what is the magnitude of its consequences. It is also unclear if restricting targeting options for housing ads is sufficient to protect vulnerable populations, especially when there are no such restrictions for related categories, such as educational institutions and legal advice. In this project we aim to investigate the effects of targeted advertising policies on the evictions problem in Philadelphia.

B. *Does Airbnb play a role in the eviction crisis? Many hosts* claim that they sign up for Airbnb to offset high rent costs. Hosting an Airbnb on a rental property is often explicitly prohibited by a lease contract, but the need for additional income can encourage a tenant to take the risk. Such violations can lead to eviction of the Airbnb host, and there is anecdotal evidence that such situations indeed happen. We propose to conduct a systematic analysis of the effect of Airbnb emergence and its policies on the eviction crisis.

C. *What is the network structure of the eviction community? What overlapping communities and sub-communities exist?* Evictions are the result of a breakage in the relationship between a landlord and tenant and cause serious hardships on tenants and the housing landscape. Government agencies, non-profits, lawyers and judges support both landlords and tenants with services, information, or enforcement. To determine the network structure, we will complete a thorough network analysis to visualize its large-scale eco-system. We will also include data regarding eviction filings to determine frequency levels and prominence in the network structure. We will perform additional analyses to determine betweenness levels among the nodes to uncover intermediary or conduit roles and outcomes. This analysis will aid in determining network-related effects regarding eviction cycles and their impact.

## III. Research Methods

The Research Methods section describes the methods this study will utilize to address our research questions.

### A. *Data Visualization*

The first step in the proposed project is to generate descriptive statistics that include data visualization. Data visualization of landlords, tenants and eviction victims can provide important insights into eviction trends, demographics and related behaviors.

### B. *Social Network Analysis*

Social network analysis takes as its starting point the premise that social life is created primarily and most importantly by relations and the patterns formed by these relations (Scott and Carrington, 2011). Numerous applications have extended social network analysis into the study of political and policy networks (Bond and Harrigan, 2011; Knoke, 2011). Analyzing eviction victims from a network perspective will determine aggregate choices with regard to frequency and geographic locations, rental payments, visualization of the evictions at site and city levels, and subnetwork patterns. Using a causal inference approach, we will create a network model assigning individuals a position in a latent space based on City of Philadelphia data and determine the network structure of eviction victims using aggregate data and predict outcomes using housing cost and income rate changes.

### C. *Quasi-Experiment*

To elicit causal effects of technological disruptions (e.g., emergence of social media, development of advertising targeting and policy interventions) we will use the longitudinal data of eviction patterns and, controlling for other relevant factors, estimate what changes can be attributed to the factors in questions.

## IV. Timeline

A. *September-October 2019* Data collection, tidying and visualization. We will use obtained insights to refine research questions within the identified directions.

B. *November 2019 - February 2020* Data analysis, visualization, network analysis and development of policy recommendations. We will first focus on the impact of advertising targeting. We will use historical data on Philadelphia eviction filings and the data on evolution of targeted advertising and policies restricting it. Controlling for other factors, we will evaluate how advertising targeting affects the evictions situation.

C. *March - May 2020* Analyzing the data related to the Airbnb effect on eviction crisis. Addressing other research questions that may emerge on the previous stage.

## References


[1] Desmond, M.. Evicted: Poverty and profit in the American city. Broadway Books, 2016.

[2] Bond, M., & Harrigan, N. Political dimensions of corporate connections. *The SAGE handbook of social network analysis*, 196-209, 2011.

[3] Knoke, D. Policy networks. *The SAGE handbook of social network analysis*, 210-222, 2011.

[4] Scott, J., & Carrington, P. J. *The SAGE handbook of social network analysis*. SAGE publications, 2011.

# Applied Urban Fire Department Incident Forecasting

Guido Legemaate*, Jeffrey de Deijn†, Sandjai Bhulai‡ and Rob van der Mei‡§

*Fire Department Amsterdam-Amstelland, Ringdijk 98, 1097 AH Amsterdam
Email: g.legemaate@brandweeraa.nl
†Vrije Universiteit Amsterdam, Faculty of Science, De Boelelaan 1081, 1081 HV Amsterdam
Email: jeffreydeijn@hotmail.com
‡Vrije Universiteit Amsterdam, Department of Mathematics, De Boelelaan 1081, 1081 HV Amsterdam
Email: s.bhulai@vu.nl
§Centrum Wiskunde en Informatica, Science Park 123, 1098 XG Amsterdam
Email: mei@cwi.nl

***Abstract*—Every day, when firefighters respond to emergencies, they and the public face an unnecessary risk due to inadequate staffing. Having too many people stand-by costs a lot of money, on the other hand, having too few people stand-by leads to unnecessary safety risks. Therefore, for adequate staffing purposes, forecasting the number of incidents that each fire station has to handle is a very relevant question. In this paper, we develop models to create a good forecast for the number of incidents that each fire station in Amsterdam-Amstelland has to handle. Previous studies mainly focused on multiplicative models containing correction factors for the weekday and the time of the year. Our main contribution is to incorporate the influence of different weather conditions in the categories of wind, temperature, rain, and visibility. We show that an ensemble model has the best predictive performance. Rain and wind typically have a strong linear influence, while temperature mainly has a non-linear influence.**

***Keywords–incident forecasting; fire department planning; generalized linear models; ensemble models.***

## I. Introduction

As for most organizations, the ability to accurately forecast demand is of "paramount importance" for emergency services, fire departments included [1]. In the 1970s, the Fire Department of the City of New York and The New York City-RAND Institute jointly conducted various groundbreaking studies [2]. More recent academic interest seems to be focused more on ambulance services. While there are obvious similarities between emergency service providers, they differ in (the number of) incident types, demand characteristics, and operational logistics.

Nevertheless, the problems that fire departments have to deal with, like loss of coverage and the degradation of response times, are similar. The same is true for possible gains. On a strategic and tactical level, improved forecasting of workload leads to a better placement of base stations, and improved staffing and scheduling. On an operational level, one may proactively relocate units to maximize coverage and minimize response times during major incidents [3]. All things considered, efficient planning of emergency service resources is considered crucial.

Demand is an important factor when models are being developed to improve the performance of emergency service providers. It is, however, not uncommon that, for instance, call arrival rates are estimated using ad-hoc or rudimentary methods such as averages based on historical data [4]. This may ultimately lead to a degradation of performance, or over- or under-staffing [5]. In most cases, reducing response times is an important performance measure since this increases the survival rate of victims [6][7].

Numerous papers have been written on the subject of forecasting forest or wildfire occurrences, many of those using weather variables and vegetation types as part of their model [8]. Forest fire forecasting is no longer a study in academia alone. In fact, in the United States, e.g., the National Interagency Coordination Center operates a predictive service which provides decision support to the U.S. Forest Service, which facilitates pro-active management and planning of fire assets on both operational and tactical levels [9].

Although the scale of wildfire occurrences in the Netherlands is smaller than in other parts of the world, it is mainly the greater interrelationship of different types of infrastructure, i.e., the wildland-urban interface, that causes concern and even lead to surface fuel models for the Netherlands [10]. For a more urban environment, like the conurbation of Western Holland, which also includes Amsterdam, forest fire occurrences are not very common.

The occurrence of certain types of incidents which fire departments in urban settings typically respond to also correlate with weather conditions. As such, incorporating this information into the planning process of emergency services yields important advantages over current practice. Typical weather and storm-related incidents that fire departments in the Netherlands respond to are fallen trees, potentially falling debris that needs securing (roofs, construction work, scaffolding), and water damage. Another important factor is that the weather also impacts fire department operations by overwhelming available resources.

At least in the Netherlands, to the best of our knowledge, there are no known applications of forecasting algorithms that are used in practice at fire departments, being urban or specialized forest services. Given this, we aim to provide an easily applicable model that can be put to use for an urban fire department. Therefore, we quantify and model the gut feeling, which tells firefighters that on stormy days they will have busy days.

The organization of this paper is as follows. In Section II, we describe the data used to obtain the forecasts. Section III describes the models used for forecasting. In Section IV, we analyze the performance of the models and state the insights. Finally, in Section V, we conclude and address a number of topics for further research.

## II. DATA

The available data contains one row for each incident that happened in the region Amsterdam-Amstelland from January 2008 up until April 2016. The most interesting information includes the incident's start- and end time, location, incident type, the concerned fire station, and the number of fire trucks used. Since the size of incidents matters for the number of people you need, the focus is on forecasting the number of trucks needed.

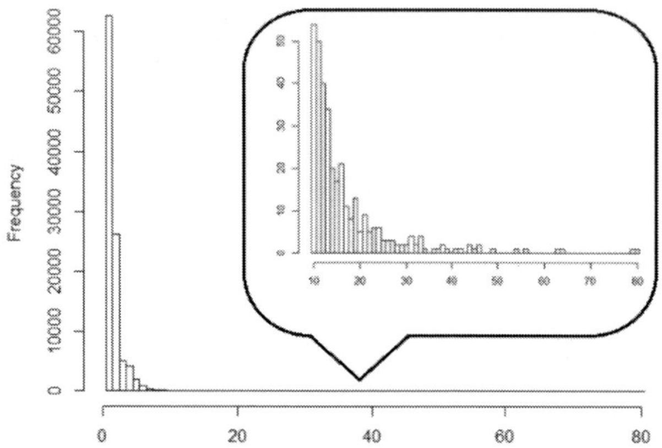


Figure 1. Histogram of the number of fire trucks per incident.

Figure 1 shows a histogram of the number of trucks per incident. The vast majority of the incidents require only one or otherwise just a few trucks. Therefore, it makes sense to distinguish between 'big' and 'small' incidents. Big incidents are mostly due to coincidences that are hard to predict. Specifically, they do not rely on bad weather conditions or a particular time of the year in the Netherlands, for example, as with forest fires in countries with a tropical climate. This arouses the expectation that the inter-incident times of big incidents can be modeled as a Poisson process.

To test the Poisson assumption, we apply the Kolmogorov-Smirnov (KS) test on the inter-incident times in cases when more than $k$ trucks are needed for several values of $k$. The KS-test shows that if we define an incident as 'big' when at least $k = 6$ trucks are used, then the KS-test does not reject exponentiality of the inter-incident times (approximate p-value $= 0.429$). However, for values of $k < 6$, the KS-test doubts (or rejects) this exponentiality (approximate p-value $=$ $0.073$ and $0.002$ when at least $k = 5$ and $k = 4$ trucks are used, respectively. Hence, according to this result, we define an incident to be big when at least 6 trucks are needed.

Now that big incidents can be modeled by a Poisson process, it is time to focus on the small incidents. The small incidents are probably easier to predict, since bad weather conditions often cause many *small* incidents to happen (like fallen trees, water damage, or police/ambulance assistance at traffic accidents). To study this, we first omit all incidents on December 31 and January 1. There are extremely many incidents around New Year's Eve, mainly caused by accidents involving fireworks. These conditions do not occur in the rest of the year, so it seems logical to analyze these days separately.

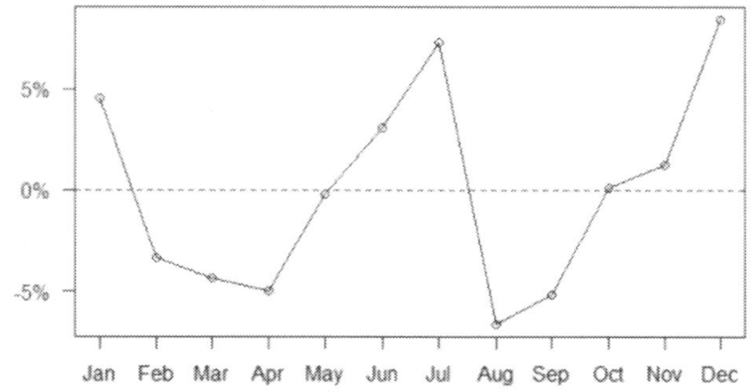


(a) Year pattern: higher during summer and winter.

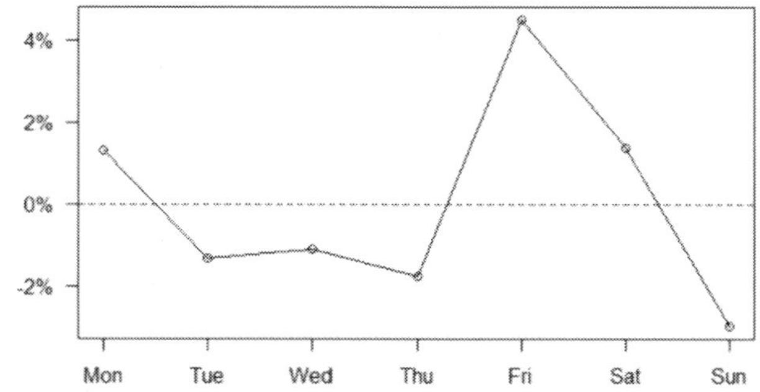


(b) Week pattern: peak on Friday.

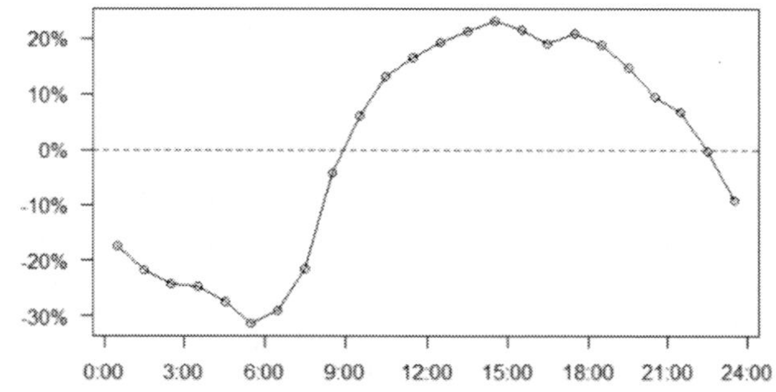


(c) Day pattern: low at night, high at midday.

Figure 2. Seasonal patterns: the given percentages represent relative differences with respect to the average (in blue).

There are clear seasonal patterns in the data for the number of trucks needed throughout each year, week, and day. The plots in Figure 2 illustrate this. The pattern in Figure 2c depicts the activity cycle that an average person goes through every day of the week. The week pattern (Figure 2b) differs per type of incident and looks a little different throughout the year. The pattern in Figure 2a can be included in the model in a more subtle way than taking factors per month. The problem here is that, for instance, the differences between the beginning and end of January are considerable. We correct for this by using a Loess-smoothed function over the factors per week. We will include all these patterns in our model, which will be discussed in the next section.

Besides the time-dependent components, we want to know which weather variables we must include in our model. Therefore, we use the Pearson correlation test to determine which weather conditions have a significant influence on the number of trucks we need. The results of these tests are summarized in Table I.

TABLE I. PEARSON'S PRODUCT-MOMENT CORRELATION TESTS BETWEEN SOME WEATHER VARIABLES AND THE NUMBER OF TRUCKS USED FOR SMALL INCIDENTS PER DAY.

| Category | Variable | p-value | Correlation |
|---|---|---|---|
| Wind | Average wind speed (FG) | $< 10^{-12}$ | 0.132 |
| | Maximum hourly mean wind speed (FHX) | $< 10^{-15}$ | 0.177 |
| | Maximum wind gust (FXX) | $< 10^{-15}$ | 0.189 |
| Temperature | Average temperature (TG) | 0.6897 | 0.007 |
| | Boolean: 1 if average $> 0$ (TG>0) | $< 10^{-8}$ | 0.105 |
| Rainfall * | Rainfall duration (DR) | 0.0004 | 0.061 |
| | Total rainfall (RH) | $< 10^{-15}$ | 0.151 |
| | Maximum hourly rainfall (RHX) | $< 10^{-12}$ | 0.132 |
| Visibility ** | Minimum visibility (VVN) | 0.2217 | -0.014 |
| | Boolean: 1 if minimum $<$ 200m (VVN<2) | 0.2893 | 0.010 |

* *In 0.1 mm and -1 for <0.05 mm;* ** *On 0-89 scale, where 0: <100 m, 89: >70 km.*

We can see from this that the minimum visibility and the average temperature both have no significant (direct) influence. However, if we consider a variable indicating whether it was on average freezing on that day, then this does have predictive value. Obviously, we also have to include some variables indicating the amount of rainfall and wind. However, the variables within these categories are highly correlated (sample correlation around 0.9) and, therefore, we may exclude some of them to simplify our model.

## III. MODELS

In this section, we will create a model that predicts directly the number of trucks that each fire station needs. In the previous section, we have shown that the big incidents (with at least six trucks needed) are very hard to predict and that we can best model them by an (inhomogeneous) Poisson process. We also showed that the daily pattern of the number of trucks used for small incidents is quite standard. So, if we know for some day how many trucks are needed in total, we can quite accurately extract from this how many trucks are needed per hour. Therefore, we will try to forecast the number of trucks needed per day per fire station.

In total, we have 9 different incident clusters or types in our dataset, some of which occur much more/less often than others. In Table II, we show the correlation with respect to one variable of each four weather categories. Looking at these correlations in detail, we can see that these are often in line with our expectations. For instance, high wind speed and rainfall obviously increase the number of incidents due to 'storm and water damage' (type 9) and decrease the likelihood of 'outside fires' occurring (type 1).

We will estimate, for each incident type $t$, a model that predicts the number of trucks used for *small* incidents $y_{t,d}$ on date $d$, i.e.,

$$y_{t,d} = f_{t,d} \cdot g_{t,d} \cdot x_{t,d}.$$

Here, $f_{t,d}$ is a correction factor for the week number based on a Loess-smoothed function as in Figure 3, and $g_{t,d}$ is a weekday

TABLE II. INCIDENT CLUSTERS AND CORRELATION WITH RESPECT TO WIND SPEED, TEMPERATURE, RAINFALL, AND VISIBILITY.

| Cluster | Type | Wind | Temp. | Rain | Visib. | # p/day |
|---|---|---|---|---|---|---|
| 1 | Outside fire | -0.135 | 0.09 | -0.193 | 0.075 | 3.46 |
| 2 | Animal in water | -0.088 | 0.134 | -0.058 | 0.013 | 1.65 |
| | Animal assistance | -0.072 | 0.129 | -0.088 | 0.069 | |
| | Person in water | -0.041 | 0.056 | -0.023 | 0.009 | |
| | Locked out | -0.006 | 0.159 | -0.043 | 0.062 | |
| 3 | Contamination / nuisance | - | -0.228 | 0.038 | -0.111 | 2.52 |
| 4 | Locked in elevator | - | -0.088 | 0.021 | -0.015 | 8.16 |
| | Automated alarm | - | -0.069 | 0.051 | -0.037 | |
| 5 | Fire rumor | - | -0.103 | - | - | 3.57 |
| | Inside fire | - | -0.038 | - | - | |
| | General assistance water | - | -0.019 | - | - | |
| 6 | Police assistance | 0.048 | -0.062 | 0.026 | - | 1.34 |
| 7 | Ambulance assistance | - | -0.065 | - | -0.039 | 8.55 |
| | Vehicle in water | - | -0.042 | - | -0.025 | |
| | Reanimation | - | -0.086 | - | -0.008 | |
| 8 | General assistance | 0.063 | 0.079 | 0.057 | 0.052 | 2.28 |
| 9 | Storm- and water damages | 0.319 | 0.028 | 0.279 | - | 2.10 |

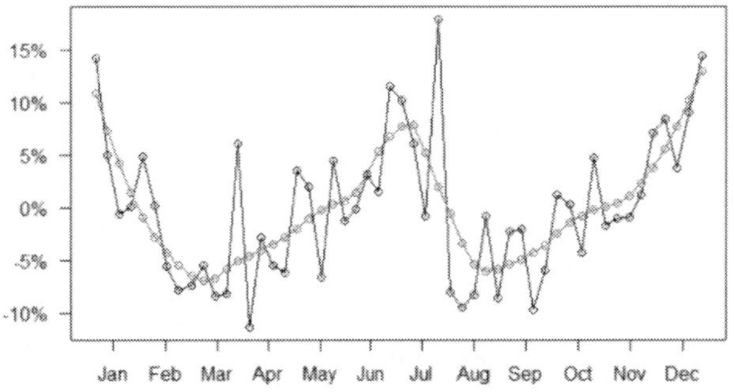


Figure 3. The year pattern per week (in black) together with its Loess-smoothed variant ($\alpha = 0.3$).

factor as in Figure 2b. Both are computed separately for each incident type. Finally, the term $x_{t,d}$ contains all remaining information. This includes the average level, dependencies on the weather, a possible trend and dependencies on all other variables that we are currently not considering, but which do exist in reality.

### A. Linear regression model

The first attempt to model $x_{t,d}$ is by means of the linear regression model (LM)

$$x_{t,d} = \beta_0 + \beta_1 \cdot d + \beta_2 \cdot \text{windspeed}_d + \beta_3 \cdot \text{temperature}_d + \beta_4 \cdot \text{rainfall}_d + \beta_5 \cdot \text{visibility}_d + \epsilon_{t,d},$$

where $\epsilon_{t,d}$ is assumed to have expectation zero and some finite variance. Note that this model includes an intercept ($\beta_0$), a linear trend ($\beta_1 \cdot d$) and (at most) four weather variables.

### B. Generalized Linear Model

Our second model, a Generalized Linear Model (GLM) arises from an observation that the largest outlier neither has the highest wind speed nor the most rainfall. However, the *combination* of wind and rainfall might be the cause. It may, therefore, be a good idea to include also cross-effects in our model, i.e.,

$$
\begin{aligned}
x_{t,d} = \beta_0 &+ \beta_1 \cdot d + \beta_2 \cdot \text{windspeed}_d + \beta_3 \cdot \text{temperature}_d \\
&+ \beta_4 \cdot \text{rainfall}_d + \beta_5 \cdot \text{visibility}_d \\
&+ \beta_6 \cdot \text{windspeed}_d \cdot \text{temperature}_d \\
&+ \beta_7 \cdot \text{windspeed}_d \cdot \text{rainfall}_d \\
&+ \beta_8 \cdot \text{windspeed}_d \cdot \text{visibility}_d \\
&+ \beta_9 \cdot \text{temperature}_d \cdot \text{rainfall}_d \\
&+ \beta_{10} \cdot \text{temperature}_d \cdot \text{visibility}_d \\
&+ \beta_{11} \cdot \text{rainfall}_d \cdot \text{visibility}_d \\
&+ \epsilon_{t,d}.
\end{aligned}
$$

Here, $\epsilon_{t,d}$ is again a residual term with zero expectation and some finite variance. Note that this is not a GLM as one may know from the literature. The only feature that causes it to be generalized is that it now also handles the cross-term relations between the weather variables. We could have called it an *expanded* linear model as well.

### C. Random Forests

The Random Forest (RF) algorithm is a machine learning algorithm that can be used for both classification and regression tasks. Compared to LM and GLM it has a large computation time, but RF is often used in practice since it generally has great performance. It will, therefore, be worth a try to implement this algorithm for our regression problem.

As input, the algorithm needs a $T \times (K + 1)$-matrix with $K$ explanatory variables and one observation variable (in this case $x_{t,d}$), all of sample size $T$. In the first iteration of the algorithm, a sample of size $T$ is drawn with replacement from the input matrix. On this sample, a decision tree (DT) algorithm is executed. This procedure is repeated $N$ times, yielding $N$ decision trees. When a new sample comes in, we can take all $N$ predictions for this sample and average these to get the final prediction.

### D. Performance measures

To evaluate the different models, we create a train and a test set. The train set contains all data up until 2015/06. The test set contains all data from 2015/07 onwards. This holds for all incident types, so all test sets contain exactly nine months of data and the quality of the forecasts can, therefore, be compared easily. We will measure the quality of a forecast on $n$ samples using the Mean Absolute Percentage Error,

$$\text{MAPE} = \frac{1}{n}\sum_{t=1}^{n}\left|\frac{y_t - \widehat{y}_t}{y_t}\right| \overset{(y_t \geq 0)}{=} \frac{1}{n}\sum_{t=1}^{n}\frac{|y_t - \widehat{y}_t|}{y_t},$$

as well as its weighted version, i.e.,

$$\text{wMAPE} = \frac{\sum_{t=1}^{n}\frac{|y_t - \widehat{y}_t|}{y_t}y_t}{\sum_{t=1}^{n} y_t} = \frac{\sum_{t=1}^{n}|y_t - \widehat{y}_t|}{\sum_{t=1}^{n} y_t}.$$

Here, $y_t$ is the true value in time period $t$ and $\widehat{y}_t$ is the prediction.

## IV. Results

In this section, we will compare the performance of the different models and evaluate the insights derived from them. The results on the MAPE and wMAPE values are given in Table III. These performance measures are based on the total daily number of trucks used for small incidents (over all fire stations and types). This enables us to compare all models through one value. It is also interesting to see how significant a parameter is on a 1 to 5 scale, as in Table IV for LM, Table V for GLM, and Table VI for RF. Here, we assign 1 when the p-value $< 0.001$ (very significant) until 5 when the p-value $\geq 0.1$ (not significant).

TABLE III. PERFORMANCE MEASURES OF THE MODELS.

| Model | MAPE | wMAPE |
|---|---|---|
| LM | 0.1886 | 0.1924 |
| GLM | 0.1865 | 0.1880 |
| RF | 0.2006 | 0.2019 |

### A. Linear regression model

For the linear model, comparing Table IV to Table II, we observe that when a weather variable has significant predictive power for some type, then their mutual correlation is relatively high as well. This is a nice result, but unfortunately, the reverse is not true. For instance, type 3 is highly correlated with one of the temperature variables, but this variable does not have predictive power for this type, which is surprising.

TABLE IV. SIGNIFICANCE OF ESTIMATED PARAMETERS FOR LM.

| Variable | Incident type 1 | 2 | 3 | 4 | 5 | 6 | 7 | 8 | 9 | Avg |
|---|---|---|---|---|---|---|---|---|---|---|
| Intercept | 1 | 1 | 1 | 1 | 1 | 4 | 1 | 1 | 1 | 1.33 |
| Trend | 1 | 5 | 1 | 4 | 3 | 5 | 5 | 5 | 5 | 3.78 |
| Wind speed | 1 | 5 | 5 | 3 | 5 | 5 | 5 | 5 | 1 | 3.89 |
| Temperature | 3 | 4 | 5 | 1 | 2 | 5 | 5 | 5 | 5 | 3.89 |
| Rainfall | 1 | 3 | 5 | 5 | 5 | 5 | 5 | 4 | 1 | 3.78 |
| Visibility | 5 | 4 | 5 | 4 | 5 | 5 | 5 | 5 | 5 | 4.78 |

Scaling: 1: $p < 0.001$, 2: $p < 0.01$, 3: $p < 0.05$, 4: $p < 0.1$, 5: $p < 1$

If we look at Table IV in more detail, it stands out that several types have no weather variables with significant predictive power. Opposed to type 3, this is not surprising for type 6 and 7, since their correlations to the weather variables are relatively low as well. On the other hand, types 1 and 9 are well predicted by the amount of wind and rainfall, which is intuitively explainable as well.

Since the wMAPE is higher, we can conclude that the LM is not very good at predicting relatively busy days (compared to predicting average days). However, the fire brigade is, of course, more interested in when they have busy days. They are prepared for average days anyway.

### B. Generalized Linear Model

Recall that the GLM model is an expanded version of the linear model, so it could be at least as good. The question is how much value it adds to the linear model. Comparing the significance of the variables in Table V to that of LM in Table IV, we observe that, in general, the single weather

TABLE V. SIGNIFICANCE OF ESTIMATED PARAMETERS FOR GLM.

| Variable | Incident type 1 | 2 | 3 | 4 | 5 | 6 | 7 | 8 | 9 | Avg |
|---|---|---|---|---|---|---|---|---|---|---|
| Intercept | 1 | 2 | 1 | 1 | 1 | 5 | 1 | 2 | 3 | 1.89 |
| Trend | 1 | 5 | 1 | 4 | 3 | 5 | 5 | 5 | 5 | 3.78 |
| Wind speed | 3 | 5 | 5 | 5 | 5 | 5 | 5 | 5 | 1 | 4.33 |
| Temperature | 5 | 5 | 5 | 3 | 2 | 5 | 5 | 5 | 4 | 4.33 |
| Rainfall | 5 | 3 | 5 | 5 | 5 | 5 | 5 | 5 | 1 | 4.33 |
| Visibility | 5 | 5 | 4 | 5 | 5 | 5 | 5 | 5 | 5 | 4.89 |
| Wind*Temp. | 5 | 5 | 5 | 5 | 5 | 5 | 5 | 5 | 5 | 5.00 |
| Wind*Rain | 3 | 3 | 5 | 5 | 5 | 5 | 5 | 5 | 1 | 4.11 |
| Wind*Visib. | 5 | 3 | 5 | 4 | 5 | 5 | 5 | 5 | 5 | 4.67 |
| Temp.*Rain | 2 | 3 | 5 | 5 | 5 | 5 | 5 | 5 | 1 | 4.00 |
| Temp.*Visib. | 5 | 5 | 5 | 5 | 5 | 5 | 5 | 5 | 5 | 5.00 |
| Rain*Visib. | 5 | 5 | 5 | 5 | 5 | 5 | 5 | 3 | 5 | 4.78 |

Scaling: 1: $p < 0.001$, 2: $p < 0.01$, 3: $p < 0.05$, 4: $p < 0.1$, 5: $p < 1$

variables have lost some importance in favor of cross-term variables they partition in. Type 1 is an excellent example of this. Here, the temperature had some predictive power in the LM, but now it turns out that it is mainly the *combination* with the amount of rainfall that matters. In addition, also wind speed and rainfall turn out to be less predictive on their own than the LM indicated. It is their cross-term effect that is important. Looking at the average column on the right, we also see that the intercept has lost some importance. Apparently, a bigger part can be modeled by the weather after adding some cross-term variables. Of all weather variables, it is even the case that two cross-term variables have the most predictive power.

Noting the influence of the cross-term variables, we expect that the performance of the GLM is better than that of the LM. If we compute the results for the totals per day, we still see that the wMAPE is somewhat higher than the MAPE, but compared to their equivalents of the LM, they are slightly better (about 2%).

## C. Random Forests

Different from the previous models, the RF algorithm does not estimate a parameter for each variable. We, therefore, have to find another measure for the importance of each variable. We will consider the 'RSS-ranking' for this purpose.

In the RF algorithm, in each decision node, the algorithm splits the remaining sample based on a decision rule on the variable that reduces the standard deviation most. In other words, it tries to improve the fit of the model to the training data as much as possible, i.e., the biggest decrease in *residual sum of squares* (RSS) between the fitted model and the observation data in the training set. Hence, we can measure the importance of a variable based on the total decrease in RSS from splitting on this variable. Table VI shows the results of the RSS ranking. As in the previous models, visibility is often the least important variable. However, the biggest difference is that in this case, the temperature is remarkably important.

When we compare the results of RF to the previous models, we see that, in general, RF gives the worst results. However, the effort for running this model is perhaps not in vain. When diving deeper into the results, we discover that the RF has the best wMAPE for type 9, which may be an indication that this algorithm is better in predicting busy days. This is confirmed by the plot of the predictions for type 9 of both GLM and RF in Figure 4. Obviously, the RF algorithm recognizes much better than GLM when the weather conditions are risky and likely to cause many incidents to happen.

TABLE VI. IMPORTANCE W.R.T. TOTAL DECREASE IN RSS.

| Variable | Type-cluster 1 | 2 | 3 | 4 | 5 | 6 | 7 | 8 | 9 | Avg |
|---|---|---|---|---|---|---|---|---|---|---|
| Wind speed | 4 | 2 | 4 | 1 | 3 | 2 | 2 | 4 | 1 | 2.56 |
| Temperature | 1 | 1 | 1 | 3 | 2 | 1 | 1 | 1 | 3 | 1.56 |
| Rainfall | 3 | 4 | 3 | 2 | 1 | 4 | 4 | 3 | 2 | 2.89 |
| Visibility | 2 | 3 | 2 | 4 | 4 | 3 | 3 | 2 | 4 | 3.00 |

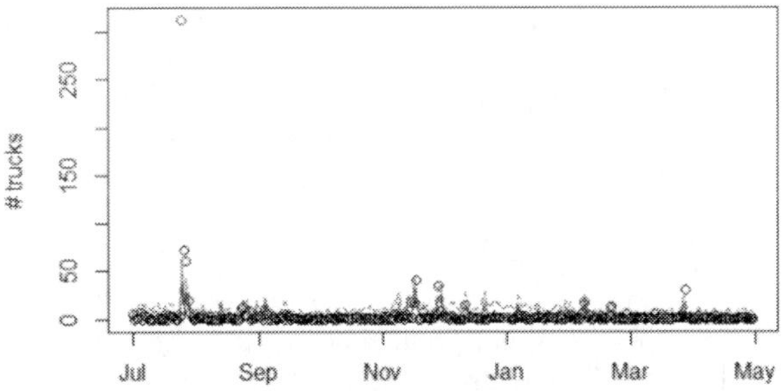


(a) Generalized Linear Model

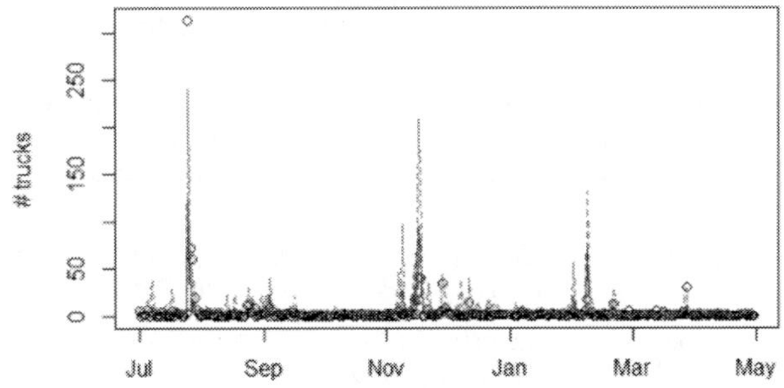


(b) Random Forest

Figure 4. Forecasts (in blue) of the number of trucks used for small incidents of type 9, including the upper bound of its 95%-prediction interval (in red).

## D. Ensemble model

From the previous discussion, we can conclude that GLM gives the best results when we look at the totals per day, but it is worse in predicting busy days than RF. If we can combine both models in such a way that we capture the good features from both models, then this may improve our forecasts. We will try to do this by applying a form of so-called *ensemble averaging* (EA). In our case, we will take a weighted average of the forecasts of RF and GLM, i.e.,

$$\text{EA} = \gamma \cdot \text{RF} + (1 - \gamma) \cdot \text{GLM},$$

for some constant $\gamma \in [0, 1]$.

We have to determine the optimal value of $\gamma$ to use in order to get the best results. Since GLM initially gives the best results, and we only need RF to be able to predict the busy days a bit better, we may expect that we have to put more weight on GLM, i.e., that $\gamma < 0.5$. When we vary $\gamma$ from 0 to 1, both the MAPE = 0.1853 and the wMAPE = 0.1860 take their minimum in $\gamma^* = 0.2$ (which is better than GLM individually; when compared with $\gamma = 0$).

### E. Practical implication

After the forecasts are complete, we extract from them the capacity we expect each fire station to need each day. For this, we want to have some certainty that the capacity is satisfying for that day. Different from a confidence interval, which only measures the uncertainty of the forecast, a prediction interval includes, in addition, the variability of the number of incidents in real life. We can, therefore, use the upper bound of the prediction interval to ensure that the predicted capacity will be satisfactory with, for instance, 95% certainty.

The $100(1-\alpha)\%$-prediction interval for the GLM model $y = X^\intercal\beta + \epsilon$ for a future observation $y_0$ can be computed as

$$\widehat{y}_0 \pm t_{n-k}^{(1-\alpha/2)}\widehat{\sigma}\sqrt{x_0^\intercal(X^\intercal X)^{-1}x_0 + 1},$$

(see [11]), where $\widehat{y}_0$ is the predicted value for $y_0$, $t_{n-k}^{(1-\alpha/2)}$ is the $(1-\alpha/2)$-quantile of the $t$-distribution with $n-k$ degrees of freedom, $n$ is the number of samples in the training set, and $k$ is the number of variables in the model.

For the RF algorithm, we have $N$ decision trees, which all yield one prediction for each future observation. The variability of these $N$ individual predictions captures the uncertainty of the final prediction (the average of the individuals). In order to capture the variability of the observations, we need again our assumption on the residuals. In this case, we will use this by adding to each of the $N$ individual predictions a random value, drawn from the empirical distribution of the residuals in the training set. Then, the resulting $N$ values include all the variation we need. Their $(\alpha/2)$- and $(1-\alpha/2)$-quantiles together directly form the desired prediction interval.

TABLE VII. CAPACITY NEEDED PER DAY AND FIRE STATION WITH CERTAINTY THIS CAPACITY SUFFICES THAT DAY.

| Fire station | Avg cap. needed | | | % of days 2 needed | | | Available cap. 1? |
|---|---|---|---|---|---|---|---|
| | 90% | 95% | 99% | 90% | 95% | 99% | |
| Aalsmeer | 0.14 | 0.17 | 0.27 | 0.0% | 0.0% | 0.0% | No |
| Amstelveen | 0.44 | 0.53 | 0.80 | 0.0% | 0.3% | 3.3% | No |
| Anton | 0.40 | 0.48 | 0.73 | 0.0% | 0.0% | 0.3% | No |
| Diemen | 0.12 | 0.15 | 0.25 | 0.0% | 0.0% | 0.0% | No |
| Dirk | 0.34 | 0.41 | 0.64 | 0.0% | 0.0% | 0.7% | No |
| Driemond | 0.04 | 0.05 | 0.10 | 0.0% | 0.0% | 0.0% | Yes |
| Duivendrecht | 0.17 | 0.20 | 0.30 | 0.0% | 0.0% | 0.0% | No |
| Hendrik | 0.59 | 0.71 | 1.07 | 0.7% | 1.7% | 67.7% | No |
| IJsbrand | 0.19 | 0.24 | 0.38 | 0.0% | 0.0% | 0.0% | Yes |
| Landelijk Noord | 0.04 | 0.06 | 0.11 | 0.0% | 0.0% | 0.0% | Yes |
| Nico | 0.35 | 0.42 | 0.64 | 0.0% | 0.0% | 0.3% | No |
| Osdorp | 0.42 | 0.51 | 0.77 | 0.0% | 0.0% | 1.0% | No |
| Ouderkerk a/d Amstel | 0.06 | 0.08 | 0.13 | 0.0% | 0.0% | 0.0% | Yes |
| Pieter | 0.41 | 0.50 | 0.75 | 0.0% | 0.0% | 1.7% | Yes |
| Teunis | 0.28 | 0.34 | 0.53 | 0.0% | 0.0% | 0.0% | No |
| Uithoorn | 0.12 | 0.15 | 0.25 | 0.0% | 0.0% | 0.0% | No |
| Victor | 0.28 | 0.34 | 0.51 | 0.0% | 0.0% | 0.0% | No |
| Willem | 0.30 | 0.36 | 0.55 | 0.0% | 0.0% | 0.0% | No |
| Zebra | 0.23 | 0.28 | 0.44 | 0.0% | 0.0% | 0.0% | Yes |

If we combine all these results, we get Table VII that gives the needed capacity for each fire station. From this, we can conclude that, on an average day, (almost) all fire stations only need a capacity of one truck. Only if we want to be 99% sure that the capacity suffices, we need a capacity of two trucks at station 'Hendrik' on an average day. Then 'Amstelveen' also needs a capacity of two on some days. Moreover, 'Pieter' does not have the required capacity in 1.7% of the days (see in red).

## V. CONCLUSIONS AND DISCUSSION

In this paper, we developed a model to create a good forecast on the number of incidents that each fire station in Amsterdam-Amstelland has to handle. Here, special interest went to the influence of several weather conditions and to the issue of dealing with the low number of incidents.

The answer is split into two parts. The forecasts created for the small incidents can be done reasonably well by ensemble averaging (EA). Big incidents can be modeled by an inhomogeneous Poisson process. Concerning the weather, (the combination of) rain and wind on average had the most influence in the linear models and temperature appeared to contain mostly non-linear relations with the number of incidents. As expected beforehand, the visibility had the least predictive power among those four weather variables.

## REFERENCES


[1] J. B. Goldberg, "Operations Research Models for the Deployment of Emergency Services Vehicles: EMS Management Journal," EMS Management Journal, vol. 1, no. 1, 2004, pp. 20–39.

[2] J. M. Chaiken and J. E. Rolph, "Predicting the demand for fire service," RAND Corporation, P-4625, 1971.

[3] P. L. van den Berg, G. A. G. Legemaate, and R. D. van der Mei, "Increasing the responsiveness of firefighter services by relocating base stations in Amsterdam," Interfaces, vol. 47, no. 4, 2017, pp. 352–361.

[4] D. S. Matteson, M. W. McLean, D. B. Woodard, and S. G. Henderson, "Forecasting emergency medical service call arrival rates," The Annals of Applied Statistics, vol. 5, no. 2B, 2011, pp. 1379–1406.

[5] H. Setzler, C. Saydam, and S. Park, "EMS call volume predictions: A comparative study," Computers & Operations Research, vol. 36, no. 6, jun 2009, pp. 1843–1851.

[6] M. P. Larsen, M. S. Eisenberg, R. O. Cummins, and A. P. Hallstrom, "Predicting survival from out-of-hospital cardiac arrest: a graphic model." Annals of emergency medicine, vol. 22, no. 11, November 1993, pp. 1652–8.

[7] M. Gendreau, G. Laporte, and F. Semet, "The Maximal Expected Coverage Relocation Problem for Emergency Vehicles," The Journal of the Operational Research Society, vol. 57, 2006, pp. 22–28.

[8] A. Ganteaume, A. Camia, M. Jappiot, J. San-Miguel-Ayanz, M. Long-Fournel, and C. Lampin, "A Review of the Main Driving Factors of Forest Fire Ignition Over Europe," Environmental Management, vol. 51, no. 3, March 2013, pp. 651–662.

[9] N. I. C. C. U.S.A. Predictive Services Program Overview. Last accessed on 07/9/2019. [Online]. Available: https://www.predictiveservices.nifc.gov

[10] B. P. Oswald, N. Brouwer, and E. Willemsen, "Initial Development of Surface Fuel Models for The Netherlands," Forest Research: Open Access, vol. 06, no. 02, 2017.

[11] J. J. Faraway, "Practical regression and ANOVA using R," University of Bath, 2002.

# Data-driven Direct Marketing via Approximate Dynamic Programming

Jesper Slik and Sandjai Bhulai

Vrije Universiteit Amsterdam
Faculty of Science, Department of Mathematics
Email: jesper.slik@pon.com and s.bhulai@vu.nl

*Abstract*—**Email marketing is a widely used business tool that is in danger of being overrun by unwanted commercial email. Therefore, direct marketing via email is usually seen as notoriously difficult. One needs to decide which email to send at what time to which customer in order to maximize the email interaction rate. Two main perspectives can be distinguished: scoring the relevancy of each email and sending the most relevant, or seeing the problem as a sequential decision problem and sending emails according to a multi-stage strategy. In this paper, we adopt the second approach and model the problem as a Markov Decision Problem (MDP). The advantage of this approach is that it can balance short- and long-term rewards and allows for complex strategies. We illustrate how the problem can be modeled such that the MDP remains tractable for large datasets. Furthermore, we numerically demonstrate by using real data that the optimal strategy has a high interaction probability, which is much higher than a greedy strategy or a random strategy. Therefore, the model leads to better relevancy to the customer and thereby generates more revenue for the company.**

*Keywords*—**email marketing; Markov decision processes; approximate dynamic programming; recommendation systems.**

## I. Introduction

Customer communication is crucial to the long-term success of any business. Research has shown communication effectiveness to be the single most powerful determinant of relationship commitment [1]. Companies can choose from multiple channels in reaching their customers. The recent rise of social media has expanded the possibilities immensely. Most research focuses on email communication though, because it is relatively easy to collect data of every email sent and every interaction resulting from the email on a customer level. Therefore, a thorough analysis of email communication effectiveness is possible.

Currently, in most companies, domain experts determine the email strategy. Customers are selected for emails based on business rules. These rules can be deterministic, such as matching the language or gender of the email with those of the customer, or stochastic, such as matching the (browsing) activity categories of a customer to the category of the email. Measurements suggest that a large fraction of the emails are unopened, a larger portion of the emails do not even direct customers to the company's website, and almost all emails are not related to direct sales. An increase in the interaction probability, therefore, directly leads to additional revenue. This probability can be increased by a better recommendation process of deciding which email to send at what time to which customer.

The challenge faced in this research can be classified within the research field of recommender systems. A recommender system has as purpose to generate meaningful recommendations of items (articles, advertisements, books, etc.) to users. It does so based on the interests and needs of the users. Such systems solve the problem of information overload. Users might have access to millions of choices but are only interested in accessing a fraction of them. For example, Amazon, YouTube, Netflix, Tripadvisor, and IMDb use recommender systems to display contents on their web pages [2]. Similarly, one can use recommender systems to recommend certain emails to users, thus, to determine when to send which email to which user.

Recommender systems have traditionally been classified into three categories: content-based filtering, collaborative filtering, and hybrid approaches [3]. Content-based filtering is a recommendation system that learns from the attributes (or the so-called contents) of items for which the user has provided feedback [4]. By doing so, it can make a prediction on the relevancy of items for which the user has not provided feedback. Collaborative filtering looks beyond the activity of the user for which a recommendation needs to be made. It recommends an item based on the ratings of similar users [3]. Hybrid recommender systems make use of a combination of the above-mentioned techniques in order to generate recommendations.

Although recommender systems might seem a good way to address the direct marketing problem, they have some shortcomings. One of the major problems for recommender systems is the so-called cold-start problem. This concerns users or items which are new to the system, thus little information is known about them. A second issue is that traditional recommender systems take into account a set of users and items and do not take into account contextual information. Contextual information might be crucial for the performance of a recommender system [5]. A third issue is overspecialization: "When the system can only recommend items that score highly against a users profile, the user is limited to being recommended items that are similar to those already rated" [3]. Lastly, recommender systems must scale to real data sets, possibly containing millions of items and users. As a consequence, algorithms often sacrifice accuracy for having a low response time [2]. When a data set increases in size, algorithms either slow down or require more computational resources.

The main contribution of this paper is that we address

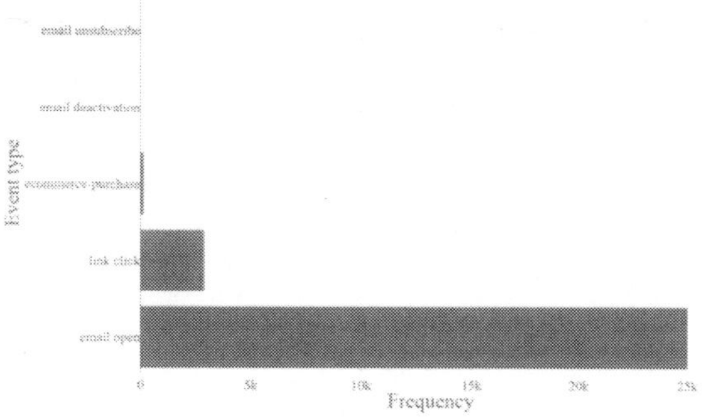


Figure 1. Frequency of event types.

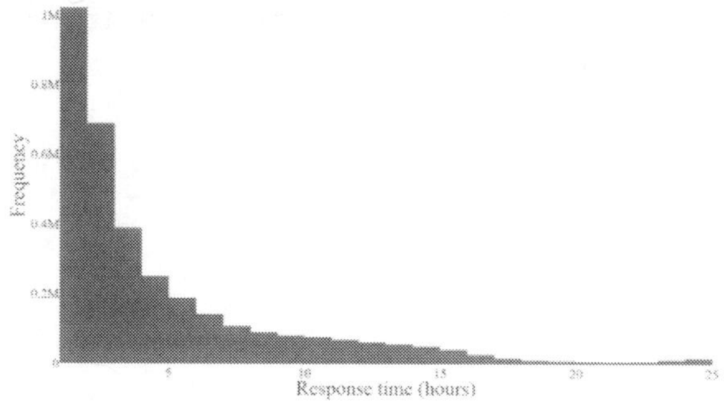


Figure 2. Distribution of time until first interaction with an email.

the mentioned shortcomings of the traditional recommender systems by formulating the direct marketing problem as a Markov Decision Process (MDP). This framework deals with context and uncertainty in a natural manner. The context (such as previous email attempts) can be specified in the state space of the MDP. The uncertainty is addressed by the optimal policy as an exploration-exploitation tradeoff. The scalability of the algorithm is addressed by limiting the history of the process to sufficient information such that the state space does not grow intractably large. Furthermore, we test our model with real data on a greedy and random policy as a benchmark. The results show that our optimal strategy has a significantly higher interaction probability than the benchmark.

The organization of this paper is as follows. In Section II, we describe the data used for our data-driven marketing algorithm. Section III describes the model and introduces the relevant notation. In Section IV, we analyze the performance of the model and state the insights from the model. Finally, in Section V we conclude and address a number of topics for further research.

## II. Data

In this section, we describe the data used for this research. The data is gathered from five tables of an international retailer from one complete year and concerns: *sales* data, *email sent* data, *email interaction* data, *customer activity* data, and *customer* data.

The *sales* table contains all orders that have been placed by each customer. This includes information on the product, price, and date. The *email sent* table contains all emails sent to each customer. An email is characterized by attributes such as title, category, type, gender, and date. The *email interaction* table is structured similarly to the *email sent* table, however, it contains an interaction type. An interaction type can be email open, link click, e-commerce purchase, email unsubscribe, or email deactivation. The *customer activity* table contains for each customer its activity on the retailer's platform, such as browsing or clicking on the website. Finally, the *customer* table contains characteristics of a customer, such as date of birth, country, city, and gender.

The retailer has over 1 million unique active customers in its database. In total, a little more than 132 million emails were sent, leading to around 34.5 million interactions. The main interaction category is 'email open', which occurs over five times more frequently than the second interaction category, 'link click'. This is intuitive, as an email needs to be opened in order to click a link. Even fewer emails are related to direct online sales and rarely an email leads to an unsubscribe or deactivation (see Figure 1). The customers that interact with an email, usually do so within a few hours. The majority even within one hour, with the number of interactions declining by the hour afterward. Only after 24 hours, there is a slight increase in the number of interacting customers (see Figure 2).

With the current email strategy, the retailer does not send the same emails to the same customers. The average customer receives an email every other day and interacts with an email every 10 days. Interestingly, some customers interact with more than 1 email per day on average. The email interaction rate varies between the email category and email type. The interaction rate of individual emails shows even larger differences. This rate ranges from 3.4% to 67%.

In this research, we are mainly interested in delivering relevant communication to the customers. Whether an email is relevant to a customer can be expressed by whether the customer interacted with the email. We investigate two correlations related to the email interaction rate. We do this by visualizing the relation with a scatter plot (plotting a random sample of the data) and including a 95% confidence interval for the mean. The confidence interval is created through a bootstrap procedure.

Figure 3 (left) visualizes the correlation between the average number of emails received and the number of interactions. The average daily interactions is positively correlated with the average daily emails. This is intuitive, as it would benefit no strategy to send more emails to a customer that does not interact with emails. Also, it is impossible for a customer to interact with 2 emails if the customer only received 1. However, sending more emails does not necessarily mean more interactions. Figure 3 (right) visualizes the correlation between the interaction probability and total order value of

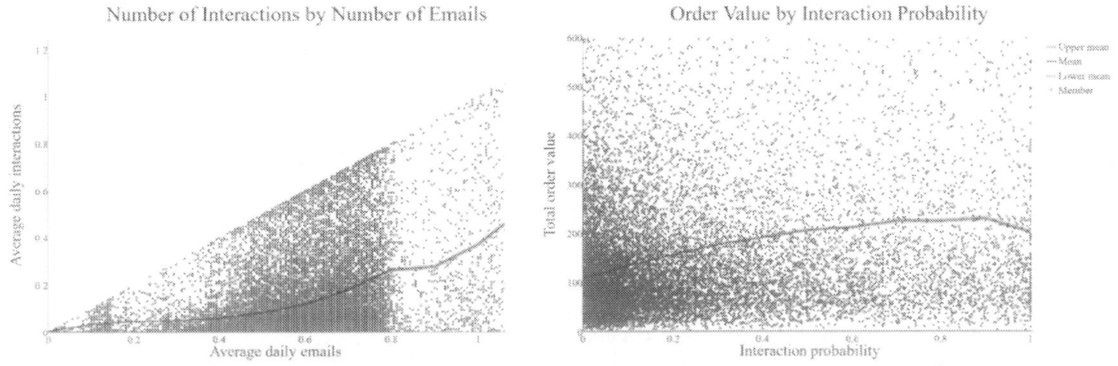


Figure 3. Scatter plots diagrams: # emails vs # interactions (left) and interaction probability vs customer order value (right).

a specific customer. The interaction probability is defined as the number of interactions divided by the number of received emails for a specific customer. The graph indicates that a higher interaction probability is correlated with a higher-order value. When looking at the interaction probabilities of 0.3 and 0.4, the confidence intervals for the mean total order value (averaged over all customers) are non-overlapping. For a probability of 0.3, the confidence interval is $[174.68, 180.71$ and for a probability of 0.4 this yields $[189.02, 195.11]$. Thus, customers that have a higher interaction probability have a higher customer value (for interaction probabilities smaller than 0.8).

## III. Model description

We implement a discrete-time MDP for our email marketing process. The MDP is defined by four entities: the state space $\mathcal{S}$, the action space $\mathcal{A}$, the reward function $r$, and the transition function $p$.

We define a state $s \in \mathcal{S}$ as a vector of the form $s = (x_0, x_1, x_2, y_0, y_1)$. Here, $x_i$ represents the $(3-i)^{\text{th}}$ previous interaction of the customer for $i \in \{0,1,2\}$. Similarly, $y_j$ is defined as:

$$y_j = \begin{cases} 1, & \text{if } (2-j)^{\text{th}} \text{ previous action lead to an interaction,} \\ 0, & \text{otherwise,} \end{cases} \tag{1}$$

for $j \in \{0,1\}$.

This choice for the state is partially inspired by [6], in which the state is defined as the sequence of the past $k$ items bought. We make a clear distinction between actions and interactions, an action meaning sending an email to a customer and an interaction meaning the customer interacting with an email. The $x_i$'s of the state space represent a customer's preference in content, and the $y_i$'s represent the customer's sensitivity to emails. The parameters $i = 3$ and $j = 2$ have been empirically chosen, leading to an approximate model. There is a trade-off between tailoring the model for individuals and more accurately estimating the model parameters. The size of the state space grows exponentially as $i$ and $j$ are increased, since $|\mathcal{S}| = |\mathcal{A}|^i 2^j$.

We define an action $a_i \in \mathcal{A}$ as an integer. This integer represents a combination of email category and email type. An example of a category is 'household products' and an example of type is 'special event'. In our data, 20 categories and 21 types exist. However, not all combinations of category and type appear in the data. Therefore, we focus on the 20 actions that occur most frequently. In this way, we reduce the size of the action set by 95% at the cost of discarding 21% of the data.

The reward function represents the reward (business value) of a customer visiting a state. We aim to maximize the communication relevancy to the customers. This can be measured by customers interacting with emails. Thus, the reward function should measure email interactions. We define the reward function as $r(s) = y_1$ for $s = (x_0, x_1, x_2, y_0, y_1)$. This function expresses whether the previous action leads to an interaction. Conveniently, the last element in the state vector already does so.

The transition probabilities are estimated by simply counting the occurrences of a transition in the data. Specifically,

$$p(s, a, s') = \frac{C(s, a, s')}{\sum_{s' \in \mathcal{S}} C(s, a, s')},$$

in which $C(s, a, s')$ is a function that counts the number of occurrences of transitioning from state $s$ to state $s'$ when applying action $a$. To create the data to estimate these probabilities, three steps are required. First, we collect on a daily level which action and interaction was registered with which customer. Next, we compute the state of each customer based on this information. Lastly, we aggregate all state changes of all customers into one final table. These steps are visualized in Figure 4.

To summarize the implementation of the MDP, we present an example. This example is visualized in Figure 5. The example highlights that when a customer is in state $s_t = (14, 6, 10, 0, 0)$ and action $a_t = 17$ is applied, we have a 19% chance of transitioning to state $s_{t+1} = (6, 10, 17, 0, 1)$ (since $p(s_t, a_t, s_{t+1}) = p\big((14, 6, 10, 0, 0), 17, (6, 10, 17, 0, 1)\big) = 0.19$) and a 81% chance of transitioning to state $s_{t+1} = (14, 6, 10, 0, 0)$. Note that for any $s_t$, only two possibilities exist for $s_{t+1}$.

| customer id | date | action | interaction |
|---|---|---|---|
| a | 1 | 18 | 0 |
| a | 3 | 15 | 15 |
| a | 5 | 3 | 3 |
| a | 6 | 14 | 0 |
| a | 7 | 6 | 6 |
| a | 10 | 20 | 0 |
| ... | ... | ... | ... |

| customer id | date | state | action | state next |
|---|---|---|---|---|
| a | 1 | (1, 1, 1, 1, 0) | 18 | (1, 1, 1, 0, 0) |
| a | 3 | (1, 1, 1, 0, 0) | 15 | (1, 1, 15, 0, 1) |
| a | 5 | (1, 1, 15, 0, 1) | 3 | (1, 15, 3, 1, 1) |
| a | 6 | (1, 15, 3, 1, 1) | 14 | (1, 15, 3, 1, 0) |
| a | 7 | (1, 15, 3, 1, 0) | 6 | (15, 3, 6, 0, 1) |
| a | 10 | (15, 3, 6, 0, 1) | 20 | (15, 3, 6, 1, 0) |
| ... | ... | ... | ... | ... |

| state | action | state next | frequency |
|---|---|---|---|
| (11, 9, 17, 1, 1) | 9 | (9, 17, 9, 1, 1) | 5197 |
| (11, 9, 17, 1, 1) | 9 | (11, 9, 17, 1, 0) | 828 |
| (11, 9, 17, 1, 1) | 11 | (9, 17, 11, 1, 1) | 6561 |
| (11, 9, 17, 1, 1) | 11 | (11, 9, 17, 1, 0) | 1042 |
| (11, 9, 17, 1, 1) | 12 | (9, 17, 12, 1, 1) | 10 |
| (11, 9, 17, 1, 1) | 12 | (11, 9, 17, 1, 0) | 2 |
| ... | ... | ... | ... |

Figure 4. The three data processing steps required for estimating the transition probabilities.

*Modeling considerations*

Multiple challenges arise when modeling the problem as an MDP. Most of these have been tackled by defining an appropriate MDP as done in the previous paragraphs. However, some modeling choices remain which are described next.

*A. The unichain condition*

In order for solution techniques to work for our model, the MDP needs to be unichain. The unichain property states that there is at least one state $s \in \mathcal{S}$, such that there is a path from any state to $s$ [7]. A path from $z_0$ to $z_k$ of length $k$ is defined as a sequence of states $z_0, z_1, \ldots, z_k$ with $z_i \in \mathcal{S}$ with the property that $p(z_0, z_1) \cdots p(z_{k-1}, z_k) > 0$.

The unichain property does not automatically hold when we take all states and state transitions directly from the data. This is because the chain is partially observed, so for some states it is not observed that a specific action causes an interaction. For some states, it might only be observed that the next possible state is the current state. We solve this problem by removing all states for which fewer than 2 next states are observed.

*B. Estimation of transition probabilities*

In our implementation, making the MDP unichain reduces the number of observed states. A problem with the estimation of the transition probabilities is that some probabilities are based upon thousands of observations, whereas others only on a few observations. This introduces noise in the transition probabilities. To tackle this challenge, we recursively remove state transitions that occur fewer than 50 times and, if this leads to states being impossible to transition to, we also remove those and transitions to those states.

The MDP is partially observed, we initially observe 86% of the theoretically possible states. After filtering, we are left with 39% of possible states. This is a large reduction in the number of observed states, however, it does ensure we focus on the most relevant and frequently observed states. Figure 6 shows the distribution of the number of observed transitions per state before filtering.

*C. Exponential growth*

Lastly, defining and solving an MDP can be difficult because of the exponential growth of the state space due to the multiple components of the state, as discussed before when setting the values of $i$ and $j$. If the state space becomes too large, solving the MDP might not be realistic. To ensure the MDP can be solved within a feasible time period, we implement a custom version of the value iteration algorithm, taking into account the following issues.

In our case, the set of possible next states, defined as $E(s, a)$, only consists of 2 states. This significantly reduces the run time of the algorithm. If we would not do this, the algorithm would have to check the transition probabilities to and values of all 32,000 possible states.

We implemented the action set, $\mathcal{A}$, as being dependent on the state, thus redefining it as $\mathcal{A}(s)$. For some states, not all 20 actions are observed. So, it is unknown to the model what the transitions would be. Not taking into account these unknown actions improves the speed of the algorithm.

Finally, we initialize $E(s)$, $\mathcal{A}(s)$, and $p(s, a, s')$ for all $s$, $a$, and $s'$ in memory, using Python dictionaries. This allows for $\mathcal{O}(1)$ lookup steps of any probability, action set, or the set of next states within the algorithm.

## IV. RESULTS

In this section, we present an analysis of the performance of the models. We analyze the strategy performance by comparing three different strategies, all based on the MDP framework:

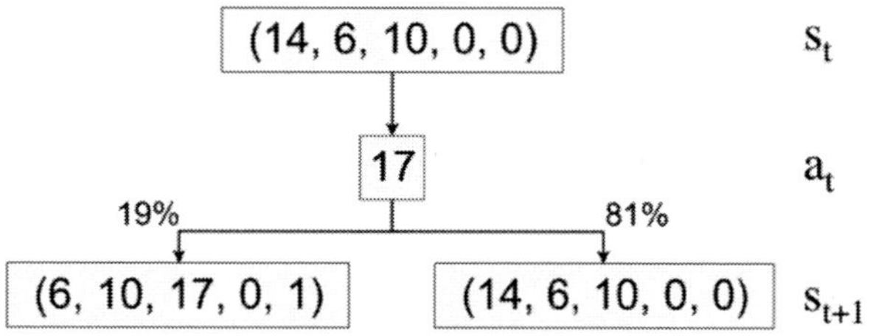


Figure 5. Example transition.

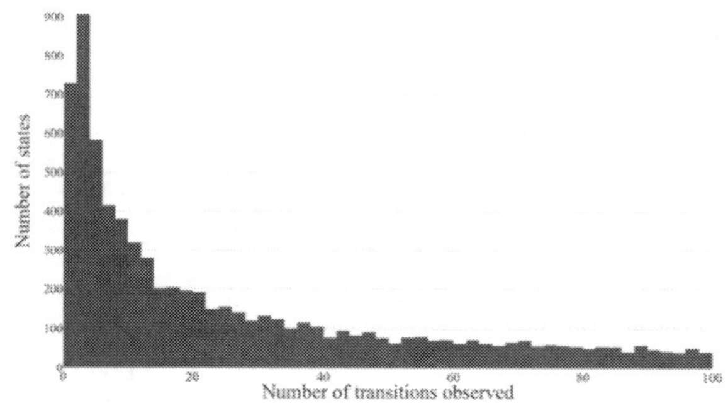


Figure 6. Distribution of the number of observed transitions per state.

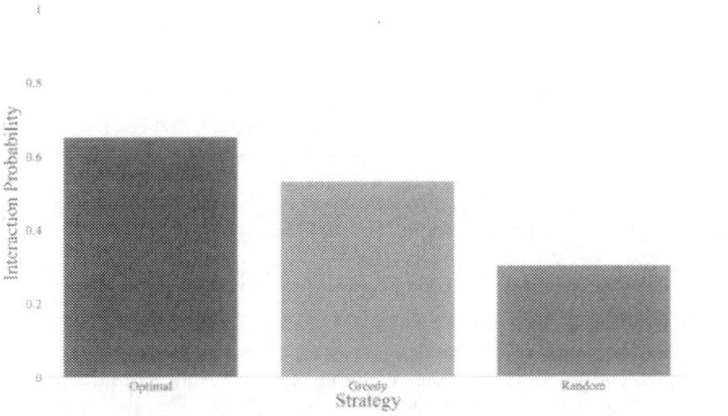


Figure 7. Comparing strategy performance: optimal vs greedy vs random.

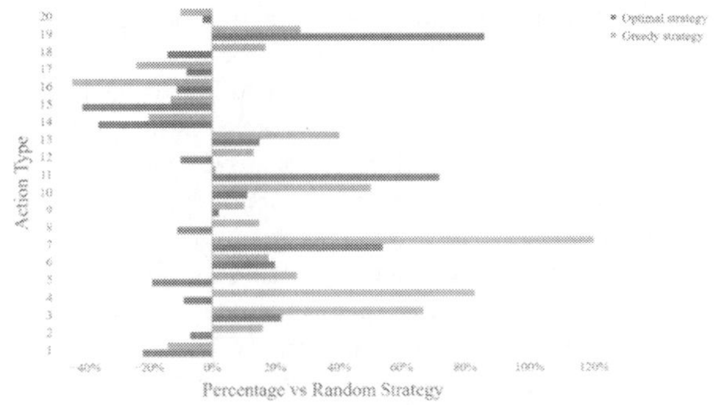


Figure 8. Action performance: frequency of an action within the optimal or greedy strategy divided by the expected frequency of that action.

the optimal strategy, a greedy strategy, and a random strategy (benchmark). The optimal strategy is calculated through value iteration, the greedy strategy through choosing in each state the action with the highest interaction probability, and the random strategy through randomly choosing an action in each state.

Figure 7 shows the resulting performance of the three strategies. The optimal strategy has the highest long-run interaction probability, corresponding to a value of 65%. The greedy strategy is second with a rate of 53%, and the random strategy with 30%. Interestingly, the interaction rate of the optimal strategy is 23% higher than the rate of the greedy strategy, showing that taking into account delayed rewards can highly increase the strategy value. Both the optimal and greedy strategy perform better than the random strategy, showing that using advanced strategies has a large impact on the interaction rate.

Figure 8 highlights the effectiveness of each action type. This effectiveness is measured by dividing the frequency of an action within the optimal or greedy strategy over the expected frequency of that action. It is measured in this way, since an absolute measure would not be accurately representing the action performance, as in some states only one action might be possible. So, the absolute measure would not represent how much the action is preferred over other actions. A comparison between the greedy and optimal strategy is made, to highlight the difference between short- and long-term rewards of the corresponding action.

Large differences are visible in action performance. Actions that perform well on both the short- and long-term are action 7: the type retail clearance, 19: weekly limited product releases in a specific category, and 6: new releases. Interestingly, some actions are highly beneficial for the long-term, but not beneficial for the short-term, see., e.g., action 4. Actions that perform poorly are action 1, 14, 15, 16, or 17, which are all weekly limited product releases. It seems that only the weekly limited product release in a specific category (action 19) performs well.

## V. Conclusions and Discussion

This research shows that the retailer can increase its relevance to its customers by applying a different email strategy. Hereby, it possibly increases the revenue it generates. However, the strategy we developed is based on the data generated from the retailer's current email strategy. If the retailer starts experimenting with different strategies, this might uncover patterns unknown to the current model and potentially improve the optimal strategy we presented.

An interesting result of this research is the difference between the optimal and the greedy strategy. The interaction rate of the optimal strategy is 23% higher, relatively. Thus, the balance between short- and long-term reward should be taken into account when dealing with similar problems. If we would have chosen to use traditional methods, such as content-based or hybrid filtering, this result would not have been directly visible. These methods do not explicitly include this balance, so during the modeling process, it will be beneficial to try to include this balance.

Moreover, the results indicate a 'reality gap' between theory and practice. The interaction rate of the random strategy (30%) is higher than the interaction rate of the retailer's current strategy (27%). This is probably because our model has fewer restrictions compared to real life. However, with the interaction rate of the optimal strategy being 65%, the model shows to have potential.

Throughout this research, all data concerns the past. However, to more accurately measure the impact of strategies, it would be better to measure the performance real-time. For example, through an A/B testing procedure. Then, reinforcement learning could be used to learn the value of strategies in real-time. Next to a balance in short- and long-term reward, this algorithm balances exploration and exploitation. Thus, it tries to both learn a better strategy and apply the best-known current strategy.

Furthermore, we can extend the model by redefining actions. In this research, we focused on emails. However, this channel is not tied to the model. In the future, the same model can optimize push notifications of mobile applications, in exactly the same manner as the current model does.

*Research opportunities*

As with any model, the model we presented in this research is a simplification of reality. The main impact is that, compared to real life, the model can choose between more actions. In reality, not every action can be undertaken in every time period. This can be improved by further restricting the action set, based upon the state. For example, incorporating the previous action in the state and restricting the action set based on this previous action.

Furthermore, the estimate of transition probabilities can be improved. At the moment, this estimation is based upon counting frequencies. However, when transitions are not observed, or observed infrequently, this estimation is unreliable and these transitions are filtered. This leads to a further restricted state space. Instead of removing these transitions, we could initialize a default probability from transitioning from a state to any other state. Or we could use machine learning techniques to estimate these probabilities, as a transition probability might say something about the transition probability of a similar action.

## REFERENCES

[1] N. Sharma and P. Patterson, "The impact of communication effectiveness and service quality on relationship commitment in consumer, professional services," *Journal of Services Marketing*, vol. 13, 1999.

[2] F. Ricci, L. Rokach, B. Shapira, and P. Kantor, *Recommender Systems Handbook*. Springer, 2011.

[3] G. Adomavicius and A. Tuzhilin, "Toward the next generation of recommender systems: A survey of the state-of-the-art and possible extensions," *IEEE Transactions on Knowledge and Data Engineering*, vol. 17, no. 6, 2005.

[4] M. Pazzani and D. Billsus, "Content-based recommendation systems," in *The adaptive web*. Springer-Verlag, 2007, pp. 325–341.

[5] G. Adomavicius, B. Mobasher, F. Ricci, and A. Tuzhilin, "Context-aware recommender systems," *AI Magazine*, 2011.

[6] G. Shani, R. Brafman, and D. Heckerman, "An MDP-based recommender system," *Journal of Machine Learning Research*, no. 6, 2005.

[7] S. Bhulai and G. Koole, "Stochastic optimization," September 2014.